All Worth Their Salt:
The People of NWI
Volume II

Jeff Manes

Copyright (etc)

Copyright © 2016 by Jeff Manes
All rights reserved. No part of this publication may be reproduced, distributed, or transmitted in any form or by any means, including photocopying, recording, or other electronic or mechanical methods, without the prior written permission of the publisher, except in the case of brief quotations embodied in critical reviews and certain other noncommercial uses permitted by copyright law. For permission requests, write to the publisher, at the address below.

Publisher; Jeff Manes 219-775-3083
6742 Ramsey Road
Hebron, IN 46341

Quantity sales. Special discounts are available on quantity purchases by corporations, associations, and others. For details, contact the publisher at the address above.
Orders by U.S. trade bookstores and wholesalers. Please contact

Publisher; Jeff Manes 219-775-3083
6742 Ramsey Road
Hebron, IN 46341

Printed in the United States of America

Manes, Jeffrey, 1957-.
All worth their salt: The people of Northwest Indiana / Jeff Manes.
p. cm.
ISBN 978-0-9970047-1-7

1. Northwest Indiana – Interviews – 21st Century. 2. Indiana – Calumet Region – Interviews – 21st Century. 3. I. Title.
977.29 –dc22

Cover designed by Conservation Mike Echterling

First Edition

"At last someone has written about working Americans in their own words, using their own language, and telling their own stories! Jeff Manes is one of the few writers who not only admires such folks, but shares their experience and concerns. Anyone who reads this book will understand why the people who are 'the salt of the earth' are more than 'worth their salt.'"

- Debby D'Amico, PhD, has spent her working life learning about worker education in unions and community programs in New York City and beyond.

"Jeff Manes has a style and candor that gets to the heart of a person's character. His working class sensibilities highlight what really matters in people from all walks of life. He truly captures what it means to be from the area in an authentic voice."

- Judy Lennon, National Writers Union, Local 1981

"Jeff Manes never disappoints his reader – nor those he profiles. For he is one of few contemporary writers who precisely captures the folks who make Northwest Indiana so beloved to him. Through inquisitive and respectful conversations, Manes crafts astute sketches of ordinary people living meaningful lives. Jeff's writing engages the reader and keenly communicates what it means to be worth one's 'salt.'"

- Regina Robinson, Philadelphia, Penn: Adult educator and working group member of "Kindred Voices: The Workers Writing Project"

"There is but one author I can compare Jeff Manes' writing to and that's Studs Terkel. Studs was a friend of mine and his passing created a vacuum. Jeff Manes has filled that space with his wonderful sense of timing and beautiful play with words. Volume I of 'All Worth Their Salt' makes me anxious for Volume II. There is nothing more enjoyable than relaxing with stories of real people that often bring tears and joy in a world in dire need of same."

- Lil' Joe Gutierrez, author of "Secrets of the Neighborhood – Where Tomorrow Begins"

"Walt Whitman heard America singing, and Jeff Manes extends the tradition by listening to America talk. In All Worth Their Salt: The People of NWI, a collection of 100 of his stunning newspaper columns, Manes invites real people to tell their stories as simple conversation, without intrusive narration or invasive sermonizing. With his spare, down-to-earth style, Manes reveals the people of Northwest Indiana as truly 'worth their salt.'"

- Constance Alexander, recipient of Kentucky Governor's Award in the Arts for her work in media and award-winning newspaper columnist

Contents

Introduction

Chapter I: Salt of the Earth

John Bianchi	2
Sharon Bolt	6
Ziggy Czerniak	10
Father Snoich	14
Garrard McClendon	18
Harmon Lisnow	22
Doc James	26
Dick Stevens	30
The Sheidt Boys	34
Jim Barrington	37
Victoria Mueller	41

Chapter II: Work

Larry Overton	46
Julius Surprise	50
Ken Travis	54
Dorine Godinez	59
Chris Wilk	62
Elizabeth Myers	65
John Gelon	69
Larry Hine	72
Carlos Aburto	75
Ken Burbridge	79
Fly Rod Jimmy	83

Chapter III: Melting Pot

Johnny Nguyen	88
Sam Quirarte	91

Dorothy Mokry	95
Barb Kubiak	99
Moanes Khawalid	103
Ken Eng	107
Jack Gross	111
Larbi Kharchaf	115
Roger Brewin	119
Wolfgang Rubsam	123
Panida Girddonfag	127
Ed van Wijk	131
Millie Rytel	135

Chapter IV: History Books

Steve McShane	139
John Hodson	143
Stanley Swanson	147
Betty Balanoff	151
Pat Tilton	155
Fern Eddy Schultz	158
Dr. Ruth Needleman	163
Dave Howkinson	167

Chapter V: Up to the Challenge

Ed Regnier	172
Rich Zmuda	175
Jason Delgado	178
Dan Reynolds	182
Cathy Wunderink	186

Chapter VI: Characters

Carl Matury	191
Linda Keichle	195
Chris Christian	199
Mary K. Emmrich	203

Glenn Novak 207
Linda Arnold 210

Chapter VII: Caregivers & Do-gooders
Val Carr 215
Buddy Bell 219
Debbie Martinez Bolanos 224
Mary Lou DeLong 228
Pat Wisniewski 233
Ann Herbert 236
Valorie Cady Dunn 239

Chapter VIII: Educators
Robert Petyko 244
David Lane 248
Dorothy Bishop 252
Paul & Angie Lowe 256
Leon Kendrick 260
Mary Cusic 264
Barb Arko-Hargrove 268
Verna Schrombeck 272
Greg Easton 276
Jimmy Holmes 280
Sophie Wojohoski 284

Chapter IX: The Arts
Gwen Calmese-Wright 289
Sam Dalkilic-Miestowski 292
Ted Kosmatka 296
Mark Spencer 300
Irene Evans 304
Jerry Edmonds 308
Scott Brandush 312
Little Chris Pabon 317

Tyler Lennox Bush 321
Mary McClelland 325

Chapter X: The Good Earth

George Bunce 331
Barb Dodge 335
Jim Hitz 339
Mike Echterling 343
Dan McDowell 347
Kip Walton 350
Alyssa Nyberg 354
Chris Salberg 357
John Barenie 361
Kim Ferraro 365
Dan Plath 369
Larry Davis 373

Chapter XI: Kindred Spirits

Josie Sturgill 377
Harvey & Alice Johnson 381
Barb & Bill Peterson 385
Sally Burns 388
Alice Gray 392
Jennie Conrad 396

A Note to the Reader

It was January of 2005 when the first of these human interest columns was published. More than 1,000 have been written since. Some of the folks featured in this collection are now deceased. Some have changed occupations since being interviewed. Their stories and photographs will appear as they did when first published – without updates.
  – JM

All Worth Their Salt:
The People of NWI
Volume II

Introduction

Salt. The human body contains about four ounces of it. Without enough salt we perish. It was for salt that Mahatma Gandhi marched.

Around 1900, certain social leaders in New York claimed there were only 400 people worth knowing. In disagreement, author O. Henry wrote a volume he called "The Four Million." He thought everybody was worth knowing.

In more recent times, Raymond Carver, dubbed the American Chekov, spoke of the laborers and service workers who formed his submerged population: "They're my people, I could never write down to them." Ray Carver grew up on a small river town of 700 souls.

I have had the advantage of growing up along the bayous of the Kankakee River and atop the carcinogenic coke batteries abutting Lake Michigan. I'd like you to get to know your neighbor, those living, sometimes eking out a living, just across the alley or down the road. Their names don't usually appear in the newspaper. The obits, maybe. But they are all worth their salt.

Everyone has a story to tell.

– Jeff Manes

Salt of the Earth

John Bianchi *(Jan. 2012)*

*"And when the night is cloudy
there is still a light that shines on me
Shine until tomorrow, let it be.
I wake up to the sound of music,
Mother Mary come to me
Speaking words of wisdom,
let it be... ."*
– Lennon/McCartney

John Bianchi is a huge Beatles fan, but one of his favorite childhood memories is watching "The Three Stooges" and "Flash Gordon" with his father while his mother cooked spaghetti.

Bianchi's dad worked at Youngstown Sheet & Tube for 35 years; his mother was a cook and a seamstress at Hoosier Boys' Town.

John retired from ArcelorMittal's No. 2 BOF in April with 38 years seniority, but spent the majority of his career in the mill's coke plants.

Bianchi, 61, lives in the Black Oak neighborhood of Gary with his wife, Shirley. He was raised in East Chicago and graduated from Bishop Noll Institute.

* * *

"Jeff, I don't know why you want to interview me; I'm not an interesting person," Bianchi began.

Talk to me.

"I grew up three blocks from East Chicago Roosevelt High School; all my friends went to Roosevelt. Because of my Italian mother, I had to go to a Catholic school. I love her."

Your parents were born in Italy.

"Yes, about 40 miles southeast of Rome. Everybody needs to go to Italy one time. It's a different lifestyle. The Italians take time at life. But there's nothin' like this country."

Your immediate family?

"Shirley and I had a regular Brady Bunch. She had four kids from her first marriage; I had one child from my first marriage and then we had Danielle and Jonnica. And now we've adopted three children, Reagan, Kennedy and Tyler. Reagan and Kennedy are 9-year old twin girls; Tyler is 6."

When did you adopt them?

"Last year, but they've been in our custody as permanent guardianship for about four or five years. They are all Shirley's granddaughter's kids."

That's really something.

"We do a lot of camping, mostly at the Dunes. Jeff, the way you feel about the Grand Kankakee Marsh is the way I feel about the Dunes. When I die, I want my ashes spread out there; it's just a beautiful place.

"We've camped at places like Potato Creek and Prophetstown in Lafayette. Nothing really out of the area, Indiana mostly.

"The greatest vacation I've ever taken was traveling all around Lake Michigan. It's just as good as going to the Grand Canyon. I went all the way up the Michigan side by Mackinac Island; it was absolutely beautiful. You can drink the water off the island, that's how clear it was. Then, we came down the Wisconsin side. If you do that, you'll never forget it."

Tell me about East Chicago in the early '60s.

"East Chicago was the best place in the world to live. It was a melting pot. Everybody cared about you. I lived on the north side. If I got in trouble on the south side, by the time I walked those eight blocks, my mother already knew about it. That's the way it was back then.

"If you had a beef with somebody, you met at the park, duked it out, and it was over with. It wasn't as crazy as it is now. I remember one time, by accident, we broke somebody's window while playing sandlot baseball. We thought about running away, but we didn't. We went up to the homeowner and said, 'Hey, we broke your window; we're sorry.'"

What happened next?

"The homeowner said, 'Don't worry about it. Go play ball.'"

Your family attended Immaculate Conception Catholic Church.

"Yes, on the corner of Olcott and 149th. In that neighborhood was a lot of Italians. My God parents, Pete and Mary Calacci, lived right across the street from the church"

"Mary was Father Campagna's administrator for 30 years at Boys' Town. Mary had a philosophy that there was good in every boy that came to live there, no matter how hard a life they had or how much trouble they'd been in. I learned a lot from Mary; she was a beautiful person.

"Pete taught me about solidarity; he was the president of United Steelworkers Local 1010 from 1956 to 1962."

That means he was president during the 116-day strike in '59. Tell me about when you worked at Zel's Roast Beef in East Chicago.

"Stan Routeman was the creator of Zel's. Great guy. Stan was in his 70s when he sold out to a corporation."

John, the beefs and chili cheese dogs at that Zel's on Columbus Drive and Euclid were hard to beat back in the 1970s.

"Stan would take like six to eight hours to cook the meat for his sandwiches. He took a lot of pride in his food and his employees."

Explain what a "mix" is.

"While working at Zel's, the kids from the neighborhood would order a mix, which was a squirt of root beer, grape, Hawaiian Punch, Coke, Sprite.... We don't eat out a lot now that I'm on a fixed income, but once in a while I'll take the kids to Subway. They'll get sandwiches and I'll order a mix. I tried it and liked it."

My buddy Lil' Joe Gutierrez has written a book entitled "The Neighborhood." Joe grew up near you.

"I went to school with Lil' Joe's sister, Esther. She was a really great person."

Our mutual friend, Jerry Edmonds, played at your wedding.

"People still talk about that. Jerry played 'Heart of Gold' by Neil Young in memory of my dad, who had passed away, and for Shirley's oldest daughter who was killed by a drunk driver. She was just shy of her 16th birthday. I love Jerry."

The mill?

"I'm glad they're pushing safety so hard. Guys at the (union) hall like Don Jones and John Gelon do a heckuva job. I don't miss the mill or the work, but I do miss the people.

"Jeff, about 15 of us were waiting for an outage. There must've been over 400 years of experience in that room. Everybody had at least 30 years seniority. A 28-year old college grad came in to line us up."

And?

"I said, 'Look, tell us what you want us to do and leave. Come see us at the end of the day.' He asked, 'Why?' I said, 'Because I don't want anybody getting hurt.' By the end of the day, all the work was done and we all went home safe."

* * *

Bianchi is a diabetic with high blood pressure and a colon cancer survivor. He also walks with a cane these days. He attributes that to years of working underneath the pusher and the door machine changing shear bolts and the countless times he carried a pair of 60-pound idlers to the top of the coal handling section of the coke plant.

John Bianchi's back might not be as strong as it was when he wore a younger man's set of flame retardant greens, but he still wears a heart of gold on his sleeve. A more likeable or interesting man, I've yet to meet."

Sharon Bolt *(Feb. 2007)*

*"The one-l lama,
he's a priest.
The two-llama,
he's a beast.
And I would bet
a silk pajama,
there isn't any
three-l lllama."
-Ogden Nash*

I drove toward sandhill crane country: Wheatfield. Sharon Jurs married Jim Bolt 43 years ago. Both graduated from Lowell High School. They have lived in Wheatfield for 20 years.

They raised two children, Bob and Kristi.

The stunningly beautiful Sharon plays numerous musical instruments and has sung in a band. She worked for the Visiting Nurses Association, is an incredible artist, a licensed beautician, an interior decorator, and on occasion, a clown.

* * *

"I still don't know why you wanted to interview me, Jeff," Bolt began. "I'm not very interesting. I'm a river rat. I grew up on a farm right near the Grand Kankakee Marsh, about a half-mile from the river bridge where the corners of Jasper, Newton and Lake counties meet.

"My Grandpa Jurs bought that farm back in 1917. We'd swim in the river after we got done baling hay. We didn't know what an air conditioner was. My mother would fry up a chicken and we'd have picnics out in the woods along the river bank. I grew up in those woods. I thought it was the best place in the world to be from.

"I'd make my brother get up at four in the morning; we'd grab a blanket in the summer time and lay in the hay in the barn.

"When the sun came up and hit us – I just loved that. The smell of the hay. The cows returning to the barn in the morning. I hated being a girl; Mom thought I was a lost cause. She put me in charm school when I was a teenager. They made me walk around with a book on my head."

You're quite an artist, I hear.

"I call this 'Peruvian Sunset.'"

You painted that?!

"I call this one 'Backyard River Garden.' I paint llamas on mailboxes, T-shirts, candles – you name it. I take my wares to the show competitions – everything sells out. What I need to do is finish texturing this ceiling. You'll have to come back when we're finished with all the construction."

Tell me about these exotic creatures.

"They're like a dog because they're very loyal. They don't have hooves, just two toes. They have the three-compartment stomach like a cow and have a prehensile lip that they use to grab things. They don't have teeth on top, just the bottom.

"Llamas have been domesticated for 2,000 years. In the wilds of their native South America, there is always a dominant male in the herd. If another male decides to challenge, there's a fight. I have to keep my males separated. Llamas live about 30 years."

Sounds like you could write a book on the subject.

"Actually, I am. I've got about five chapters finished."

How much does a llama cost?

"Anywhere from $500 to $500,000. We've had as many as 21. I sold five llamas last year."

Adds Jim, "Sharon's out in that show ring with some big names."

"That's the best part, Jeff. I get out there with these rich retired lawyers, who have 200 or 300 llamas to choose from. They're doing it for a hobby; it's just a tax write-off for them. Here I am, this little old blonde peon lady, and I beat 'em.

"They get so mad! There was a doctor who wrote a nasty letter to the judge because he lost to me and Rocky. Rocky was deemed second-best llama in Indiana and won grand champion four times."

They seem to be intelligent animals.

"I teach my llamas 15 command words. They know their names. If they're together in a group and I say, 'Roxanna, come here,' Roxanna will come. They all go potty in one spot – on a tarp. I sell the poop. Master gardeners use it for fertilizer."

Stud service?

"Rocky is 10 years old now but he's still good for stud fees. I have people who bring these great big honkin' female llamas to breed with my little guy. I dig a hole and place the female in it.

"Then, I make sure everything goes right where it's supposed to. It's no big deal. After the breeding, I'll reintroduce the female to Rocky a couple days later. If she spits on him, that means she took.

"After they're bred, the females want nothing to with the male. Some of my girls wave their tails at Rocky to get his attention after they've been bred. He'll come a runnin' up to the fence and they'll spit on him."

That's not very nice.

"Well, actually, llamas are very gentle. I've taken them to nursery schools and old folks' homes. For years, I've taught 10 or more kids here twice a week, year-round, about llamas and how to show them.

"I've helped children out financially who come from families that can't afford for their kids to be in 4-H.

"It has cost me a pretty penny. Some people spend their money at the casino or on lavish vacations. I spend mine on these kids, many of whom start out shy and have low self-confidence.

"I took my llamas to visit a young woman who was a hospice patient. I remember a special-needs child who had not spoken a single word in six years – he uttered, 'Llama.' The looks on the faces of that young woman and boy were worth a million bucks, Jeff.

"My llamas let out this real high-pitched whinny, almost like a horse when a coyote comes around. Out West, the sheepherders use llamas to help protect the flock.

"They'll put themselves in between the sheep and the predator. They'll spit at the coyote and then spike them with their feet.

"Moochie's a chicken. He'd run through a fence and hightail it if a coyote came. Now, Rocky, he would take the coyote on."

Sharon, there's something about Rocky. I can't help but like that beast.

* * *

I said my goodbyes to Rocky, Roxanna, Sheeza Surprise, Sir Star Rider, Pebbles, Topaz, We Be Fancy, Karisma, Liza, and to one of the most interesting human beings I've ever met – a llama mama by the name of Sharon Bolt.

Ziggy Czerniak *(Nov. 2005)*

"...In the name of your sacred dead, strike! Let no heart be faint. Let every arm be steeled."
-Gen. Douglas MacArthur

I showed up a little early at The Lake of the Red Cedars Museum located on the shore of Cedar Lake. It was a Thursday morning, drizzling rain. It wasn't red cedars that caught my eye, but five huge catalpa trees bordering the south side of the nostalgic building. They must have been nearly a century old. Walking down to the pier, I watched a charcoal-colored cat paw mercilessly at a hapless vole. Survival of the fittest.

Zigmund Czerniak was born in Chicago on Jan. 15, 1915. He attended an elementary school for the children of Polish immigrants. His teachers told him to change his first name to Sigmund. The lifelong bachelor is nearly 91 and hard of hearing – steel mills and cannons could not have helped.

Czerniak moved to Cedar Lake in 1974. In 2003, he was named Grand Marshall of the 4th of July parade, and also was voted Cedar Lake's Citizen of the Year. He is a member of Holy Name Catholic Church choir.

Being the caretaker of the museum, Czerniak carries the key. Closed for the season, it's kind of eerie inside and vaguely reminds me of the hotel in "The Shining."

* * *

"My folks had three children in Poland, but two died before they came across," Czerniak began. "From there, they had another eight children. I grew up by the mills on the south side of Chicago, near the lake and St. Michael's Catholic Church.

"My father died when I started high school. He was gassed while working in the blast furnace at US Steel's Southworks. He didn't die right away, but stayed sick for a long time after it happened. I'm sure it contributed to his early death. My mother raised eight of us by herself. I took a two-year course at Bowen High School – architectural and mechanical drawing – but it was hard times, and my first job was with the Civilian Conservation Corps out in Oregon.

"I eventually ended up at US Steel like my father; I became an electrician. I worked nearly 35 years in that mill. Things were shaky in the steel mills back in '30s. We had a lot of trouble trying to get the union in. If the boss didn't like you; he'd fire you. I remember a bunch of guys getting shot at Republic Steel."

The Memorial Day Massacre; 10 steel workers were murdered by the Chicago Police Department. What did you think about Franklin Roosevelt?

"He was a good man."

I noticed a bumper sticker on your car that promotes the Special Olympics.

"I do a lot of volunteering at the handicapped school. They don't like to call it handicap – disabilities. I had trouble with my speech when I was a boy. Kids were always picking on me. I slurred my speech."

Would you care to tell me about your experience in World War II?

"I've brought some photographs. This is me sitting on top of Mauna Kea, a dormant volcano in Hawaii. Hawaii was my first mission. This photo is of a 75 mm. See the single rail and wagon wheels; it was horse-drawn. They motorized them just before the war, put rubber wheels on them. Eventually, we went to the 105 mm. When I was first inducted, we used World War I equipment. I was qualified as a cannoneer."

"Actually, I was in two outfits. The first three years, I was in the 131st Infantry; a machine gunner. After my term was over, I joined the 124th field artillery. They're both in the same regiment. I was reconnaissance.

"During the war, I graduated from combat ranger school; it was a special unit just like the Marines. They taught us to be proficient in judo and karate – killing blows. They also taught us how to use a Thompson submachine gun and a Browning automatic rifle. I was given a rating of 'very satisfactory.'"

I bet you were in the best shape of your life.

"I was a commando."

What is this photo of?

"We found a Jap cannon hidden in the weeds; I figured out how to use it. There were two rounds. On the second round, I hit my target."

You used a Japanese cannon on the Japanese?

"Better than the Japanese using it on us. Let me show you something. (Czerniak shuffles down a dark corridor. I follow him into one of the museum's many rooms. In a glass case is a photograph, a certificate, and a medal. The photo shows a general pinning a bronze star onto the chest of a young GI. The certificate is written to the mother of said GI, namely, the widow Hattie Czerniak).

PFC Sigmund F. Czerniak 20615796, field artillery United States Army for heroism and action against the enemy at Galliano Le Union Luzon Philippine Islands. On the 29th of March, 1945, Private Czerniak was a member of a forward observer party whose mission was to adjust artillery fire in support of the infantry. While moving forward across a rice paddy, the party was subjected to machine gun fire, killing two members of the party. With utter disregard for his own personal safety, Private Czerniak moved forward under enemy fire and recovered valuable radio equipment.

"We were on the tail end, making our way along a path in the rice paddies. They killed our radioman. We had to scatter. We left the dead men lay. When the machine gun fire settled down a bit toward evening, we had to retrieve the radio. That radio was our contact with the artillery unit. We dug in. Then we retrieved the radio and informed our heavy artillery.

"The enemy opened fire on our position with their cannon; we expected that. Our unit zeroed in on them by the flash of their cannon fire in the darkness. Those boys put the Japanese out of commission. If not, our whole unit would have been shot to pieces."

What you guys endured. Maybe we should change the subject. Do you ever visit friends and family from Chicago?

"Everybody's dead. I used to have golfing buddies. Now, I drive the ball and I can't see where it goes – I lose it. I used to be a good athlete, swimming, baseball, bowling... .

"When I was about 3 years old, I lived right next to the US Steel gates. Suddenly all these horns and sirens started blaring from the mill. The bells of St. Michael's started ringing. The steel workers hung a likeness of the Kaiser in infamy from one of the stacks. It was 11 or 12 o'clock. I can still remember that."

World War I was over.

"Yes; the war that was supposed to end all wars."

* * *

I asked Czerniak if I could take his picture. He didn't mind, but made me wait until he changed hats. The old Pole doffed his depression cap and donned that of the American Legion.

I left and he stayed. A relic, at home in a museum.

Father Snoich *(Sept. 2007)*

*"Daddy died a miner and grandpa he did too,
I'll bet this coal will kill me
before my working days is through...
...There's fire in our hearts and fire in our soul
but there ain't gonna be no fire in the hole..."*
-Hazel Dickens

A small Catholic church stands at Indiana 10 and U.S. 41 in Lake Village. When I was a boy, the pastor at St. Augusta was the Rev. Scholl. There never has been a Betty Crocker, but there was a Dr. Scholl. The pastor was his cousin.

The Rev. Stephen Snoich, 78, has been the pastor at St. Augusta since 2004. He was born and raised in Shenandoah, Pa., during the Great Depression.

* * *

"Shenandoah was an anthracite coal mining town," Snoich began. "Anthracite is a hard coal; it burns very hot – it has a blue flame to it. You use soft coal in the steel mill; you'll get an orange or yellow flame from soft coal."

Your family?

"My grandfathers on both sides of the family were killed in the mines. One was a Lithuanian immigrant, the other migrated here from the Ukraine. My dad started in the mines at the age of 9. He died from black lung (disease). It's a very dangerous job. There were some miners killed just recently out in Utah – cave in. They couldn't locate them.

"My mother was a seamstress; she made all of my trousers. She worked in a factory where they made hunting shirts – those plaid shirts."

Flannel shirts like lumberjacks wear?

"Yes, they made a lot of those shirts way back. They were paid by the dozen. Some ladies sewed the arms on, some shoulders, collars – there were always extra pieces left over. Mother would go from pile to pile, and that's how I got my shirts. They would have thrown away the scrap pieces. She did the same for my sisters' dresses. Both my sisters went on to be nurses. One of them, she's older than me, is still living in the same homestead built in 1885."

Was it mostly Eastern Europeans living in Shenandoah during the '30s and '40s?

"We had just about everything: Slovaks, Polish, Lithuanian, German, Irish, Little Italy. During the boom time, we had about 30,000 people. Today there are less than 4,000."

Did you work in the mines?

"No; I started working at age 10 as a delivery boy for a butcher shop. Then, the owner's son was called into the service during World War II.

"I was the only other employee; I was cutting meat by the time I was 12. I could barely lift a quarter round of beef up to the block, but I did.

"After I graduated from high school, I went to college for one year in Philadelphia, a liberal arts course.

"I had a chance to stay with a widow and her family. She rented to students for extra money. I eventually moved on and took a carpentry apprenticeship in Philadelphia. I became a journeyman carpenter. I soon was running many of the jobs, although only in my 20s."

Were you salaried?

"Oh, no; I paid my union dues. When I started in the trade, we wore full-bib coveralls with a nail apron in the front. But you didn't get your own nails, even if you were working right next to the barrel. You could put a laborer out of a job that way.

"We had a bad winter, and they said to take some time off from work. I visited an uncle and his family who lived in Kentucky. I also visited a Trappist monastery that was close by. They were a contemplative monastery; they're vegetarians and a little more strict than what I'm part of now.

"They had some construction going on. Those brothers were up on a scaffold laughing, joking, and talking... . I thought to myself, 'They're doing the same work I do, but look how much fun they're having.'

"One thing led to another, and my uncle wrote to one of the priests at St. Meinrad, a Benedictine monastery and seminary in southern Indiana. I was invited to visit them in 1955; they needed somebody with a construction background. Shall we say they laid the red carpet out for me?

"I joined the community as a novice. I learned the Benedictine way of life. Almost immediately, they sent me to the carpenter shop. I was given the job of making 50 oak tables for a group of sisters.

"Once I'd finished that task, the abbot called me into the office. He said, 'Our water has been condemned and, if we don't build a filter plant, we are going to have to send our entire student body home. Can you build it?' I said, 'Well, if I had a blueprint.'

"The abbot gave me one piece of paper; it was merely a floor-plan sketch. I had no skilled labor for help. My crew consisted of men who didn't know the difference between a hammer and a hatchet. We built the filter plant.

"I also built a guest house. Then, I was sent to California to build another guest house.

"When I finished that up in 1965, I asked to go into the seminary. It was then that I was relieved of my maintenance responsibilities."

Let's back up a bit. What does OSB stand for?

"Order of St. Benedict. You make your vows as a Benedictine monk. Some monks remain brothers for the rest of their lives; some go on for ordination."

"Once I'd obtained my masters degree, I was given many assignments at St. Meinrad and was eventually assigned to St. Benedict's in Evansville as an associate pastor for 17 years... to '92. Today, it's a cathedral.

"I was reassigned as a chaplain to a community of Benedictine sisters in Ferdinand – the Convent of the Immaculate Conception. I was there for 12 years. I came up here in 2004."

I hear you have an artistic side.

"I love to carve wood and etch glass. I've done some stained-glass work, as a hobby.

"When I was about to leave St. Benedict, the Men's Club wanted to give me something that I could remember them by. They bought me a very powerful drill – 4,000 rpms. It's so fast you can drill holes in an egg without damaging the shell. It was designed by a dentist. I set up a little shop in the back of the monastery and started carving eggs."

How many parishioners do you have here?
"About 400 souls."

* * *

Father Snoich told me that he's always believed in preventive maintenance, that he likes to catch a problem before it becomes too serious. He also told me he brought his tools to Lake Village.

Appropriately, for his photograph, Snoich stood next to the patron saint of workers – St. Joseph. Just to their right was yet another former carpenter, nailed to a cross.

Garrard McClendon *(May 2011)*

"Congress shall make no law respecting an establishment of religion, or prohibiting the free exercise thereof; or abridging the freedom of speech, or the press; or the right of the people peaceably to assemble, and to petition the Government for a redress of grievances."
– The First Amendment

I first met Garrard McClendon at Calumet College of St. Joseph in Hammond where he was emceeing an event put on by professor Ruth Needleman regarding the current labor situation in Northwest Indiana.

McClendon, 45, has been married to Quanica for 14 years; they are vegans who have raised two children, Jocelyn and Tristin Russell. Jocelyn is a Dominican University graduate and Tristin is a freshman at The Ohio State University.

McClendon is the host of the WYCC- Ch.20 PBS Chicago program "Off 63rd."

* * *

You live in Merrillville, but you're a Hammond guy.

"Born and raised, man," he said. "I had a really good experience there with public schools. I went to Bethany Child Care, Wallace Elementary School, Edison Middle School and graduated from Hammond High School in 1984."

Did you play sports for Hammond High?

"I was a hurdler on the track team; I also was on the speech and debate team and senior class president."

College?

"I went to college on a speech-and-debate scholarship. I started off at Wabash College – the Little Giants – as an English major. I attended Valparaiso University for my masters in English and history and I earned my Ph.D. at Loyola University in Chicago."

Garrard, I'm embarrassed. Except for Chicago White Sox games and a select number of PBS programs, I haven't watched television in 25 years.

"Ha! You're a good man."

But I have friends from Lowell to Valparaiso who love your TV show. I'm going to make it a point to start watching your program. I've been told you call 'em like you see 'em. I noticed that at Calumet College; you brought up some interesting points of view that most emcees wouldn't have dared to expound upon in the presence of a room filled with unionists and liberals.

"Yes, we discussed things such as whether labor unions are a thing of the past because there are so many businesses fighting for right-to-work (legislation). I wasn't there to spout an opinion that particular day, but I strongly believe that a person can't live a life totally on the left or the right. It's an unbalanced life if you always say, 'I'm a Democrat until the day I die' or 'I'm a Republican until the day I die.'"

Garrard, I agree. On Tuesday, May 3, while voting in the primaries, I asked the ladies working the polls if they had an "S" (Socialist) when they told me to pick a "D" or an "R."

"I'm asking for people to think. If you wake up in the morning and you're not thinking, you're going to be manipulated by a politician, a school representative, a labor union leader, the television news.... .

"We saw it happen with Donald Trump (recently), calling for a birth certificate. That was the most ridiculous, asinine thing, arguably, in U.S. history I've ever seen."

It seems like I read in the National Enquirer or Wikipedia that Trump was born in Iceland.

"I don't necessarily think like white people or Hispanic or black people. It's not even about that. It's about being a thinking human being.

"People say, 'Well. Garrard, you're black and you think a ceratin way.' No, it's about me being a human being. I have a family to care for, I have contracts to fulfill; that has nothing to do with being black. You can't let politics always be your skin color "

Garrard, I'm grateful the Post-Tribune includes photos of its columnists. Otherwise, most readers would mistakenly assume that the

Rev. Raymond Dix is the conservative white guy and Jeff Manes is the angry black man.

"I love it. Rev. Dix is a good friend of mine. When we start to compartmentalize, like, 'OK, you're black, so that means you're a liberal Democrat, you're poor, you play basketball and eat fried chicken and collard greens. When we put people in boxes like that, that's when the diversity of America is torn down.

"If I assume that you're rich because you're Jewish or assume that you're a restaurant owner because you're Greek, I'm cutting myself off at the knees and I'm cutting you off at the knees."

Sounds sensible.

"We are three-dimensional human beings with feelings and emotions. This is why media must show responsibility, whether it be print media, electronic media or visual media. We have a responsibility to not only show the truth, but to give a point of view that is accurate and fair – not necessarily balanced – but gives the opportunity for people to agree, disagree or be somewhere in between.

"On my TV program, we try to give the people the First Amendment. I strongly believe in freedom of speech. The First Amendment is such a powerful amendment. Here we are, in the new millennium, and people don't take advantage of the First Amendment.

"And it's not just freedom of speech; it's freedom of the press and freedom to peaceably assemble. Those powers are so strong. To be able to write a newspaper article, to be able to give your opinion on television or radio, that's why I exist."

A fresh perspective, one might say.

"My whole point in this media game is to give people an alternative to what they're going to see on other networks and to not lie to people, whether it's on my TV show, whether it's my book, 'Axe or Ask: The African-American Guide to Better English,' or whether it's the lectures and workshops I give."

When does "Off 63rd" appear?

"At 6:30 every Thursday night on channel 20 or 25. We've been on the air for five months now. All the past episodes are on YouTube. I have multiple guests on 'Off 63rd' and I also take phone calls, Facebook, Twitter, email messages – the works."

What are some of the hottest topics you've discussed on your show?

"Political topics always seem to be the hottest. The (Rod) Blagojevich trial, Mayor (Richard M.) Daley deciding to resign, Chicago not getting the Olympics, the murders in Chicago... .

"I try to bring a magnifying glass to things that people look at and ignore. When somebody gets murdered, that's not just a news story at 10 o'clock; that's a whole family that is being affected.

"I want people to take action. I don't want people to just sit there and say, 'That's a good TV show.' If you're pissed off about somebody being killed on your street, I'm calling you to action."

Garrard, I wasn't going to bring it up, but we're heading in that direction. The murder of your parents? Brother, I can't imagine.

"Tough blow to have both parents murdered like that – over $70 and some jewelry. What's sad, the two perpetrators, you know, these are babies, man – teenagers. These are two African-American kids who should have been playing sports and having fun getting ready for prom. Instead, they're looking at senior citizens as prey."

I doubt if they were raised like you were.

"It really doesn't matter. A lot of people grow up in precarious situations and don't perpetrate crimes. I know a lot of poor people who don't commit crimes."

So do I, Garrard.

"You know what? I've forgiven the perpetrators. When I found out about the tragedy (while) in the WGN newsroom, I said, 'Let it go' because Garrard won't do anyone any good if he harbors that hatred."

You're a better man than I.

"Garrard is still angry. I can't go to a Cubs or Sox game with my dad and I can't eat my mom's lemon meringue pie anymore. But I know my parents raised us to love people."

* * *

I've met some extraordinary people thanks to this media game.

Garrard McClendon is an eloquent, passionate, intelligent, forgiving, angry, brutally honest, opinionated human being with feelings.

He's in-your-face First Amendment.

Harmon Lisnow *(March 2005)*

"Don't walk in front of me; I may not follow. Don't walk behind me; I may not lead. Just walk beside me and be my friend."
-Albert Camus

Harmon Lisnow lives in Crown Point. He is 64 and 6-feet, 4 inches tall. A gentle giant with caring eyes that stand guard atop a nose with character. His remaining hair and perfectly trimmed beard are white now. He stays in good physical condition. Harmon exercises everyday. To a Midwesterner, his Brooklynese is detectable; he pronounces the word "saw" with an "r" (sawr) and New York without an r (New Yawk).

Lisnow is the Executive Director of the Institute for Career Development, USWA & Participating Steel Companies. The national headquarters are in Merrillville. He also helped organize the National Association of Joint Labor/Management Educational Programs, and he's currently on the board of ALMA (Adult Literacy Media Alliance).

During the 70's Lisnow worked to help oppressed Mexican-Americans along the Texas border regarding issues such as economic development and Visa packaging. He has run three state agencies for three different elected officials in Texas. Harmon Lisnow has worked for, or with, such notables as Jesse Jackson and Texans Ann Richards, Jim Hightower, and Bob Bullock. He has managed political campaigns in California.

Yet, other than a quick cup of coffee in California, he spent 30 years living in Texas before moving to the Hoosier State in '94. He and his wife Virginia are the proud parents of two adult children, Patricia Ann and Ian Tomas. Ian's middle name serves as a reminder of his Hispanic heritage, states Harmon. Virginia is of Mexican-Italian ancestry.

The native New Yorker has traveled the globe. He has whaled with Eskimos. He spent almost two years in the jungles of West Africa after graduating college, ala John F. Kennedy's Peace Corps. He was recently involved with "The Gates" in Central Park which exemplified the importance of collaboration between art and industry. The Amish of Shipshewana are handcrafting Harmon a buggy. Via horse and buggy, Lisnow will travel through the National Forests of Colorado.

Putting his arm around me, Harmon states, "My friend, you look hungry. Come with me... ."

* * *

"I'll have a Diet Pepsi," he said.

"*I'm sorry sir, we serve Coca Cola.*"

"I won't buy Coke products. Union people in South America have been murdered trying to organize their plants. Give me an iced tea, please."

Harmon, tell me about growing up in The Big Apple... Thanks to you, I've been to New York City twice once to receive an award for my writing and once to act in the play "Steel & Roses." I realize that Brooklyn is one of the boroughs, of course, but tell me about your particular niche in Brooklyn...

"Bensonhurst, next to Coney Island. Mostly Italians and Jews. Half my friends were Catholics. Half were Jewish. In our neighborhood, although it was Brooklyn, there were both Yankee fans and Dodger fans. I became a Yankee fan because my father liked the Yanks. My mother became a Dodger fan because she loved Jackie Robinson and what he stood for. We were all baseball fanatics back in those days. I remember when the Dodgers blew something like a 13-game lead late in the season. Bobby Thompson hit a home run. I think it was off Ralph Branca. 'The shot heard round the world'. Clinched the pennant. My mother froze. We started laughing at her, teasing her, because the Dodgers lost. She didn't say a word.
She just sat there. Staring... After a while, we started getting worried, two hours went by. She hadn't moved..."

Probably how Cub fans felt '69.

"My dad had gone to college and became a pharmacist but never used it. He wanted to be a writer or a baseball player. He was a tremendous baseball player. My grandpa told him those professions were for bums. That's why he never pursued baseball. He ended up taking over my grandfather's very small retail store. He sold linoleum and floor coverings on Avenue U, the Italian section of Brooklyn... My father drank."

Tell me more about your childhood.

"I was born in 1941. I was a very impressionable child. I can remember people coming home from the concentration camps. Jews with tattoos on their arms, ones that had settled in New York, in our neighborhood. It made an indelible mark. It was incomprehensible to me that this could have happened. It was a very interesting childhood.

"It also was a very community-oriented neighborhood. I ran around during my earliest years with a wonderful bunch of guys; it was kind of the way you survived there. But we weren't a gang, we were athletic. I remember playing a lot of stick ball, using old discarded brooms and rubber balls. We played sewer ball. The four corners of the street served as bases.

"They also could be mean streets. You had to be very conscious of where you were and who you were with, whether it was daylight or dark. With that said, I grew up in a very intellectually stimulating family. The best part of my childhood, the best part of my family life, was eating dinner everyday at the same time. There were five of us in the family. We lived in an 800-square foot apartment. We'd sit at that small table, always in the same seats, and we'd talk about issues of the day. About things in the newspaper. We'd talk about our Judaism, what it meant. We didn't know we were poor. It was a very rich childhood."

Let's fast forward to current events.

"Wal-Mart. They're putting all the mom-and-pop shops out of business. Many of their own workers qualify for food stamps."

Yeah, but the poor don't shop Gucci, Harmon. They need to go where prices are lowest.

"The point is, we need to establish standards so that the very poor, who have jobs, don't have to be poor. Then, they can afford paying an extra dime for a mop. We're rushing to the bottom. Yes, our workforce makes cheaper and cheaper goods, but, they make less and less for their jobs. People who work hard should be protected with a decent income."

Point well-taken.

"Jeff, my parents met on a picket line running from the cops. My father asked my mother if he could carry her picket sign while they fled.

Dad became a union leader. Both my grandpas were union members. Meat cutters. Garment workers. My brother's name is Franklin Delano Roosevelt Lisnow. My parents thought Roosevelt was a savior. When nothing else seemed to work in this country, along came Roosevelt with all his social programs of the '30s. Programs that lifted this country out of poverty. My father thought the creation of Social Security was the greatest thing ever done in the history of social programs in this country. Maybe mankind... That's why, to see it so easily disregarded now, is a tragedy."

I think Social Security can be straightened out, don't you?

"Of course it can. But the powers that be don't want it fixed. They want to eliminate it. They believe everything should be free market. The problem is, it's *not* a free market; it always benefits the wealthy. You see, in this country we have a growing disparity between the rich and poor. We're seeing the elimination of the middle class.

"Workers salaries and incomes have been frozen since 1973, when you consider inflation. We see corporate salaries going up and up. In 1970 the average CEO made 40 times what the average worker made. Today, it's over 500 times what the average worker makes. And the working class becomes smaller and smaller because we're shipping our jobs overseas. These corporate leaders wave the American flag, but they don't believe in America. They don't believe in the principles that made this country great. They believe in lining their own coffers. If something happens in this country they take off, flee to the Bahamas, to Switzerland. They don't care about this country and what it stands for. My parents did. And I'm proud of my parents values. I have the same values. They believed in working America. They believed that you should be paid well for a day's hard work!"

Harmon, has it been worth it? I mean, the struggle... .

"Struggle? I care about people. When I look back, I guess I could have gone a different direction, and made a lot of money. I think I have strong administrative and management skills. If I had worked in a corporation, I would've probably been successful as a corporate bureaucrat. I've never cared about making a lot of money. I care about helping people."

That you do, my friend..

Doc James *(Aug. 2008)*

*"...I get up each morning, dust off my wits,
Pick up the paper and read the obits.
If my name is missing, I know I'm not dead.
So I eat a good breakfast and go back to bed."
-Traditional*

Ernest K. James, D.D.S., is an octogenarian humanitarian and a Lowellian.

Longtime friends and former clients fondly refer to him as "Doc" James. The retired dentist had been referred as a possible interview for this column a year or so ago. It was decided that our chat would have to wait because his wife's health was failing.

* * *

"Nell and I were married for 65 years (since 1943)," James began. "There were a lot of memories. I had a wonderful wife; she was beautiful inside and beautiful outside.

"We met while I was attending Indiana University in Bloomington; it was 1942 or '43. I'm 13 years shy of a century now; sometimes I forget things. Anyway, I was working for my meals, serving tables for the women's sorority that she was a part of. We fell in love right there on the spot.

"Nell asked one of her sorority sisters who I was. Her friend said, 'Why that's Ernie James from Crawfordsville; I've known him from way back.' Nell said, 'Well, I want to meet him.'"

Where was Nell from?

"Gary, near Emerson High School. Her maiden name was Higgenbotham."

Childhood memories of Crawfordsville?

"Crawfordsville is a small farming community about 30 miles south of Lafayette and about 75 miles from Bloomington; I used to hitchhike to the campus and back on weekends.

"My dad was the principal of Crawfordsville High School, so I had to toe the mark. I was one of four children. Kids were to be seen and not heard in that era. Folks were frugal back in the 1920s and '30s; they had to be. My dad was on a $3,000 salary.

"Early on, I was a Cub Scout, then I was a Boy Scout. I was almost an Eagle Scout, but didn't quite make my swimming badge. At about the age of 16, I became a 'girl' scout – you have to keep joking, you know."

College days?

"I went for $50 per semester – $5 chemistry fee. College tuition is ridiculously high today."

Doc, one of my three daughters is in her final year at Indiana University's School of Dentistry in Indianapolis. She's studying to be a dental hygienist. She probably will have her student loans paid off when she's your age. She also has been steadily dating a nice young man who will become a dentist.

"Very good!"

Thought you'd like that.

"We went straight through at IU because it was wartime. You moved from being a sophomore on Saturday to a junior on Monday morning; I got through dental school in 32 months.

"I graduated on a Saturday at noon and, at 2 that afternoon, the Navy grabbed me by the back of the neck and said, 'You're in'.

"I went on duty until '46; then I came here to Lowell and started practice. I wasn't discharged; I was released. They still had my name in the program, you see. In '52, I got called back for duty in the Army. I'm not the only one who served in two different branches of the service; I'm not complaining."

How did your tours of duty affect family life?

"Nell and my daughter stayed with her parents when I was sent to medical field service school at Fort Sam Houston in San Antonio. I wound up in Korea for a year-and-a-half with the Army's 3rd Division – the one (Gen. Dwight D.) Eisenhower was famous for in the war before.

"I sewed up a lot of guys in M*A*S*H hospitals. I prefer not to talk about those experiences. The chow was a lot better in the Navy. It took the Army boys, fighting in mud and snow, to do it, though – I have the highest respect for them. Everybody had to do their part."

The weather in Korea?

"There were beautiful days and there were days I thought we were going to freeze death; some did."

GI "Mickey Mouse" boots?

"They were the warmest and best-fitting boots I ever wore. We lived in tents and bunkers. We tangled with the Chinese once in a while; I had to be on duty for that. But, praise the Lord, I came back with two eyes, arms and feet; some didn't."

What made you decide to become a dentist?

"I made many trips to the dentist in my early life; I had to have a lot of service done. I attached myself to a family dentist who encouraged me to follow dentistry."

How did you end up in Lowell?

"I wanted to practice dentistry, so I needed to find a place where I might join up with someone who would enable me to associate with them. Dr. Dinwiddie took me in as an associate and I eventually bought his practice out. In '54, I moved my practice to West Commercial near Anco TV. I've been retired for 21 years now."

Where was Dinwiddie's practice located?

"Above the Sears and Roebuck in downtown Lowell on the south side of Commercial Avenue."

Those old buildings in that area are fascinating. Just northwest of where you're talking about is a facade with 'Dr. Death: 1899' etched into it.

"He pronounced it 'Deeth.'"

Doc, if I were an M.D., I'd pronounce it "Deeth," too. Tell me about pulling teeth back in the day.

"We did things the hard way in the '40s; we stood at the chair and worked all day. Finally, we decided we could work from stools. And by the way, I didn't pull teeth; I removed teeth. Doesn't that sound a little better? I practiced general dentistry – everything from restorations to removals. Some oral surgery, too."

As far as patients, are kids the toughest?

"No, kids are the best. I've had children go to sleep right in the chair. Fear is instilled in some children. That is why I didn't get an Eagle

Scout swimming badge; I was warned as a child to never go near water."

You are a religious man.

"I was instrumental in the start of Bethany Chapel in 1966. We had a little group that met for Bible studies in this living room. Today, the church is located on the north side of town; it's nondenominational.

"My mission has always been to help people, to love them, and to encourage them. With that said, Heaven's looking a little better to me; terrible things happen in the world today. Look at your newspaper: rapes, murders, babies being shot in the streets.

"We can't write these children off. Jesus didn't write me off. I've made a mess of my life many times, but God comes right back and takes you on again; he never gives up. I'm not a preacher or anything like that; I'm just sharing."

Is that a photograph of you and Nell displayed on the coffee table?

"Yes, it was taken at P.H. Ho Photography in Indianapolis a couple of days after we were wed. The chain has been broken with her gone. I miss her."

Talk a little about aging.

"Getting old is inescapable. Life not only happens; it happens fast. Everybody is very concerned about me. They won't let me mow the yard. Sometimes, they catch me working. They all have these cell numbers; they tell on me.

"I'm not vain, but I don't carry a cane; I forget where I set them down. It's embarrassing when I'm in the grocery store and I can't recall someone's name. I'll stare at them while they're speaking to me and all that comes to mind is 'second bicuspid on the upper left' – that's how I remember them.

"Everything seems larger when you're young. The lawn I mowed as a boy seemed huge; it wasn't. The sunfish we'd catch in the streams were all trophies; they weren't. Everything shrinks when you get old.

"And, Jeff, my apologies for not being better prepared for this; I'm not conducive to interviews."

Doc, I beg to differ.

Dick Stephens *(Nov. 2010)*

Wilbur Post: "What are you going to do with that straw hat?"
Mr. Ed: "I'll wear it until it goes out of style. Then I'll eat it!"
– From the 1960s sitcom "Mr. Ed"

I interviewed Dick Stephens on an absolutely gorgeous fall afternoon in Jackson Township when The oaks and maples provided a colorful canopy of red, orange and yellow.

Shirley came along for our hour-long ride. Actually, Shirley provided the ride and occasionally joined our conversation with a whinny as she clippity-clopped along the bucolic backroads. Shirley, 10, is a Percheron mare.

Stephens, 60, is the owner-operator of Buggies & Things, a horse drawn carriage service. He has been married to Judy for 25 years; they have raised three children; Dick has a son and daughter from a previous marriage.

* * *

"I'm originally from Medaryville," Stephens began. "Bethlehem Steel started building new homes in South Haven and Westville back in the late '60s and early '70s because they had so much work for people. My first wife and I bought like the fourth new home in Westville because I got a job at Bethlehem in 1969. But I couldn't handle the shift work and got divorced. The mills will work you three shifts in one week; it was terrible.

"I got myself an associate's degree in welding from Ivy Tech and then went to work at Union Tank in East Chicago. I worked there until two years ago; they closed the plant up. I had 31 years in."

How long have you lived at this location?

"We built this place in 1988. We own five acres of this is 75-acre farmstead; it's been in Judy's family for quite a few years."

Let's back up a little bit. High school?

"I started out at Medaryville High School, but they consolidated my senior year in 1968. The Francesville kids came on down to Medaryville; that boosted our class up to about 80 kids. So, I graduated from West Central High School."

Medaryville in the 1950s?

"My dad moved up from Kentucky in 1952 and bought 300 acres out there by Jasper-Pulaski game farm. It was all swamp. About 1955, he bought himself an old bulldozer and started clearing all that land and putting drainage tile in it. You go by there now and you can see it's all farmland."

Dick, let's talk horses.

"It wasn't that long ago, in the early 1900s, that they had to farm and truck everything with horses. My mother-in-law remembers when they plowed the fields in this area with horses."

The horse or mule commands "haw" and "gee" frequently come up in crossword puzzles.

"Left and right; I had an old Amish man tell me the way to always remember that is gee is for God and your on the 'right' path."

Dick, I guess I was destined to go down the wrong path in life. Being a lefty, I'm just a haw kind of guy.

"When we moved into this place, I decided to get back into horses. I bought a standard-bred horse with a surrey. I was giving people rides and everybody said, 'Why don't you start a business?' I said, 'Naw.' But that was in '91 and here I am. I'd just do it on the weekends while working at Union Tank, but now I do it full time."

Hey, with your pension, this is a nice set up for you.

"I don't get a lot of work. Last year was the first time in 10 years the town of Valparaiso didn't hire me for its Christmas party. I used to give rides around the courthouse. When I would show up with my carriage on a Friday night we would have people lined up."

What happened?

"With the economy the way it is, I guess the town just didn't have the funds. I still do the Christmas stuff for Chesterton; I've done the Local 150 Operating Engineers Christmas party for the last 15 years and Sand Creek Country Club's as well. Believe it or not, Christmastime is my busiest season."

Other events?

"Parades, parties and anniversaries... . I do weddings in the summer on Saturdays. And I do a lot of those – I can't think of the word – when an Hispanic girl turns 15... ."

Quinceanera.

"Yeah, that's it; I have one of those scheduled in May in South Bend."

How many horses do you own?

"Three drafts and a mini. Bonita, the miniature, will shake hands with you. American miniature horses are really a hot item right now."

How much does a miniature horse cost?

"It depends; you can buy one for $50, on the other hand, one of the top stallions just sold for $160,000. It all depends on the quality of the horse."

Tell me about Shirley.

"She's a Percheron draft horse. Shirley is black; when we get back home I can show you, Bob, he's snow white. Some Percherons stay black and some of them turn white. My dapple grey will be white when he gets older. Shirley is already 10; she'll stay black."

It's like the hair on our heads. My Great-uncle Ed Magliola lived to be about 80 and had pitch-black hair the day he died; then, there are folks whose hair turns grey or white by the time they're 35.

"Bob turned completely white by the time he was 13. People like a white horse for weddings. When I do Indian weddings, I have to have a white horse; it's a sign of purity. Those are pretty neat; the Indian people dress up in costumes and play their special brand of music. Usually it's the man who rides in on the horse with the carriage."

Have you ever used Shirley for funerals? I think of the riderless horse, Black Jack, that followed the caisson carrying the casket of President John F. Kennedy on the way to Arlington National Cemetery.

"I did a funeral up by Wrigley Field; they wanted a horse following the hearse. The deceased was a military man.

"For the Oz parade this year, I did the 'horse of a different color.' I started that years ago on my own. I paint Bob green, orange, red and yellow with hair coloring kids use today. It washes right out."

How old are your other two Percherons?

"Paul, the dapple, is 8; Bob is 20."

Dick, I'll whisper so she can't hear me: How much does Shirley weigh?

"About 1,800 pounds; she's getting fat."

"Neigh!" (Shirley said)

Whoa, she has great hearing. Hey, Shirley just stopped.

"She's just followin' your command."

Gee, I didn't realize.... Dick, why is Shirley veering off to the right?

* * *

Dick taught me a lot about equines during our ride in his wagonette. I learned the difference between a horse and a pony, what withers were, that a pinto and a palomino are not breeds of horses but colors of horses, and much more.

I also learned that Dick Stephens loves his animals and he's a man with good horse sense.

The Scheidt Boys *(Sept. 2005)*

"Twigs in a bundle are unbreakable."
- Kenyan Proverb

Rich, Ryan, and Reid Scheidt live with their parents, Bernie and Roberta, on 10 acres south of Lake Village. They are seniors at North Newton High School. The Scheidt boys are big, strong, blond-haired, blue-eyed, good-looking sons of guns who make good grades in school and are exceptional athletes.

I remember when they were born. There was quite a to-do down in Lake Village. I'd long since moved out of Newton County, but news of the triplets' birth traveled fast.

Yet, I'd never seen them and quite frankly had forgotten about them when I entered North Newton's gym for Lowell's basketball season opener last year. When the three sibs strode out onto the hardwood, I blinked a couple of times – thrice probably – and said to myself, "It's them – Roberta's triplets. The Scheidt boys have grown up."

* * *

What's your favorite sport?
"Football," answered the Scheidt boys in stereo.
Which one of you is the oldest?
"I am," stated Rich. "By a minute; I'm the fraternal triplet."
And you're also the quarterback, right?
"Yes."
And you two, Reid and Ryan, are the identical pair.
"Yes. Yes."
Your mother explained to me that you're not only identical, but you're what is known as 'mirror image' twins, the most similar type of twins there are.
"Yes, that's why I'm left-handed," Ryan said.

"And that's why I'm right-handed," Reid concluded.

What about you, Rich?

"Lefty, like Ryan."

I'm trying real hard to keep you guys straight here. I mean, your dad told my dad he still can't tell Ryan and Reid apart at times.

"Awesome, Dad," chided either Rich, Ryan or Reid. (I give up)

Got any humorous triplet stories, Mom?

"Well, Dean and Barb Dawson still laugh hysterically about the time when one of the boys called the other ugly. And there was the time when they went to kindergarten and one astonished little guy went home and told his mother that there were three boys in his class who had the same face."

Roberta, I don't know how you did it. Teething, diapers... times three!

"The pediatrician in Bourbonnais worked it out with us and donated Pampers," Roberta said.

Back to you guys. What are some of your pet peeves?

"No one ever knows our first name," said Ryan.

"They call us twin or triplet a lot," said Reid.

I bet. And if the coach yells out 'Scheidt' all three of you probably turn around. I must say, you fellas are high-spirited, red-blooded, all-American boys. And very competitive when playing sports. Why, I remember last summer at Railcats Stadium when you lined out against Hebron, Reid. You sure let that batting helmet fly in the dugout.

"Yeah, I shouldn't have done that."

Hey, I ducked. Missed me by a good inch. I walked over and picked it up for you. In fact, I wore it for the rest of the game. Dangerous job, sports writer. (The Scheidt boys say nothing aloud, but six mischievously sparkling eyeballs speak volumes as the three simultaneously grin like possums. They're starting to make me dizzy).

I've heard through the grapevine that on an occasional midsummer's night, the athletic director has been known to receive an anonymous phone call claiming the football stadium was all lit up.

Apparently three tow-headed hooligans had mysteriously gotten out onto the field and were throwing a pigskin to one another at 1 a.m. before an audience of corn stalks and crickets. Know anything about that? Cat got your tongues?

* * *

The Scheidt Boys. They are definitely hardy Midwestern stock. Although Rich will miss a week of football with a banged up knee, the three of them have pretty much played injury free since Pop Warner and Little League. Ma Scheidt has nourished them well.

The band of brothers play both ways on the football team as is the case with most small high schools, but they like offense the best – putting points on the board. If you get a chance, check them out at this year's Lowell-North Newton basketball game; they're very good. And very scrappy.

They're not shy, but hold their cards close. Not the easiest Salt interview by any means. Something tells me the big, little rascals enjoyed my frustration at not being able to tell them apart, and the occasional silent treatment they'd give me when asked to elaborate or expound.

As I got up to leave, I had to ask them if they've had a few donnybrooks amongst themselves.

Rich begins the sentence with an ornery grin.

"Sure, we fight... ."

Ryan ends the sentence with an ornery grin.

"...all the time."

And reminiscent of three rough-and-tumble brothers from along ago – by the names of Morgan, Virgil and Wyatt – Reid, not grinning whatsoever, concludes... .

"But if any outsiders try to mess with one of us, or try to cheap shot one of us on the field, best believe, two more Scheidts are comin' at 'em."

I believe it.

Jim Barrington *(Jan. 2011)*

"...He was the last man to wear a respirator when the government finally enforced it. He would wash his tools with benzene, a by-product of the coke plant, and he didn't wear rubber gloves while he washed the tools. And he ripped asbestos insulation from rotted out pipelines so he could demolish them with his torch; he preferred a No. 6 tip in the torch. And he used it like a bazooka."
 – *Jeff Manes, from the short story "Appalachian Apologia"*

I met Jim Barrington at the Aukiki River Festival by Baum's Bridge near Kouts in August. We talked only for a minute or so, but I jotted down his name and number. Our interview marked the second time we had met.

Barrington, 85, has been married to Dorothy for 50 years; they live in Chesterton. The Barringtons have raised two adult sons, Byron and Jim.

Barrington graduated from Valparaiso High School, attended Valparaiso University for two years, then earned a degree in chemical engineering at Purdue University in West Lafayette. He is a member of the Kankakee Valley Historical Society.

* * *

You visited the Baum's Bridge area as a boy.

"Yes, in the '30s, we camped out in a tent behind Collier's Lodge," he began. "Old man Collier was still alive. The son, Jim Collier, would trade gum balls and jawbreakers for the arrowheads us kids would find."

The Collier Lodge was somewhat different then the other hunt clubs that stood near it a century ago.

"Yeah, it evolved into a general store. When they dredged the river, that pretty much was the end of the good hunting. When they built Indiana 2 south through Kouts, that cut off Collier's business. I believe Old Man Collier originally was from Momence, (Ill.)."

Tell me about your ancestors.

"My great-grandfather was born in Ireland. His older brother, Nicholas Barrington, was studying law. He got involved with an Irish freedom society, and found himself in a conflict with the British government; they pronounced a sentence of transportation to an Australian penal colony."

What happened?

"Somebody tipped him off. He had to flee the country. Nicholas came to the United States just before the potato famine. Just before he left, his mother said, 'You have to get out, but you'll not go to America alone; you'll take your little brother with you.' That 12-year-old boy, Peter Barrington, was my great-grandfather."

Then what?

"They skedaddled and settled in Staten Island. Peter Barrington lived to be 100."

Your paternal grandfather?

"John Barrington ended up in South Dakota, during the Depression, they got hit by the drouth (archaic form of the word "drought"). Everything turned to dust. It wiped out the farmers. I was out there in '36 or '37 and a dust storm came through; it was like a black wall a comin'. Worst dust storm you ever saw; it blotted out the sun.

"My grandmother ran around with wet towels, puttin' 'em on the window sills and under the doors."

Did that work?

"Didn't do a bit of good."

Your father?

"That would be Byron Barrington; he ran off to fight in World War I at the age of 16."

The war to end all wars.

"My grandfather got him out twice. The third time, Dad got clear over to France. Dad was still 16; he threatened to join the French army. The Americans decided to keep him until he turned 17, then signed him up."

What did your dad do for a living after the war?

"He practiced law in Valparaiso; he handled the Collier estate. I still have my father's World War I helmet, bayonet and gas mask."

Tell me what it was like growing up during the Great Depression.

"There was no money; 25 percent of the population was out of work. In Valparaiso, they had a hobo camp along the Nickel Plate Railroad on the back end of Sager's Lake. The hobos would come into town and mooch meals. My mother would usually give them food.

"Then, they'd put a little chalk X under the window sill to show the other hobos that this place would feed you. At that time, they could ride the boxcars."

Jim, if the unemployment rate goes much higher and gasoline prices soar to $5 per gallon like some people predict, we could find ourselves in a similar situation.

"Could happen."

You're a World War II veteran.

"Yes, I was drafted during my first year of college. I was in the 10th Armored Division and attached to the 90th Calvary Reconnaissance Squadron. We went all over checking roads and bridges.

"We landed at Normandy about five weeks after the original D-Day landing. There were still a lot of Germans on the loose.

"Our first job was to pick up mines; they were everywhere – thousands of them. We'd put them in piles of 100, and at the end of the day, we'd blow them up."

Our troops continue to deal with that in Iraq and Afghanistan.

"Oh, yeah, and some of those mines are booby trapped. Anyway, we were in winter quarters near Metz and got orders to move north about 40 miles."

And?

"There were a whole lot of Germans waiting for us. There were German units in front of us and behind us. We were getting bombed and strafed the whole time. There was nothing nice about it.

"That went on for two months. We were in the front lines for nine straight months altogether, including the Battle of the Bulge. The weather was just like it is here today during that battle."

My hat's off to all you guys.

"The infantry units had it a lot worse than us. We followed just behind them."

Your career as a chemical engineer?

"I worked at U.S. Steel as an engineer for a while, but I've pretty much worked for myself through the years."

Did you ever have jobs inside a coke plant?

"The coke plant at U.S. Steel was where I worked the most."

Any pleasant coke plant memories?

"No, I eventually got out of there; it was virtually intolerable. It was gassy and smoky. Some of those coal chemicals are carcinogens."

Jim, it seems like more people I knew who worked in the by-products department of the coke plant died of cancer than the guys who worked on the battery or the coal handling sections of the coke plant.

"Benzene was a real bad carcinogen; you can go right down the list: benzene, xylene, napthalene, sulphuric acid... . Benzene was used as aviation fuel to get it up to 100 octane."

Those old-timers I worked with would fill their cigarette lighters with benzene. With bare hands, they'd wash their tools with it; they didn't know any better. We didn't have to wear respirators when I first hired in. Let's switch gears. How long have you lived in this neighborhood?

"I built this house in 1962; there wasn't anything here – it was a big swamp. What's your name again?"

Jeff Manes.

"Well, Jeff Manes, you come by and visit me any time. Hey, we made it out of the coke plant, didn't we?"

That we did, Jim Barrington.

* * *

You can learn a lot from a person in an hour. I'm glad I jotted down the old-timer's phone number last August. In my book, Jim Barrington and the Barringtons before him are salt of the earth.

Victoria Mueller *(June 2005)*

"When I was a young girl well, I had me a cowboy
He weren't much to look at, just a free rambling man
But that was a long time and no matter how I try
The years just flow by like a broken down dam.
...Make me an angel that flies from Montgom'ry
Make me a poster of an old Rodeo
Just give me one thing that I can hold on to
To believe in this livin' is just a hard way to go."
-John Prine

East Street is a dead-end street about two-and-a-half football fields long. There are four adjoining apartments on East Street. In one of them lives Victoria Mueller of Lowell.

I knocked on her back door. Mrs. Mueller doesn't have a front door. In her postage stamp yard are many treasures, including a 16-pound Brunswick painted yellow, with a pair of black eyes and a smile. Mrs. Mueller likes to paint things.

On the window of her back door is a placard that reads: "You are a stranger here but once."

Mrs. Mueller graduated from East Chicago Roosevelt High School in 1946. Vickie Dunn, as she was known back then, was 16 when her parents died. They were only in their thirties. She was voted runner-up in a 'Prettiest Lips' contest, has green eyes like Pocahontas, and has raven black hair – her mother's maiden name was Sir-May. She was of French-Iroquois extraction.

Mrs. Mueller wears a baseball cap and cannot walk without forearm crutches. She was married for 29 years to Roger Mueller, a World War II veteran and construction worker. He died in 1977 after a prolonged illness.

Mrs. Mueller does not own a car. She has no living children. She has had rheumatic fever, numerous heart attacks, and 39 cobalt treatments. She currently suffers from muscular disease, hemophilia, diabetes, arthritis and glaucoma.

* * *

How did you meet your husband?

"I was working for Pullman Standard, making shells for the Navy," she began. "Roger's sister worked there, too. I brought her a cake for her birthday. Roger was there at his sister's Hammond apartment in full uniform. He hadn't had a furlough in three-and-a-half years. Roger was a paratrooper during World War II. He was on 15 missions. I didn't see him again for about a month.

"One afternoon, I lived in Whiting at the time; I decided to take in a movie at the Paramount. I walked out of the theater and waited for a bus. Roger walked by and recognized me. He asked me if I'd like to see a movie. I accepted and watched the same show over again, unbeknownst to Roger. We started seeing each other regularly after that."

How romantic. How long have you lived in this apartment?

"For 11 years now; before that, we lived in Sumava Resorts. Roger and I lived in the last resort on the road that runs past Lukes Restaurant. Roger was dying. After he passed, the place flooded. I had 38 inches of water in my house. I used Roger's hip waders to get around."

That had to be a mess.

"I erected a little plaque that read, 'The Last Resort.' Me staying there alone, in the woods, during a flood, was truly the last resort."

Meals on Wheels brings you food.

"Five days a week. They charge you according to your income. Roger and I never had much, but we always had breakfast, lunch, and supper. When we lived on the farm in Cedar Lake, the first thing I'd do was bake bread – every day. Even when we moved to Sumava, after our farmhouse burned down in Cedar Lake, I baked bread. I still do some canning. I quilt, too."

You have a nice ramp outside.

"I've put $2,000 into it. I borrowed against my cremation money to build that ramp. I've tried to pay back the account, but it's almost empty. That's good; I have to keep living so I can afford a funeral.

"I'm a rock hound. I want to have my ashes put into that big rock in my yard. Roger brought it home for me. It came from Monticello, where we used to fish. It costs $995 to be cremated. If you donate your body to science you can have a free funeral, but my parts aren't any good."

Are you making it financially?

"I'm not on welfare. I worked. I'm drawing my disability. I get a small widow's VA pension. I was still working 10 years ago. I didn't even have a chair three years ago. No place for the priest to sit. This apartment was a garage. That's why there's no door in front. Nothing underneath either. Cold. Cold. Cold. I'm getting the hell out of here. And I'm gonna take my big rocks with me."

Besides the Meals on Wheels people, do you get many visitors?

"Jeff, when you become disabled, aren't active anymore, and you're broke, the Good Time Charlies aren't there. I had to pay someone to take me to my husband's funeral. Gus, from the Moose (Lodge), has been comin' here for eight years. He brings me food every Christmas. First thing he does is heads right for the portrait I painted of Roger in his uniform. He's so proud of my artwork. When I die, Gus will get that painting."

Gus Gustafson was the third person I interviewed for this column.

"Yes. I read it. When we lived in Schneider somebody put our name in for a care package. The organization, which I won't mention, called me up and asked what I needed. I told them whatever they brought would be appreciated. He mentioned cookies. I told him I'd rather have some sugar, flour, and margarine.

"Roger was gravely ill, I thought he'd like it if I baked him homemade cookies. They came by with a box on Christmas Eve and left in a hurry. I opened the box up and saw that it contained twenty-three cans of dog food. I called them up asking if they'd made some kind of mistake. He told me people eats dog food and hung up the phone. The Bible says I have to love these people, but I don't have to like 'em, honey! Roger only weighed 62 pounds at the time."

I'm sorry... .

"Life goes on, baby. Last winter, I saw my neighbor working out in the snow in tennis shoes. I charged a pair of cowboy boots for him. He worked all his life in one of those factories, breathing all that stuff, and now he's paying for it, like all them others. Has to be on oxygen. We're all in this together. Jeff, remember, life is a gift. Live it, don't grieve it."

* * *

I've given Mrs. Mueller a few packages of soup, you know. Actually, they were given to me when I was out of work. And I've shoveled snow from her ramp once or twice – once probably. When I began interviewing her, I mistakenly called her Virginia.

I didn't get in my truck to drive away from this interview. I walked 15 feet to my meager apartment.

Victoria Mueller is my next door neighbor.

WORK

Larry Overton *(March 2011)*

*"...Well now, Jesus just left Chicago and he's bound for New Orleans.
Yeah, yeah.
Workin' from one end to the other and all points in between."
– Billy Gibbons, Dusty Hill, Frank Beard (ZZ Top)*

Larry Overton left Chicago in 1979 for Sauk Village, Ill., and was bound for Lake Dalecarlia by 1985.

Overton and his wife, Mary, have lived in Cedar Lake for a year-and-a-half. They've raised one son and have been married 37 years.

Overton, 59, is a retired Local 150 operating engineer.

* * *

Where were you born and raised?

"Chicago; the Roseland-Pullman area," he said. "I grew up in a mixed area that was mostly Italian, Polish and Mexican."

Are you a White Sox fan?

"I'm not a big sports fan, but if I was, I'd be a Sox fan. I hate the North Side. They don't even have good taverns there."

Did you go to Fenger High School?

"Yeah."

Rough area in the late '60s?

"The roughest in the city of Chicago. The only school that was competition for Fenger was (Chicago Vocational School)."

You were in a band.

"Yeah, 'Cold Sweat,' but that ended in 1968 after I decided to quit playing the guitar for them. We were an R&B band for the most part. In 2000, I started 'Cold Sweat Chicago.' But we never quite made it because we couldn't find the right singer."

A couple of your favorite bands?

"ZZ Top and Gov't Mule."

Indiana?

"I'm not crazy about this state, but my old lady loves it. Mary is one helluva a lady. She still eats my cookin'. I do all the cookin'."

Your years as an operating engineer?

"I was pretty much strictly downtown Chicago on tower cranes and crawlers."

Tell me more about the life of a guy who worked high in the sky.

"I've been as high as 1,000 feet. One time the Thunderbirds were doing their free-flight stuff for a water-and-air show and kind of went over my tower a little bit. They kinda threw some ironworkers and me off a little bit. The ironworkers were ready to jump. The Thunderbirds' sonic boom shook the crane for about a half-hour or so. But, later on, I met the crew chief at Pippen's Tavern, downtown. We settled our differences."

What did your father do for a living?

"He was an operator, too."

Today, your life is filled with seven Saturdays a week.

"Yeah, after retirement, you know, you have to do somethin'. And as much as I love playin' the blues and stuff, there's a lot more for me to do.

"I'm very active as an officer on the executive board of American Legion Post 261 in Cedar Lake. I'm also an American Legion rider and a Patriot Guard rider.

What does that involve?

"We do all the parades for Lowell and Cedar Lake. We escort servicemen home – alive and dead. I'm not in the Army anymore, but I still perform a service for this country out of respect."

What kind of bike do you have?

"A 2006, 35th-anniversary Super Glide."

How fast have you gone on that Harley-Davidson?

"I'm not so much into the speed anymore as I'm into comfort. I've done my share of drag racing and stuff. I try to contain myself. On this bike, about 100 mph. That's plenty fast."

My dad had a couple of Harleys back in the late '40s and early '50s. He said when a June bug splatters against your forehead at 110 mph, it feels like you got hit with a croquet ball.

"That's why they have windshields on them now."

Remember the black-and-white movie, "The Wild One" and the documentary "Gimme Shelter"? Is there still a stigma regarding bikers? I mean, today, there are female schoolteachers who own Harleys.

"Bikers got a notorious name because of my generation. That biker look and some of their actions in the '50s and '60s scared a lot of people. Some of that has still carried over. The American Legion and Patriot Guard are not motorcycle clubs; we ride in honor of veterans. This is the first motorcycle I've owned.

"I have a wild side that dictated to me that I didn't ride a bike during my working career. I like my saloons. I lived the construction worker's life. Firearms are not allowed in this house. There are some sides to me that maybe shouldn't be let loose."

Larry, you've done all right.

"I don't have a high school diploma, but I have a degree; I'm an engineer. There wasn't a day went by in 37 years that wasn't memorable working downtown. I had the time of my life working with all the trades and building the tall buildings. It don't get no better than that."

Were you ever on a job where someone got killed?

"I was fortunate; nobody got hurt and everything got finished. When you're working in the blind and depending on other people's signals, things can happen.

"In 1982, I ran the crane on the State of Illinois Building. They called that crane the kangaroo; it had about 300 foot of boom on it. Before I got there, a crew of ironworkers and the operator that was on that crane fell 160 feet and died."

Your thoughts on Indiana possibly becoming a right-to-work state?

"Who you talkin' to? I'm retired out of Local 150 and still pay my union dues. I wanna pay those dues."

Why's that?

"I want my gold watch."

* * *

Overton can't ride his Harley at the moment; he recently had three cervicals fused in his neck and a steel plate put in. He was wearing a neck brace a few days before I interviewed him.

Overton said his neck problems are from years of running cranes, watching mirrors and looking up at the boom. Occupational hazards are part of the trade.

I hadn't met him before our interview. But I'd wager Overton is the kind of guy you'd want watching your back if you found yourself in a hostile venue where games of 8-ball are played for blood and "I Got a Tear in My Beer" is played repeatedly on the juke box.

Let the cowboys ride.

Julius Surprise *(Jan. 2009)*

"Saturday's child works hard for his living."
-Traditional

A white guy named George was president of the United States the year (1794) Pierre Surprenant was born in Canada.

During the 1830s, Surprenant and his wife, LaRosa, an American Indian, built themselves a log cabin in Cedar Lake. Today, that piece of land is the second green of South Shore golf course.

LaRosa is buried southwest of Cedar Lake in Creston. She gave birth to 14 children; six died as infants. Pierre lived for 109 years, six months and three days.   Julius Guy Surprise was born Saturday, Jan. 25, 1919. He is the great-grandson of Pierre Surprenant; also known as Peter Surprise.

Surprise lives with his daughter in Cedar Lake. It was decided our interview would take place at Jenn McBride's house in Crown Point – Jenn loves hearing her grandpa's stories. The soon-to-be nonagenarian was washing down fried chicken with a can of Miller High Life when I pulled up a chair next to him.

* * *

Julius, I was at a White Sox game last summer and heard a guy tell the man hawking Miller Lite, "Life's too short to drink light beer."

"I drink two beers a day; one with lunch and one with supper," he said.

Were you born and raised in Cedar Lake?

"Yes, but I went to Lowell High School. Had a classmate call me up the other day, hadn't heard from him in 70 years. He went down to Purdue to become a pharmacist; I went to Indiana University to become a big shot.

"I had never spent one night away from home. My folks wanted me to go to Valparaiso University and become a lawyer; I was a straight-A student. After five or six weeks, I called my parents and told them I wanted to come home. My mother cried on the phone, trying to get me to stay. They came and got me, and that was the extent of my college education.

"I took a job at Inland Steel's employment office as a doctor's secretary in 1938. I was drafted by the Army in '41. I spent 3 years, 3 months and 11 days in the medical corps."

You owned a Tastee Freez located at the intersection of 145th Avenue and Morse Street in Cedar Lake.

"I operated my ice cream store for 40 years – from 1953 to '93. I was 73 when I retired and never missed a day of work in 40 years. I worked seven days a week for seven months every year."

That's amazing. What about the other five months?

"Two weeks in the fall to close the place down, two weeks in the spring to open it up, and when the kids were small – four months on the beach in Florida."

That's also amazing.

"I've had a wonderful life."

You mentioned your parents earlier; tell me more about your family.

"My mother was full-blooded German; her maiden name was von Ribbentrop. Her first-cousin was Joachim von Ribbentrop, Hitler's foreign minister. They hung him at Nuremberg."

Julius, like they say, you can pick your friends, not your relatives.

"My mother was a fanatic on cleanliness. That's why I was successful in that ice cream store for 40 years; I had a reputation for cleanliness. In 40 years, I never knew when the Health Department was going to knock on the backdoor – I never had one bum report.

"Not too long ago, I was at the barbershop in Shelby; I thought I remembered one of the men who was waiting to get his hair cut – he was my milkman! He remarked about how clean my walk-in cooler was.

I said, 'Yes, that's because I got down on my hands and knees every night and washed the floor.' No matter how I tired I was – I scrubbed that floor every night for 40 years."

Your dad, Cass Surprise, was of French and American Indian descent.

"Yes; my brother Roy, who owned Surprise Hardware across the street from my ice cream store, took after my dad's side of the family. We looked nothing alike; he had jet-black hair, high cheekbones and no facial hair.

"As a young man, my father harvested ice on Cedar Lake. Later, he and his two brothers-in-law got into the manufactured ice business up in Hammond. Of course, refrigeration came in, so they sold their business.

"Dad brought his money to the Lowell National Bank; my two uncles took their monies to banks in Hammond and Calumet City, Ill. Those banks went bust. But my dad did not lose a penny to the Lowell National Bank. And that was the start of the Great Depression.

"When I was a kid, we'd ice skate in the evening. All around the lake, there might have been a half-dozen lights on – very few permanent residents."

The Chicagoans had battened down their summer bungalows for a long winter's nap. I believe Sumava Resorts was much the same during the Roaring Twenties. Marriage?

"I took care of my parents in their sicknesses. I didn't marry until I was 38 because I was too involved with them. After my dad passed, I started looking for a woman who came to my store with no wedding ring.

"I had several women who would've gladly given up their husbands because I drove Mercuries, had a nice home, and I spent my winters south. I was prosperous.

"Anyway, Dorothy had two children but no wedding ring. Her husband had been killed in the Korean War. We married. I adopted little Debbie; John was 11 years old and chose not to be adopted. Dorothy and I had one child together, Susan, she's the one I live with. Dorothy and I were married 50 years; she died in October."

You enjoyed what you did for a living.

"I had a lot of fun with the kids. They were shocked when they'd get to the bottom of a cone and find a dill pickle slice."

Julius, those kids weren't shocked, they were "Surprised."

"When we weren't too busy, they'd come up to the window, and ask, 'Mr. Surprise, can we have a contest today?'

"And I say, 'Sure.' I'd line them up outside of the store, and have them run down to the first sand trap of the golf course and back. The one who made it back the quickest got a free banana split.

"The Misch brothers, Jon and Joe, used to come to my ice cream store every night after school and buy chocolate shakes. Years later, when Jon finished his residency up in Grand Rapids, Mich., he pulled into my lot driving a fancy red sports car. My ice cream store was the first place he stopped; he wanted to introduce me to his lovely wife. Jon has taken care of me ever since; he's my primary care doctor."

* * *

Surprise told me another story about a car that pulled into his parking lot, but conked out. It was an old beater owned by a poor man. The man's wife walked up to the window, but didn't order a pizza burger or banana split; she was distraught.

Although reasonably young, her husband's heart also conked out while he tried to push-start his car. Surprise drove the woman and her children to their home near Buck Hill, south of Crown Point. When she got out of his car, Surprise handed her $40. He said, "You're probably going to need this."

That Christmas, Surprise asked his children to give up some of their presents so those kids living on Buck Hill could have presents, too.

That was 40 years ago. Surprise hadn't heard from the widow since – until last month when he received a Christmas card with a letter enclosed. She had read in the newspaper that the wife of the man who showed her such kindness had passed away.

The widow simply wanted to return the favor.

Ken Travis *(March 2005)*

*"...Truckin', I'm a goin' home. Whoa whoa baby,
back where I belong..."*
– Jerome J. Garcia, Philip Lesh, Robert C. Hunter, Robert Hall Weir

It was 6:59 a.m. when Ken Travis pulled up to my Lowell apartment. I jumped in. He's used to driving. Travis has driven all his life. Our destination? Beaners.

En route to Merrillville, I didn't say much. Wasn't with it yet. Nothing a quadruple latte triple decker creme de la creme wouldn't cure... Actually, I always let Kenny order first, "Yeah, I'll have what he's drinking, and, ah, give us a couple of those orange-colored sconce things to go with them Joes..." (the cappuccinos are accompanied with apricot scones)

I slept-walked to our table... .

* * *

When did you start driving a truck, Ken?
"When I was a kid, my dad owned a lumber yard and a saw mill. I was the late bloomer. My brothers started driving a fork lift when they were 6. I didn't start until I was 9. They followed my dad around like a shadow. I liked to read... Whenever one of us turned 12, after sixth grade, that's when we had to go to work. Summers, after school, Saturdays – we worked."

You were a teenager in the 60's and early 70's. Were you drafted?

"No. I was classified 1A, my number was 59. They abolished the draft on my 19th birthday. I was willing to go with the flow. I'd already decided if I was drafted, I would go. My folks didn't understand the sit-ins, all the activism that was going on. They were really bothered by what they saw. The vandalism part of it. It was like watching Dr. Martin Luther King. Wherever he went, the riots followed. The media covered the riots instead of what he was saying. A lot of people didn't want to hear his message."

If I remember correctly, when he was assassinated he was trying to help the–

"Garbage workers. After graduating from Lowell High School in '72, dad was into stone, I started hauling fill sand and different things for him. My dad always had trucks. So driving a truck was just jumping in it, and driving it. We grew up around the business; I'd answer the phone when I was 9 or 10 years old and take orders for him."

"When my dad finally retired, he left the business to me and my brother. I was 31 by then. I saw no future in the man-made limestone business. I looked at my wife Eileen, and said, 'This is what I'm going to do for the rest of my life?'

"In '85, the year my son Nick was born, I went to work for this small outfit in Hammond, where Central Rent-a-Crane is now, on Kennedy Avenue. It was called Harnic Trucking. Harnic was my first truck driving job away from my dad. At 31 years of age, I had no verifiable experience. I worked for Harnic for two years just to establish experience."

"My daughter Shay was born at home. Shortly thereafter, I started working for Gary Transfer, but I was driving a broker's truck. From Harvey, Ill. to Medina, Ohio. I did that for a year. Gary Transfer finally hired me as one of their own."

"About three years later, Gary Transfer decided to get rid of all their trucks. So I had to buy a truck. I did that for several years. I was still an employee of Gary Transfer but owned my own truck. I supported my family. I could still be doing that. But then I had the opportunity to start at Gas City in '98. There's been some down sides, but overall, I'm glad I made the switch. I'm fortunate, outside of my dad, most of the companies I've driven for have been union companies."

Teamsters?

"Oh yeah. I'm building on my old pension."

You mentioned reading as a boy; what's one of your favorite books?

"*'Destined to Witness'*, the true story of Hans J. Massaquoi, the grandson of a Liberian diplomat. His mother was German. Because of World War II, Liberian diplomats were recalled. So he stayed in Nazi Germany with his mother. The man is simply amazing. He's still alive today. I heard him on one of Terri Grosses' on-air interviews."

So, you enjoy WBEZ?

"I'm in a truck, that's where I pick up a lot of stuff. I'm a big NPR listener. It really helps break the day down".

Travis. Do you know much about your roots?

"My folks moved up from Alabama. Mostly Irish and some Native American, they tell me. There's no doubt that the older I get the more I respect what my father accomplished. Sure, he made a few bad business decisions, but I really believe that it would take me and my four siblings, working together, to accomplish the things he did. He was really an interesting guy. He juggled all those different businesses around without a high school education. He was born in Hunstville, and my mother was born in Scotsboro, Alabama."

Home of the ill-fated "Scotsboro Boys" Scotsboro?

"Yes. My parents moved to Cedar Lake when I was six months old. About nine months later they moved to Creston, which is where I grew up."

How many people lived there when you were growing up?

"We figure it was a community of about 120 people. We lost our status as a town December 29, 1967 – when the post office and the store closed."

You remember that date.

"Yes. It was a big day."

Besides your father, who are some other people that you've really admired in life?

"I really respect what Martin Luther King, Jr. did. And the man Nixon fired – Archibald Cox. The guy was a true American. When he was called by President Kennedy to serve, he went. For Archie, it wasn't about money, it was about service. It was during the '80s when politicians had to be paid whatever they would have been paid in the private sector. Service to your country is your civic duty and honor. Cox was supposed to have gotten a Supreme Court nomination, but Jimmy

Carter messed that up. Geography came into play. Archibald Cox was a New Englander."

I always liked Carter. Voted for him twice.

"I liked him too, but he was not a good president. I think he's a great human being, but those are things we have to separate. I don't think Ronald Reagan was a good president and I don't think he was a particularly great human being. We'll just have to wait for history to decide that.

"We're in a very strange, difficult time, politically. I think this president has not been the unifier that is talked about. The media really irks me. Roughly, 50 percent of the America people were opposed to the invasion of Iraq."

The European Union?

"You have all these countries that are changing their governments, changing their human rights situations, improving their standard of living so they can join the European economic community. Now, the thing is, they're not firing a shot to do that. I have a much more European view of the way the world should be.

"I don't know when socialism became a bad word. When is it evil to care about your fellow human being? Bush has said that one of his heroes was Teddy Roosevelt. 'Walk softly and carry a big stick'. Well, that's not bad advice. But we don't walk softly. We walk very loudly. And we're swingin' a big stick. I cringe every time 'Dubya' gets up there and says democracies are peaceful societies. Iraq didn't invade us!"

The presidential election? I knew it was going to be close...

"My hats off to Carl Rove. The man's a diabolical genius. He knew it was going to come down to Ohio. They knew that they could play the gay card, that people are homophobic. For the life of me, I don't know how homosexuals can mess up marriage worse than heterosexuals can."

Education?

"A country that wants to guarantee a class society is the only one that cuts education. Education is not the great equalizer, it's the only one."

Gun control?

"Our country is still relatively young. It's going to take us another 100 years before we don't see handguns as a good thing. It's unfortunate that it takes some people to be personally afflicted before they can be compassionate. I think of Brady and gun control, Nancy Reagan and stem cell research, Steve Buyer and Gulf War Syndrome..."

Pipe dreams?

"I'd love to refurbish The Palo (indoor movie theater sitting idle in Lowell) and make it into a community theater."

The life of a trucker?

"You know, it's like one of those refrigerator magnet quips, 'I didn't know what I wanted to be when I grew up, but I know it wasn't this.' I don't hate the job anymore. I try to find the interesting things about it. Right now, it's the best way I can support my family. I've been on the road for 20 years.

"I did have a delivery to the Grand Canyon. Dad had semis that were leased to this company called Hunt's Super Service out of Kankakee (Ill.). They were in 48 states. In a period of a couple years I was in 40 of them. I never went anyplace for the first time and not love it."

* * *

So, if ever you're in Beaners, and you spot a burly, beer-bellied brute with a pack of Lucky Strikes rolled up in the sleeve of his gravy-stained T-shirt, revealing a heart tattoo in memory of Mom, while washing down a handful of bennies with a cup of mud; be assured, it's not Travis.

My friend is the trucker tooling down I-65, 80-94, or Cline Avenue, keeping an eye on the road while hauling a volatile, virtual bomb directly behind him. He told me hauling steel bars and coils was even more dangerous.

Envision him listening to Nation Public Radio and savoring a cup of cappuccino while musing about human rights. The Grand Canyon, maybe.

Ken Travis keeps on truckin'.

Dorine Godinez *(May 2007)*

"I would rather die standing up, than live life on my knees."
- Emiliano Zapata

The Kankakee River, she leads me upstream toward her little sister; the Yellow River in Starke County... .

Dorine and Jesus Godinez live in Knox. Dorine works in East Chicago. She has made the 78-mile drive (one way) for 13 years now. She was born Dorine Barbara Hendrick in East Chicago 50 years ago.

* * *

"I spent most of my youth between East Chicago, Hammond, Gary, and the Chesapeake Bay area in Virginia," Godinez began. "By the time I was 18, I had attended 22 schools, most of those several times each. I was the oldest of six children.

"Jesus and I had both been married before. When we met, he had three children of his own and I had two. We also raised six of my sister's children, plus four other children for parts of their lives."

Did your sister pass away?

"For a while. Then, they brought her back to life at St. Margaret's Hospital. She was air-lifted to Christ Hospital in Illinois where she remained in a coma for a month. She woke up on Christmas Day. My sister was hit by a car. She's in a nursing home."

You graduated an East Chicago Roosevelt Rough Rider, class of '76. Then what?

"I worked as a secretary for the East Chicago Administrative Office by day and Shrimp Harbor by night.

"I saw an ad in the newspaper: 'Are you a woman? Have you ever thought of doing something for a living that most women would never consider, like driving a truck or working as a mechanic?' Well, I knew that was me. I had worked long hours, but no matter how hard a woman worked or how much a woman knew, her pay and benefits could not compare to the salaries men were making in those days. Even a man without a clue could earn enough to raise his family in most cases."

Continue, please.

"I attended classes by and for women in the basement of a house in the old historic section of Hammond in Harrison Park. I hired into the labor gang of Inland Steel's 24-inch Bar Mill back in June of '78. There, I painted, shoveled, and used a jackhammer. I weighed 102 pounds. With a pitch fork, I turned red hot bars coming out the furnace like fresh crusted bread from an oven. Large welts from the intense heat would remain on my neck for days. I eventually got an electrical apprenticeship."

All my children?

"My home in Gary wouldn't fit all the children. In this area, there's no gang for 45 minutes in any direction. We had as many as 14 kids here at once. Everybody helped. They all learned to cook, wash dishes, and mow grass. Thanksgiving or Christmas, it was like an assembly line. They learned how to build a roof – girls and guys. When you have that many people in the house, there is no other way to survive. The downside, that many teenagers can be very expensive."

Are you going to work more than 30 years in the mill?

"Yes, I like working. And I like learning. I made this guitar for Jesus at career development classes. I can't sit around and do nothing. I need to try to make a difference."

Who is the photo of hanging above the mantel?

"He was one of my sister's children that I helped raise. He was living with another sister of mine when he was robbed and murdered on Guthrie Street in East Chicago. His brother also was shot, but survived. The police caught all of the guys who did it; they're all in jail. He was such a good boy. Sixteen years old... ."

Religious beliefs?

"Jesus is Catholic. I'm Baptist. We made sure all the children went to church. We told them they need to put God first, health second. If you don't take care of yourself, you're not going to be able to help anybody else."

A major turning point in your life?

"I attended the Midwest School For Women in Milwaukee for a week. I needed a vacation – a break. I didn't get any break. But it changed my life. I met women from all over the world wanting to make good changes."

People you've looked up to?

"Off the top of my head; Abraham Lincoln, Josephine Brooks, Jim Robinson, Betty Balanoff, Sal and Louie Aguilar, Ruth Needleman, Linda Chavez, Brother Jack Hyles from Hammond Baptist, and my husband."

Parents?

"My mother's maiden name was Martinez. She helped put a good work ethic in her daughters. She came from a large family. Her parents made her quit school. They told her women didn't need education; men would support them.

"My mother begged to go to school but to no avail. She worked two jobs – at a Laundromat and a restaurant. She had to give her parents seven of the eight paychecks she earned every month. She got married; she took care of us."

Your father?

"He was a drunk and a womanizer. He also was very intelligent. I saw alcohol destroy my father and my family. There came a time when I thought there was no hope. That he'd gone too bad.

"But my father did change. He gave me his coin for 25 years of sobriety. That was my inheritance from him. That was very important to me, because through it all, I thought the world revolved around my father. He was able to help others. That's what it's all about, right? Finding yourself. Helping make change. Making a difference."

* * *

As a little girl, she said the electricity was turned off a lot. She would later become an electrician. She is currently a union training coordinator. She is also the chairwoman for human and civil rights for United Steelworkers Local 1010. She founded Women of Steel. President Bill Clinton invited her to the Northwest Economic Council Meetings for Families. If given the chance, she will work to help Bill Clinton's wife become President of the United States.

Dorine knows something about firsts; she was the first woman to be elected to the union griever position at Local 1010.

It took 100 years.

Chris Wilk *(Jan. 2010)*

"...If I do not stop to help the sanitation workers, what will happen to them?"
– The Rev. Martin Luther King, Jr.,
April 1968, Memphis, Tenn.

Chris Wilk lives in a gorgeous 3,200-square-foot home in Wheatfield with a finished 1,200-square-foot basement. He and his wife, Gina, also have acreage. Their back yard features a gigantic swing set, sand box and an in-ground trampoline for their 9-year-old son, Ben.

Wilk, 36, can afford it; he pulls down $80,000-plus per year with benefits.

He's a garbage man.

* * *

"I grew up in Crown Point," Wilk began. "I wrestled (at 125 pounds) for Crown Point High School."

Chris, wrestling for coach Scott Vlink's Bulldogs might be part of the reason you can endure the job you do. Talk to me.

"I'm a commercial front-load driver for Waste Management. I work out of the Portage shop. I do gas stations, restaurants, the malls..."

Do you have a partner?

"No, everybody works by themselves now, whether you're on a commercial or residential route.

"When I started, I was on the back of a rear loader, pitching. It took 15 years of 'throwing homes' before I was able to get a commercial route."

Do move-ups go by seniority?

"Oh, yeah. Age-wise, I'm still the youngest guy there. But I'm about in the middle as far as seniority."

Union?

"Teamsters Local 142 out of Gary. That's why I make the drive. I could get a job closer to home, but with the union, I make better money.

"I usually work about 56 hours per week. The Indiana Department of Transportation won't permit us to work any more than 60."

Where do your routes take you?

"Gary, Griffith and Highland. I usually start work at 4 a.m.; today, I started at 3 a.m. Nobody goes home until all the garbage is off the ground, whether the delay is because of a breakdown or inclement weather. I also have to clean up my truck at the end of the day."

Injuries?

"I laid my leg open on one of those thick plates that go inside a microwave. It was inside a plastic garbage bag. I still have the scar, but I patched myself up and finished the route. Waste Management really focuses on safety, which is good; it keeps me disciplined."

Odd occurrences on the job?

"(One place) in Highland had an eight-yard can that always was overloaded. I couldn't get to it without picking up refuse off the ground and tossing it back into the box."

Yeah?

"All of a sudden, the garbage started flying back at me."

Raccoons don't normally throw things.

"A dirty man wearing a tight, black dress jumped out at me. It was like 4 a.m. Kinda freaked me out."

What did you do?

"I got back in my truck and hit the rest of the complex so he'd have a chance to gather his worldly possessions from the can before I dumped it. I think he was living in there.

"And there was the day I lost my 'pop stop' in Merrillville."

Pop stop?

"I'd been doing that particular route for a long time. There was an old man who took a liking to me. Every time I'd pick up his garbage, he'd have a can of pop waiting for me.

"Sometimes, older people look for you. He had a vacant lot next to his house where he'd dump his grass. When I got there, his mower was running, but he was nowhere around."

Yeah?

"I wanted my soda. I started calling out his name, then I saw him in the vacant lot; he was blue. It must have just happened; his wife was inside the house; I phoned for help, but he was already dead."

Poor old fella. Chris, let's switch gears. Tell me about some of the fringe benefits.

"If I want something, I'll have the customer put it aside and go back for it. I have a pickup and a trailer. I've salvaged lawn tractors, Weedeaters, a 60-year-old Schwinn bicycle built for two... .

"Some people can be very wasteful. In this household, we recycle and also keep a compost pile for our garden."

You said you push a button after every stop to compress your load. What happens to the remaining garbage?

"We had a landfill in Wheeler, but it's full. Same with the one in Michigan City. Now, I take my loads to our transfer in Gary on 15th Avenue, where it's loaded into tractor-trailers and taken down south."

The smell?

"You get used to it or ignore it. Nothing really grosses me out. Don't get me wrong; it's there. The maggots are bad in the summer."

Winter?

"This Christmas Eve was one of the worst – the ice. My nerves were shot. My truck weighs 20 tons empty. You're within inches of power lines. I also have to thaw out the locks and latches of the enclosures on my commercial route with a torch."

Occupational pet peeves?

"People seem to love to park in front of Dumpsters; that's how I met you last summer at Glen Park Academy."

Sorry.

"When I first started, I was like, 'Man, I don't know if I want to do this for a living.' Now, 18 years later, I'm proud to say I work for 'Waste.'"

* * *

Chris Wilk is a hard worker who is living proof that one man's garbage is another man's treasure.

And I'm glad to have met him.

Elizabeth Myers *(March 2008)*

"...Lions and tigers and bears – oh my!..."
- Dorothy Gale

Goose feather snowflakes paint my windshield. It's a February afternoon and I'm driving along that 25-mile stretch of Highway 12 connecting I-65 and Michigan City. My destination is Washington Park Zoological Gardens nestled along Lake Michigan's sandy shore. My interview is with zookeeper Elizabeth Myers. She is 29 years of age, engaged to be wed, and a native of Michigan who now resides in Michigan City.

* * *

"I take care of the large carnivores and omnivores," Myers began. "My job title is general curator of the zoo."

Is the zoo closed to the public right now?

"Yes, we closed Nov.1 and we'll reopen April 1."

How long has the Washington Park Zoological Gardens been here?

"Since 1928. We had 69,000 visitors last year."

Did you go to school to be a zookeeper?

"Actually, I didn't. I applied for a seasonal position back 2000. As a seasonal keeper you don't work with the large exotics that much. Mostly, I started out working with birds of prey and in the pet barn area where we have our domestic stock, but that's how I got my foot in the door. Since I've been working here, I've been sent to classes through the AZA (American Zoological Association).

"Besides the big cats, I also look after the aviary and the hoof stock animals such as the zebras. There are actually five full-time zookeepers here now. We divide the duties up."

What are some of the duties?

"We clean up after them, give them fresh feed, and look them over to make sure nobody is sick. Each zookeeper is responsible for a certain area every day."

Job safety must be a concern.

"We will go into the cage with some animals like the ring-tailed lemurs and bobcats. But we have protected contact with the more dangerous animals like the baboons and tigers, which means we can touch them or manipulate them through the bars, but we'll never be in the cage with them.

"My Bengal tigers were bottle babies. They like to play like any other animal. But we cease going in the cage with them once they develop the habit of wanting to stalk you. We don't want to show the public that it's okay to have them as pets. You cannot believe their muscle mass."

Have you ever been injured?

"Yeah, I've been bitten by parrots and prairie dogs, and scratched by a cougar. Nothing serious."

Liz, what was the name of that famous alligator guy who died a while back?

"Steve Irwin. Come on, the crocodile hunter on Animal Planet! He was my hero. Steve had an awesome way of teaching people about animals."

Forgive me; I don't watch much TV these days. Used to like Mutual of Omaha's Wild Kingdom with Marlin Perkins. Yeah, ol' Mar-

lin would call the play by play while sipping on a banana daiquiri from the shade of a tent while his aide de camp, Jim Fowler, wrestled rhinos in heat or was being suffocated by a 30-foot long boa constrictor the diameter of a large oak tree.

"Marlin who?"

It's a generational thing. Elizabeth, I realize you get up close to the animals, but do you become close emotionally? I mean, like someone who would mourn the loss of their cocker spaniel to an age-related illness?

"Yes. I'm with these animals every single day. You build a relationship with them. Maggie, my lioness, is going to be 19. You wouldn't know it by looking at her – she's as playful as a kitten."

A very big kitty. Do they all have names?

"Yeah, I can't call Maggie 'MO87205.'"

Is there anything here at the zoo that kind of creeps you out?

"I'm not too crazy about the hissing cockroaches."

Liz, I've never been too fond of spiders. Nothing should have eight legs – let alone eight eyes! Tell me more about the two Bengal tigers. How much do the they weigh?

"None of our scales at the zoo are big enough to weigh them. The biggest scale maxes out at 300 pounds. I'd guess they weigh about 500 pounds each. Stars and Stripes are five year-old twin brothers.

"All of our big cats eat once a day. Each tiger gets about 11 pounds of food. But we do have fasting days. They also get a big beef leg bone once a week with some meat and gristle on it which is like us brushing our teeth.

"I've had people tell me they've seen tigers on TV, but when they see them eye to eye, hear them chuffing, smell them –"

Chuffing?

"It's how they say hello. It's not a purr. Big cats can't purr. They do it to each other. I chuff at them and they chuff right back, 'How is it going?' 'Everything's alright.'

"The animals are not here at the zoo just to be displayed or to educate the public. A lot of people come to the zoos and don't realize we have enrichment programs for these animals. They are getting top quality care with top-notch diets fed to them. We offer them things to play with to stimulate their minds and bring out their natural behaviors and instincts. They are not just rotting away in their cages. We try to make their lives enjoyable. With the exception of the bears, these animals have never been in the wild."

There are those who do not approve of circuses, county fairs and zoos. What's the story on the two grizzlies?

"They were going to be euthanized. And, yes, there are radicals who will say they would have been better off killed than brought to the zoo. Visitors are only separated from these girls by an inch of glass. It's our new exhibit. They're from Montana.

"The Department of Fish and Game out there had relocated their mother about five or six times. She had a radio collar. She was a problem bear, getting into people's farms and feed barns. She taught her cubs to do the same thing. The mother eventually was euthanized. The girls were eight months old at the time. Anything under a year, officials try to place. If a home hadn't been found for them they were destined to be euthanized as well. They are about five years old now.

"Some of these animals are highly endangered. Zoos have breeding programs; we try to reintroduce species back into the wild. We have a species survival plan. We're trying to get the gene pool as authentic as we can. There's only a few tigers left out there. And their numbers keep dwindling.

"I'd like to do this for the rest of my life. It doesn't seem like work, being around the animals everyday."

* * *

Elizabeth Myers. Tending creatures great and small.

John Gelon *(Aug. 2005)*

*"...Shithouse poets nom de plume.
Ladies wearin' cheap perfume.
Inland Steel Christmas trees.
Occasional fatalities.
Plant Protection. Staff Infection.
Fall protection. No direction.
General foreman at the door...
'Is this home of Widow Parr?'
'I'm no widow.'
'Now you are.'
'Woman don't you cry, don't you stew,
in time we take your pension too...'*
– Jeff Manes, from the poem "Thirty" (years in the mill)

Labor Day nears. I opt to interview a union safety advocate by the name of John Gelon.

Gelon, 45, lives north of Lowell in a beautiful house on a lake with his wife Gina and their dog, Buddy.

It hasn't always been so cozy for John Gelon. There was a day when he stood alone watching five feet of Little Calumet River water flow into his slab home in Highland. His first wife had left him a month before. Insurance didn't cover the house's contents nor the destruction of his vehicle.

Without a car and homeless, Gelon lived out of a Coleman cooler and a Weber barbeque grill. Life's experiences have taught him to appreciate what he has.

We've known each other for a quarter of a century. We met in the bowels of Inland Steel – #2 Coke Plant. We've fished, drank beer,

played ball, and sweat blood together. The coke battery was hell.
You had to be there.

* * *

Thanks for the Zel's Roast Beef, my friend. Reminds me of our younger days.

"Picked 'em up in Crown Point. Not quite the same taste as the Zel's in East Chicago."

You're right, the Harbor had flavor. John, your fish tanks look great. They really do. Shedd Aquarium has nothin' on handsome John Gelon. It's like being at Sea World down here.

"Thanks, Jeff. And please don't call me handsome John Gelon in the newspaper."

You have my word on it. How did it go in the steel mill today?

"Safety training. I do it two or three days a week. Jeff, I always tell everybody, 'You are your own last line of defense.'"

Brother, I could use a laugh. What's one of the tougher comments or questions they've thrown at you? I know there's some real characters out there in the mill.

"The toughest question? I've had 1,200 people come through for safety training in 73 eight-hour classes. I was talking about railroad safety one day, and a guy actually asked who had the right of way, him or the train. After a moment of silence, I remembered what they taught me in training, 'There are no stupid questions.'"

There'll be a moment of silence all right – for him, if he fails to yield for one of those remote-controlled locomotives.

"One of the questions I ask is, 'How many of you lock out and verify every time you get in a position where you could be injured by an unexpected start-up or energizing of equipment or machinery?' Jeff, only 177 out of 740 said they locked out and verified every time. Yes, management has to provide a safe workplace for us; that's the law. But we have responsibilities, too."

Johnny, what do you think conditions would be like if there were no union?

"It would be much worse. The worker has to stand up to management and say, 'This is unsafe, I can't do the job unless we make it safe.' Management might choose to send them home; sometimes they consider that insubordination. The union calls it asking for safety relief. More often than not, we get them paid. Without the union, there would be no safety relief."

How many workers have lost their lives at Inland Steel?

"There have been 387 fatalities since 1903. That doesn't include outside contractors."

Last fatality?

"June 5, 2004. Tony Parker fell at 2 BOF working on an unprotected ledge. We fought with management for 18 months; people kept going up there working, and then Parker falls."

I bet the company has hand railing now.

"They got hand railing now."

* * *

Three John Gelons have worked for what is now known as MittalSteel, my friend, his father, and his grandfather. John was not named after his dad, he was named after his grandfather. An old yellowed newspaper clipping explains... .

"The face of John Gelon, of 3515 Hemlock Street, Indiana Harbor, was in grins as he reported to work at Inland Steel Company, March 30, 1946. Early that morning, his wife had given birth to a third son at St Catherine Hospital. John was still getting congratulatory pats on the back at noon. At 12:30 p.m., John Gelon, #10654, a 39-year old pipe fitter leader, was carrying four lengths of half-inch pipe, south on the west side of the 76-inch Hot Strip mill roller line. Gelon walked through a cloud of steam and stepped into a hole where floor plates had been removed. He fell into a conveyor, then into a crop box containing about five feet of water – 200 degrees Fahrenheit. Deputy Coroner John L. Zivich said he was scalded or suffocated by the steam. A plant spokesman stated the victim was the first plant fatality in almost seven months. He is survived by his widow Anna, two daughters, Margaret and Verna, and three sons, John Jr, Richard, and an infant, unnamed. Compensation paid $7,026. Gelon was employed with Inland Steel for 20 years."

John once told me that his father turned 16 shortly after his grandfather was killed. Being the eldest child, John's dad quit school and took a job at Inland Steel to support his brothers and sisters. The owners back then, the Block family, guaranteed any member of the Gelon family employment.

On her hands and knees, the widow Gelon scrubbed floors at Inland Steel's main office.

Larry Hine *(Feb. 2010)*

"It's too bad that all the people who know how to run the country are busy driving taxi cabs and cutting hair."
–George Burns

It is a testament to my faith in mankind that I can enter that bastion of conservatism, Crown Point, exit my car with its Obama bumper sticker, and while sporting a White Sox sweatshirt, allow an ultraconservative Cub fan to wield razor-sharp instruments near my jugular vein.

But, Larry Hine, proprietor of Larry's Barber Shop, is a friend of my brother, also a self-employed conservative from Crown Point.

Hine, 69, lives on the section of Indiana 55 between Lowell and Crown Point known as the "Nine-Mile Stretch." He has a Lowell phone number.

Larry and Pat Hine have been married 48 years and have raised five children.

* * *

"While in high school, my parents moved to Lake County from Starke County," Hine began.

What part of Starke County?

"San Pierre; it was a self-sufficient little town back then. It had two grocery stores, a couple of restaurants, a hardware store, lumberyard, butcher shop... . The two bars are still there; they always survive.

"My first job was at age 11 – weeding pine tree seedlings for 25 cents per hour at Jasper-Pulaski state nursery."

San Pierre probably had a barber shop.

"Two of them; my father was a barber in the late '20s and early '30s, but he slipped on the ice and ran his hand through a window. That kind of took care of his barbering career.

"I graduated from Lowell High School in 1960, worked that summer to save up some money, then began attending Weeden's Barber College at 1231 W. Madison Street in Chicago."

A few blocks from old Chicago Stadium; that was a rough neighborhood.

"That was skid row. Twice, I found guys lying dead in the alley, which kinda freaked me out; I was just a country boy.

"As of a few years ago, there wasn't a barber college in Chicago. The barbering trade went downhill; nobody wanted to be a barber."

But you've remained in the business through thick and thin.

"It'll be 50 years this August. From the time I was a sophomore in high school, I wanted to be a barber. My dad told me: 'You're never going to get rich being a barber, but you'll always be able to feed your family.' He told me, 'People will always need a haircut.' Well, my dad died in the late 1960s."

Yeah?

"Nobody got a haircut from 1970 to 1980. It was tough; I was trying to raise five kids. I worked as a carpenter for my father-in-law on my days off for a couple of years. After that, I worked for my neighbor who was a concrete contractor for about eight years until 1980."

Any quirky occurrences through the years, while lowering a man's ears?

"I had a guy come knocking at the door after hours; I always closed at 4 p.m. on Saturdays."

Go on?

"He was very persistent; he also was bombed. He slurred, 'I have to get a haircut.'

"I said, 'We're closed.'"

"'It's a matter of life and death.'"

"'Life and death?'"

"'I left the house at 8 o'clock this morning to get a haircut; if I don't come home with a haircut, my wife's gonna (hiccup) kill me.'"

What did you do?

"I said, 'Come on in.'

"He snored through the entire haircut. I woke him up, he paid me, and I never saw him again. Maybe his wife did kill him, I don't know."

The significance of the striped pole.

"The red and white represents blood and bandages; the blue signifies veins. In the Middle Ages, hair was not the only thing that barbers cut; they performed surgery, tooth extractions and blood letting."

Speaking of blood letting, do you still get requests for shaves?

"No, I haven't had to hone and strop my straight razor for 20 years; I just display these razor straps for old time's sake."

You charge $11 for a haircut today; how much did you charge back in the summer of '62?

"Two bucks."

Compared to a lot of things, $9 isn't that great of an increase in nearly 50 years.

"A guy came in here the other day saying he paid $17 for a regular haircut in Munster. We've kind of fallen behind here in Crown Point."

Larry, your place really has flavor with all the novelties, knick-knacks, words of wisdom and witticisms on the walls. I mean, you've got it all – everything from 'Big-Mouth Billy Bass' to an original Ron Santo Bobblehead to a fake drake mallard that quacks the question, "Did somebody step on a duck?"

What happened to this signed 8-by-10 photograph of this extremely attractive woman? Some of her teeth have been blackened out?

"The brat who did that isn't allowed in here anymore."

I couldn't help but notice this particular piece of advice: "I'd rather hunt with Dick Cheney than ride with Ted Kennedy."

"I'm an ultraconservative member of the National Rifle Association who enjoys upland game hunting. Here's a photo of the last time I went bird hunting -- killed three quail on that covey rise. What about you?"

Larry, I display my Limbaugh bumper sticker with pride. Go Cubbies!

* * *

Larry Hine considers himself luckier than most people because he really loves what he does for a living; he will continue to cut hair as long as his health permits.

Carlos Aburto *(May 2010)*

*"In a world where you can be anything,
try being yourself."*
-Author unknown

While coaching boys cross country at Highland High School, Carlos Aburto brought his Trojan horses once came to "our house," Lowell High School, and dethroned my Red Devil harriers by one point for the Lake Athletic Conference championship.

It was a tough pill to swallow, but if our team was going to get beat, I'm glad it was a blue-collar coach like Aburto who did the job on us.

Aburto, 51, lives in Highland with Kathy, his wife of 24 years. Carlos is the father of four; his youngest just graduated from Highland High School and will attend Purdue University in West Lafayette on a full academic scholarship.

Aburto has worked for the East Chicago Fire Department for 21 years; I interviewed him at his parents' house on Homerlee Avenue in E.C.

* * *

Always lived in Highland?

"I was born in the Harbor (section of East Chicago)," Aburto said. "Then, my dad moved us to the Brunswick neighborhood of Gary. He built a house there with his own two hands; it's still standing. I'm very proud of that. We eventually moved to this house in '74, so I could attend Bishop Noll. My dad worked very hard to put five of us through Noll."

Where did your father work?

"For Inland (Steel Co.). He was at No. 2 Open Hearth for a good portion of his career, but ended up being a millwright at the blast furnace. He was a minimally educated man who made a lot of himself. He had a very traditional work ethic and can count on one hand the days of work he missed in 35 years."

Carlos, it sounds like you're talking about my dad.

"Right out of high school, I worked at Republic Steel in Chicago for 10 years; I was trying to raise a family, but kept getting laid off."

What did you do?

"While laid off, I worked for Marshall Fields at River Oaks (shopping center in Calumet City, Ill.); I was a ladies shoe salesman."

I can picture you doing that.

"Yeah, that was a great job. In '84, I answered an ad to become a flight attendant for TWA and worked there for five years."

I can't picture you doing that.

"But in '89, I got the chance to become a firefighter for the city of East Chicago. It was my calling. I took a $10,000 cut in pay."

As a boy, did you want to be a firefighter?

"Actually, no. I never thought of being a firefighter. However, I always wanted to do something honorable for a living, I've found that with the fire service. It's been a privilege to serve the community. I can't say enough about the brotherhood we share – the tradition of the fire department."

Job description?

"I'm a maintenance chief; I take care of all our rigs by scheduling servicing. I'm also in charge of the upkeep of four firehouses and the grounds. Early on, I was a chauffeur before promoting myself to captain."

Chauffeur?

"The engineer or the driver of the apparatus. It's a very important job. He has to know the territory; get you there safely and provide water for suppression without interruption while the crew is inside beating a fire."

You mentioned promoting yourself to captain.

"We test out for our promotions. And through attrition, we move up. It's very fair."

Union?

"Absolutely; Local 365 represents our firemen. I served as president of Local 365 from '94 until '00.

"I'd say our department is probably progressively the best in the area; I'm biased, of course. But I've seen my guys in action. There is nothing they can't do or won't attempt to saves lives and property. I say that with a lot of pride."

Carlos, I've been involved in a few fires and explosions in the mill where men died. My hat goes off to you guys.

"In my opinion, firefighters have a rough exterior, but, at the end of the day the reason why we do it is because we're compassionate people and we want to serve."

And you have to continue to stay in shape.

"I've always been a fitness-orientated guy. Anything that would get my sweat up, I'd try."

You've been to known to spar in the ring.

"Yeah, that was in the '80s. But for the most part, I stayed in shape by training for marathons and running road races."

What are your personal bests for the marathon and half marathon?

"I ran a 2:56 and a 1:11 when I was in my early 30s."

You've been boys cross country coach at Highland for the past decade and served as the Trojan's assistant track coach for the last eight years. The kids today?

"As a whole, we're living in era of obesity in this nation. There's a lot of distractions for kids: iPods, iPhones, all kinds of electronic devices.

"I believe it's a detriment; they don't experience a lot of the things that you and I did, like sandlot baseball, pick-up basketball games – just hanging out and socializing face to face without a cell phone."

Did you say something? I was texting a friend.

"Jeff, I was in an antique shop in Sullivan a few weeks ago, and there was this saying on the wall that read: 'In a world where you can be anything, try being yourself.' That really touched me because that's how I see life.

"When you work with teenagers, identity is a big thing. They're not always sure of themselves; sometimes their self-esteem is low. If you can help as a coach to facilitate some of that confidence and character, they quickly find out who they are."

Any final thoughts about your full-time job?

"We find a lot of humor among ourselves; maybe that helps keep us level-headed. We see a lot of tragedy and heartache. You have to know how to process that, how to bounce back for the next call."

It has to be very tough at times.

"It's not for everybody. I remember when I was a young firefighter. There was a head-on collision between two automobiles; I got to one of the cars first. While evaluating the situation, I saw a woman and a boy in the front seat, then, I spotted an infant on the floorboard in the back. I reached down to find a pulse and I thought I had one."

And?

"I shouted out to the medic, 'Hey, we gotta pulse here!' He reached down, and then looked up at me, and matter-of-factly replied, 'No, we don't.'

"That was a reality check. I didn't want to believe that baby was dead. I did not want to believe that. It was my first real initiation of what I'd signed up for. The job entails more than just putting the wet stuff on the red stuff."

* * *

Carlos Aburto said he didn't grow up with thoughts of becoming a firefighter.

I say, he was born to be a firefighter.

Ken Burbridge *(Feb. 2012)*

Evelyn Mulwray: "Hollis seems to think you're an innocent man."

Jake Gittes: Well, I've been accused of a lot things before, Mrs. Mulwray, but never that."

– from the 1974 film "Chinatown"

Ken Burbridge is a hard-edged private dick who has seen it all. He's the president of Burbridge Detective Agency.

Burbridge's Merrillville office is located on the second floor of what looks like a mob apartment; there are large rooms all around him with nothing in them.

Burbridge, 45, is married and lives in an unincorporated area near Valparaiso. He doesn't like to detail his personal life because he's received several death threats through the years.

* * *

Did you grow up around here?

"Yeah, I went to Lake Central (High School)," he said.

College?

"I attended St. Joseph's College in Rensselaer and Calumet College in Whiting. I have a degree in criminal justice and business management."

Were you ever a police officer?

"Yes, I was a Lansing, (Ill.) police officer for about four years. From there, I got into corporate security; I supervised a staff of 14 guards for NiSource."

When did you go into business for yourself?

"January of 2000. When I first got into this business, it was mostly workman's comp cases. As the years went by, the market kind of dried up. The insurance companies started using their own employees instead of an outside firm like mine."

Other types of work you do?

"Background checks, surveillance, people searches, skip tracing, process service and criminal, civil and domestic investigations. I also locate witnesses for attorneys and fugitives for bounty hunters."

Surveillance?

"Surveillance can be boring. I remember sitting in a car more than 30 hours straight... There's an art to surveillance; it's not just watching people.

"I get a lot of employee theft cases. Parking by an exit door; that's a flag. It's usually a supervisor – someone who can drive in and out at will."

What takes up most of your work time?

"Right now, my main business is background checks all over the United States, Pakistan, Afghanistan, United Kingdom... . I do background checks on refinery and utility workers for security purposes.

"About one out of every 20 background checks somebody is using somebody else's Social Security number. It's usually illegal immigrants trying to find a job. I do a lot of background checks in Texas."

You probably use video equipment quite a bit.

"Yeah, up until a few years ago, we were still using 8 millimeter. Now, we have the HD cameras. I can zoom in from a quarter-mile away. I don't even have to be on the block and can be videotaping you."

Cases of infidelity?

"Those are usually interesting cases. When you're dealing with domestic issues, you have a lot of emotion involved. I've had some unusual cases."

I'm all ears.

"I had a case in the area where the husband claimed he was playing in a band, while the wife was staying at home with the kid. She told me she needed me to follow him at certain times. She said: 'I don't know what he's doing; he's coming home late. He's getting strange phone calls.'

"I followed him to Chicago about 2 a.m. and videotaped him. It didn't take us too long to realize he was a drug dealer. We had a couple scary moments because he caught us and chased us – him and his buddy and one of his 'clients,' but we lost them."

What did the wife have to say?

"I told her, 'Lady, I have some bad news.' She said: 'Oh, no. Who is he seeing?' I explained, 'It's not who he's seeing, it's what he's doing. I want you to watch this video; your husband is dealing drugs.' She said: 'But is he cheating?' She was OK with the fact that he was a drug dealer as long as wasn't cheating on her."

Hell hath no fury.

"Cheaters are pretty easy to figure; they're always going to go to a meeting place. They fall into patterns. They're usually both married. They like to use their cell phones.

"But the technology for that has gotten more sophisticated, too. We have software to see where phones are at; we have GPS vehicles. Now, there are GSM bugs. They're illegal bugs with a cell chip. You dial the phone number to your bug and then you can listen on your cell phone. You can get them in China."

Privacy laws?

"You can take video as long as you're on public property. For instance, if someone is in the back yard and they have an open fence, I can videotape the person from the street. But, let's say this person has a privacy fence and I actually have to climb a tree to videotape (him or her); that would be illegal."

Employees?

"I have three or four people I use as needed. For surveillance, I use off-duty police officers. For investigations, police officers are the worst. The best person for investigation work is someone with a background in sales. A salesperson makes a great P.I. A cop will help you in a surveillance car and can deal with confrontations. When you serve people they're never happy."

Serve people?

"Things like court documents or evictions. You get more information when you're a salesperson. You have to get them to believe you're on their side; then, they open up. Jeff, as a reporter, you understand that."

Ken, I always wanted to be a sleazy, wisecracking sleuth. Live fast, die young, and make a good lookin' corpse.

"Cops can come off as abrasive. It's like a me-against-you thing. People seem to shut down during an interview with cops. It can really be touchy, especially when you're working on, say, a child molesting case."

Explain, please.

"Some of the questions you have to ask. First of all, it's very difficult to investigate something like that. Your schools aren't going to talk to you; they're not allowed. The police, during investigations, aren't going to tell you how the case is going."

Do you make a pretty good buck at this gig?

"You don't make much money; it's a living. Anybody who thinks they're going to get rich being a P.I. is nuts. The normal rate in Indiana is about $45 per hour."

Are you licensed to carry a gun?

"Yes, I have a SIG Sauer semi-automatic 9 mm concealed as we speak. I've had to draw a few times. For example, I served a guy, and he came at me with a baseball bat. I told him that he better not come any closer with the bat or I'd have to do something."

* * *

Burbridge also mentioned the perils of not doing a background check regarding internet dating. He told me he received a call from a woman who was dating a guy she'd met online. Ten minutes later, the same woman called Burbridge again saying she changed her mind about the background check on her new boyfriend.

She said, "I gotta trust him; that's what a relationship is all about – trust."

Burbridge told her, "Look, lady, you got kids."

He talked her into running the check. The guy turned out to be a convicted sexual molester who was in the registry.

Fly Rod Jimmy *(Aug. 2012)*

"...Tell them to be patient and ask death for speed; for they are all there but one – I, Chingachgook – last of the Mohicans..."
– James Fenimore Cooper

James Anthony Manes, 81, lives in Lake Village with his companion of nearly 30 years, Nadia D'Apice.

During the Korean War, Manes was a gunner in the 58th Field Artillery, 3rd Division. He also is a retired steel worker and a lifelong outdoorsman who spends his winters in Florida fly fishing and playing Texas Hold 'em.

And, "Jimmy" Manes, is my dad.

* * *

"When I was 5, we moved from Chicago to Lake Village," Manes began. "It was hard times; we lost our home in Chicago. My father gathered up what money he had and bought 38 acres for $19 per acre. He built a house out of whatever he could get a hold of so we'd have something to live in."

You always said Grandpa Vito could do anything with his hands. How old was he when he emigrated from Italy?

"About 10."

What part of Chicago did the family come from?

"Around 87th (Street) & Cottage Grove (Avenue). It was a neighborhood known as Burnside which was filled with nice little brick bungalows. My maternal grandfather, Genaro DeBartolo, resided in the Grand Crossing neighborhood of Chicago. Grandpa 'Jim' outlived three wives."

Growing up during the Great Depression?

"Your grandfather didn't believe in welfare; he was too proud. I remember when a school lunch was a dime. It was 4 cents for the main dish, 3 cents for dessert, and 3 cents for the drink. There were times when Ma could only dole out the 4 cents each for all us kids.

"It wasn't so much being a little hungry; it was the embarrassment of not having the full meal like the kids whose parents had money or were on relief."

That had to be tough, living on the outskirts of Lake Village, near the state line.

"We didn't know what a chainsaw was. Believe me, your Uncle Mike and I spent our weekends wearing out crosscut saws and double-bit axes. My poor mother did all the cooking on a wood stove – no coal."

Lake Village, post-World War II?

"Our town was really prosperous; we had three grocery stores, three or four gas stations... . Old U.S. 41 went right through the middle of Lake Village. When they moved the highway, all the small towns like Lake Village and Schneider went dead. Right now, we're lucky to have one grocery store."

Let's switch gears. You remember seeing prairie chickens while hunting as a young man.

"There were two places that still had prairie chickens back in the 1940s. Jarvis' farm near the Raff Ranch and Iry Porter's place about five or six miles southeast of here. You couldn't shoot them; they were almost completely extirpated by then. They looked like a hen pheasant with a short tail."

You befriended one of the last of the market hunters.

"Carl Mattocks from Roselawn; he was in his late 60s when I was a teenager. Some of those guys killed ducks by the wagon loads. Carl told me they'd get a quarter for large ducks and 15 cents for small ones.

"Carl once took me duck hunting at his brother's place on the Wabash River. We were setting out decoys when a big flock of mallards flew by and landed in the water not too far from us. Carl said, 'Jimmy, you get on the far side of those ducks and maybe you'll be able to sneak in there and get a shot off.'"

Then what?

"I must have spooked them while trying to walk through the tall weeds and brush. The ducks flew toward Carl."

And?

"Well, Carl always carried his duck plug in the front pocket of his vest in case a game warden showed up."

A duck plug prevents a hunter from loading more than three shells.

"That's right. Old Carl 'spoke' five times with that Remington automatic and put five ducks on the water."

Fly fishing?

"I've been fly fishing for more than 60 years. I like to fish top-water for bass and bluegill. Bluegills just taste better when you catch 'em on the fly rod; that's why they call me 'Fly Rod Jimmy.'"

How long have you been deer hunting with the bow and arrow?

"This will be my 53rd year. I'd have more years bow hunting, but we didn't have deer in this area at that time.

"In 1959, we all laughed at my friend Don Stone when he said he was going to deer hunt using a bow and arrow. Well, wouldn't you know it, Stone killed a 190-pound, eight-point buck at Willow Slough with the bow. That started it. In 1960, we all bought bows and arrows."

Inland Steel Co.?

"I hired in at No. 2 Open Hearth in April 1950. It was something else – hot, dirty, shift work. I started out in the labor gang, then worked third helper, second helper and eventually first helper.

"Second helping was hell; I did that for 12 or 13 years. A shovel and a wheel barrow were the tools of the trade – digging out tap holes. Because of the heat, we had to wear long underwear year-round."

How much did you make in the '50s?

"I remember when we got up to $15 per day, we really thought we were in the money. About the time I was working first helper steadily, automation came in. When they built No. 3 Open Hearth, that hurt us. When they built No. 4 (Basic Oxygen Furnace), that paralyzed us. With 24 furnaces, No. 2 Open Hearth was the longest open hearth in the world. We went from 24 furnaces to sometimes nine furnaces. I was bumped down to third helper."

Then what?

"I saw the handwriting on the wall; they asked me if I'd like to try my hand at melting."

And?

"I took the job; in 18 years as a melter foreman, I made that company a lot of steel."

You had the first-hand experience because you worked your way up through the ranks.

"Tapped steel runs anywhere from 2,850 degrees to 3,050 degrees. Just by looking into the furnace, I could tell you the temperature within 20 degrees."

How's that?

"By the color of the steel and the slag on top of the furnace."

When I first hired into the labor gang, I used to ride with you and Uncle Junior. After a 3 to 11 shift, the three of us stopped at John's Place in Griffith for cold quarts of beer. Uncle Junior was in the passenger seat reminiscing about the best year of his life. Remember that classic?

"Sure do, Jr. said: '1959, best year of my life. My only son was born, the White Sox won the pennant and I didn't have go out to that fuckin' mill for 116 days.'"

Uncle Junior was referring to the big strike.

"That's right. For more than 30 years, us guys from Newton County car-pooled to the open hearth. Smitty, Geezie, Gordon 'Flash' Gervais, Todd Smart, Bud Cool, your Uncle Junior... . They're all dead now.

I'm the last one left."

* * *

In 37 years, my father can count on one hand the days he called off work. As a salaried employee the last half of his career, he would have been paid whether or not he showed up.

I was a little kid during the steel strike of '59, but I've been told Dad baled hay that summer for a buck an hour so I could have some milk with my corn flakes.

I guess he wanted to make sure I got the full meal.

Melting Pot

Johnny Nguyen *(Sept. 2012)*

"I trained you to become a very special manicurist, not just a plain manicurist... Because you make more money."
– Tippi Hedren

Johnny Nguyen wasn't the easiest interview. He is a humble man who speaks softly and prefers not to talk about himself. The only way he'd allow me to take his photo was with a customer.

Nguyen, 35, along with his wife, Amy, are the owner-operators of Sassy Nails in Portage. The Nguyens also live in the city.

I've never had a manicure and felt self-conscious while talking to Johnny because, the night before, I'd been loading up stink bait onto treble hooks while tight-lining for catfish in the Kankakee River.

My nails were a mess.

* * *

"I came to Sacramento, Calif., from South Vietnam when I was 10," Nguyen began. "I went to school in California to learn English.

"I go back to Vietnam on occasion. Financially, Vietnam is doing a lot better. It was a much more primitive life for my parents."

It's a warmer climate in Vietnam.

"Yes, very hot and humid. I don't want to talk too much about Vietnam."

No problem.

"We came to this country with nothing. We start from scratch and were doing OK until the economy in California took a tailspin. It is very high cost of living in California."

Do you find the folks of Northwest Indiana different than the people of north-central California?

"People are more friendly in Northwest Indiana – more open. They share their stories with me. When customers come into the salon, it's more about conversation and relaxation. When they walk out of here, they feel great. Our place is very popular.

"The only thing I dislike about Northwest Indiana is the cold weather, but I've learned to deal with it."

Have you grown accustomed to American food?

"Oh, yeah. But we still eat a lot of fried rice and dishes like beef noodle soup."

Tell me about Sassy Nails.

" We are a full-service salon. We do manicures, pedicures and much more."

It seems an inordinate percentage of manicurists are of Vietnamese descent.

"Most cultures have a niche; the Chinese operate restaurants and Koreans do a lot of dry-cleaning."

I feel you; a lot of Italians came to this country as shoemakers.

"Vietnamese people like jobs that are of service to others; we like to make people happy. The economy drove a lot of Vietnamese people into the nail business."

Explain, please.

"Some people might have tried to attend, say, medical school, but had to drop out for financial reasons; they turned to the nail business. It doesn't make any difference what you do for a living, as long as you are happy doing it."

From your mouth to God's ear. Johnny, I made good money in the steel mill, but hated it. I don't make any money as a writer, but I love it.

"It can be difficult running a business and trying to make everyone happy."

How many days per week are you open?

"Seven. I work from 9:30 a.m. to 7:30 p.m. Monday through Saturday and I work from 10 a.m. to 5 p.m. on Sundays."

Ever take a day off?

"Rarely."

How long can you keep up that pace?

"I choose to be here for a long time. We don't know what the future holds."

You have to make hay while the sun shines.

"Exactly."

Do you and Amy have children?

"Not yet."

How many people do you employ?

"Ten."

What percentage of your customers are women?

"I'd say at least 95 percent. The customers are of all ages."

How long have you been in the nail business?

"Five years; Amy has been doing it for 15 years."

Bear with me, are all pedicures the same?

"We have nine different kinds of pedicures. The most popular ones are milk & honey and lavender. I've added a new one to the menu list called chocolate martini. Customers like choices."

Clients soak their feet in these concoctions?

"Yes, a lot of people have thick callouses on the bottoms of their feet; the milk and honey will take all that away. Lavender is good for people who are on their feet all day; it relaxes them."

The deluxe manicure?

"It includes an exfoliating sea salt scrub, moisturizing mask wrapped in a warm towel and an extended massage with polish."

* * *

A couple of years before Nguyen was born, Saigon fell. Throngs of Vietnamese people emigrated to the United States – in a hurry.

At the time, when Hollywood actress Tippi Hedren wasn't plying her trade on a movie set, she served as an international relief coordinator working with Vietnamese women in a relief camp near Sacramento.

Hedren asked her manicurist, Dusty, if she would teach the Vietnamese women nail technology. The manicurist agreed; a niche for Vietnamese-Americans was born.

Johnny Nguyen is the epitome of the American Dream come true. It makes me happy to share his story.

Sam Quirarte *(Dec. 2008)*

¡Prospero Año Nuevo!

The parking lot of Lowell's extremely popular Mexican restaurant, Mi Ranchito, was empty when I arrived.

It was 10 a.m.; the place doesn't open for business until 11.

One by one, bussers, dishwashers and servers also arrived – by foot.

It was bitter cold.

Anyone who has bussed or served tables didn't need to speak Spanish to understand what was going on – hard work.

I had come to see their boss, Sam Quirarte. When I was a steel worker, I found the best bosses were the ones who came up through the ranks.

Quirarte, 49, is a good boss.

He has been married to Rosa for 25 years; they have six children. I happened to attend Spanish Mass at St Edward Catholic Church when their youngest was baptized a couple of years ago.

Quirarte's favorite beer is Pacifico. Because of his nuances and mannerisms, I felt like I was interviewing the actor Joe Mantegna. Maybe it was his eyes.

* * *

"I was born in Guadalajara, but raised on a farm," Quirarte began.

What crops were raised on the family farm?
"Beans and corn."
Soy beans and field corn like farmers grow in Indiana?

"No; from the ages of 5 to 15, I don't remember my dad selling anything; it was for survival. The corn was used to make our own tortillas; our pigs were used for meat and lard. We milked our cows and raised chickens for eggs.

"We had our own little house; I'm one of eight children. When I was 14, my dad got his first car. We rode horses."

At what age did you leave Mexico?

"When I was 15, I decided to come to the United States. The first time I tried entering the U.S., I got caught by immigration. The very next night, I tried again; I got across the border.

"I never worked for somebody else in Mexico; I worked for my dad. Since he don't give me no money, just work, I decided to leave."

Where did you enter the U.S.?

"California; I got a job as a dishwasher, then I switched to busboy. After a year in California, I decided to fly to Chicago because I heard there were more opportunities. I got caught at the airport; they sent me back to Mexico. When I was 18, I came here for good."

Illegally?

"Yes; I'm not afraid to say it. I became a legal resident of this country in '86; five years later, I became an American citizen.

"Jeff, at 15, I came to this country; I sent money made from washing dishes in California to my father to help him support our family.

"Once I became a citizen, I saw to it that my parents, brother and sisters could move here, too. Now, they are residents of the United States.

Was Rosa from the same part of Mexico as you?

"No, she's from Aguascalientes."

Hot waters.

"Yes, the water comes out of the ground hot because of the volcanos. Aguascalientes is about four hours from Guadalajara; I met Rosa in Blue Island."

Isla Azul en Mexico?

"Blue Island in Illinois."

My bad.

"I was working as a waiter at a restaurant called El Cortez; Rosa was my busgirl. I started in 1978 and worked there until '94. We got married in '83.

"I began to look for a business of my own. I wanted to make

sure my family had work. I had a friend who was a pipe fitter. He lived in Lowell, but worked all over Chicago. He would come into El Cortez to eat. He told me that I should open up a Mexican restaurant in Lowell, because there wasn't one."

What happened next?

"I told him to give me a call if there was a place that was closed down, but had good size, a liquor license and potential. The Haymarket, a restaurant in Lowell, became available.

"I had bought a house in Blue Island in 1986 for $50,000. I put more money into the house; it was eventually appraised at $96,000. I refinanced, which gave me enough money to start the business. My mortgage payment went from $250 to $750 – for 15 more years. I paid it off in 12 years."

How long were you at the original Lowell location before obtaining your current location?

"From '94 to '05, we worked at the old Mi Ranchito. We made the deal for the new Mi Ranchito in Jan. of '06; we weren't done fixing up the place until the end of '06.

"I sold the house in '06 to purchase and remodel the new Mi Ranchito (formerly Zuni's). So, that house in Blue Island put me in two different restaurants.

"I bought a house in Lowell back in 2000; I lived there while my wife and kids lived in Blue Island. They would visit me on the weekends.

"I'm having a new house built across the street from where we're living now; I bought 28 acres."

The Mi Ranchito float, dancers and horsemen are always a big hit at the Labor Day parade here in Lowell.

"We have had as many as 60 people on the float; the women in their colorful dresses are professional folk dancers."

And you're always duded up, doing lariat tricks atop your black stallion.

"I've been riding horses since I was 4 years old. I was in the Mexican rodeo from ages 12 to 15. The charro wears a suit and big sombrero; he is a showman. The vaquero is a working man; he wears a small hat and denim jeans."

You've been both.

"You become a vaquero or cowboy by working on your own

farm or ranch. You saddle your horse and work your cattle."

Sam, are the dishes you serve at Mi Ranchito the same as the meals you ate as a boy?

"The type of food that we serve cannot really be called authentic Mexican food. Down in Mexico, my mother would use a stone bowl and clay pots. Authentic is the food you eat at home.

"We use the same ingredients, but we use a blender. The Board of Health will not permit us to use stone, clay or copper."

What would a person find on the menu of a mom-and-pop restaurant in Mexico?

"Traditional food in a small restaurant in Mexico would feature enchiladas, pozole, sopes, tamales, flautas, pork meat with chili, beef or chicken soup, and fideo (spaghetti)."

Burritos?

"No burritos. Nowadays things have changed; tourist places like Cancun will serve filet mignon and red snapper. You can buy pizza, hamburgers and hot dogs."

Do you like Lowell?

"I like any place where I can make a living. I've had three steps in my life. The first 15 years were in Mexico, then 17 years in Blue Island, and the last 17 in Lowell."

How's business been lately?

"The economy is not really helping too much; it's tough times for everybody. We are just trying to survive."

Hermano, you've been a survivor all your life.

* * *

A steady stream of folks hoping to raise funds for reasons ad infinitum walk through the doors of Quirarte's "Little Ranch." They include churches, schools, Little League teams, police and fire departments or kids from Lowell who have qualified to become foreign-exchange students.

He might not give the most, but Quirarte gives to all.

"How can I give $500 to one and nothing for another?" he asked.

Quirarte employs about 20 people; a good portion of them are relatives. They all work hard, serving their native food to the hungry Americano just like 15-yearold Sam Quirarte did in California – a place once known as Mexico.

Dorothy Mokry *(June 2008)*

"...Give me your tired, your poor,
Your huddled masses yearning to breathe free,
The wretched refuse of your teeming shore.
Send these, the homeless, tempest-tost to me,
I lift my lamp beside the golden door!"
   -Emma Lazarus, 1883

Dorothy Mokry is the secretary of Minority Studies at IUN. She doesn't do Dottie and don't call her Dot. But there was a day when she answered to Dragica Dragic.

Mokry is the mother of 22 year-old twin sons, Alex and Chris. She lives in Portage with husband Larry who works for the Chicago Transit Authority.

* * *

"I met Larry back in 1976 – on Friday the 13th at Jackson's nightclub in Miller," Mokry began. "I was almost 26 years old; he was only 20. We dated long distance for two years. I was living in Merrillville; he was living up near Wrigley Field. We eventually lived together for about five years. We got married during our seven year itch in '83.

"I thought I wanted six kids, but after having the twins I changed my mind – I was 35 when I had them."

What road did you take to IUN?

"I worked as a keypunch operator for nine years at US Steel Gary works, then I transferred to the downtown office – almost 14 years total. I was laid off in '82. I've been at IUN for five years; I love my job. I'm also a member of Local 4730 (Communications Workers of

America) and part of their negotiating team."

Serbian Orthodox?

"Yes, I'm a member of St. Sava's in Merrillville."

Tell me about your roots, Dragica.

"My sister goes by Sasha these days. Her birth name is Smilka; she got teased a lot in high school."

You were born in Europe?

"Yes, my youngest sister, Borka, is the only one of us born in the United States. My parents fled from Yugoslavia on foot in 1946. They were eventually put on trains and shipped to Germany. My brother, George (Djuro), was born in the refugee camps of Italy in '46. Smilka was born in the German camps in '47. I was born in 1950, just outside of Hamburg – in the camps. I was 18 months old when we came to the U.S."

That had to be tough, your mother giving birth in refugee camps.

"Yeah, my mother didn't like the way they birthed babies in Germany – which was similar to the way they do it in the United States."

What are you talking about?

"German and American women usually give birth lying on their backs in a bed. When my mother was born in the hills of Yugoslavia they would put hay or straw on the floor and the woman would give birth from a standing or squatting position – gravity.

"I don't know what level of education my mother received; it wasn't a lot. She knows her alphabet. I thought it was interesting when she told me that in Yugoslavia a friend would stay for two weeks with the woman who had just given birth. I asked my mom why, and she said, 'depressia'. They knew about post-partem blues even way back then."

Coming to America.

"Serbian churches here in the US had families that sponsored refugees like us. We were sponsored by the Bundalo family; they had a farm on 49th Avenue.

"In Gary, during the 1950s, you had a lot of Serbs around Froebel (high school) and the Midtown area, but there were also Serbs on the west and east sides.

"Our church was on 13th and Connecticut. When we first came here we lived at 8th and Van Buren, but we moved around a lot. Our landlord was a Serbian man who had relatives here who gave him enough money to buy his own house. In turn, what he did was rent parts of it out to all these Chetniks who had come to America without their wives. This man had like a boarding house for all those guys; we were the only family living there. My mother did all the cooking and cleaning so we didn't pay any rent. My father got a job at US Steel in Gary."

Chetniks?

"Serbian soldiers who fought communism were called Chetniks. My father was a freedom fighter with the Chetnik secret police. During World War II, the Serbs and Croatians had this thing going on, kind of like the Arabs and the Jews. Croatian guerrillas who sided with the Nazis were called Ustase.

"It's sad; we're the same country, same language, same alphabet. The only difference – they're Catholic, we're Orthodox. And then there were my mother's brothers who were Partisan soldiers; they fought under (Marshal) Tito."

Let's return to growing up in the Great Melting Pot.

"We served as translators for our parents. I know Serbs who learned English by watching 'Gunsmoke,' 'I Love Lucy,' and The Three Stooges.'

"They had their ways. For example, my parents were in denial about me being almost totally deaf in one ear. When I was about 9 years old, my mother had a fit when the hearing specialist put a 'telephone' (hearing aid) in my ear. Being from the old country, there was that stigma that I would never find a husband or a job if I had a birth defect."

High school?

"I attended Horace Mann. Sometimes we took advantage of our parents not knowing the language. My mother did know the English A, B, C, D, F. I brought home an F once on my report card. She asked me in Serbian, 'What's this grade for?' I pointed to the abbreviation in the subject column which had a 'G' typed in it. I explained to her that I was failing gym. My parents didn't consider athletics important. In reality, the 'G' was for geometry. I fibbed."

Gee, sounds like that 'G' eventually symbolized Guilt. Penance?

"I went to summer school that year."

Have you ever been back to visit your roots?

"No; in 1965, my mother and two of my sisters went back to

Yugoslavia. I was a teenager and didn't want to go – I regret it today.

"Although Tito was a communist, my father has never denied the fact that he held Yugoslavia together."

The Chetniks and Partisans of Yugoslavia differed politically, but shared a common enemy during World War II.

"Yes, there were Chetniks – my father was one of them – who saved something like 500 American paratroopers, many of whom had landed into Croatian hands and were going to be turned over to the Nazis. The Chetniks loved the Americans. Years later, my father felt America betrayed the Serbs during the whole Kosovo thing."

Dorothy, we're not going there. I know too many Macedonian, Croatian and Serbian Americans with differing opinions on that particular subject – not to mention I have a pint of Albanian blood in these veins. You are obviously proud of your Serbian heritage. Was it always that way?

"When I living with my parents, I didn't want to hear about what my father did during the war. When he would try to tell me that it was a Serb who invented electricity (Nicola Tesla), I told him, 'Yeah, yeah. It was Thomas Edison!'

"Have you ever seen 'My Big Fat Greek Wedding'? Although they were Greeks, I could so relate to that movie. We got made fun of just because of our food. My dad would eat these sandwiches on Vienna bread sliced like eight inches thick. Growing up, I wanted American food!"

"Then you get a little older, you move to Chicago, and you're calling long distance... ."

Calling who and why, Dragica?

"'...Ma, how do you make sarma? I'm hungry for it.'"

Barb Kubiak *(Sept. 2010)*

"This is a nice place you got here, Joe. I'd like to live in this neighborhood, but colored folks aren't allowed to live in Glen Park."
– Odette Perkins talking to her Polish-American friend Joe Wolek, from the play "Steel Waters" by Ben Clement

Barb Kubiak lives in Glen Park with her brother. She never has been married. Our interview took place at Indiana University Northwest in Gary where she works part time as a reference librarian.

Kubiak, 67, is a member of St. Joseph the Worker Croatian Catholic Church in Gary's Glen Park neighborhood. She also is a self-proclaimed "reading junkie" who loves novels, magazines and newspapers, including the Wall Street Journal and New York Times.

* * *

"My paternal grandfather emigrated from Poland to Chicago around 1895 to work in the steel mills," Kubiak began. "When the plant in Gary was built, about 10 years later, he took a job there."

Did the family move from Chicago to Gary?

"Yes, my grandfather built a two-story house. My grandmother took in boarders. They lived on the ground floor; the boarders lived upstairs."

And the Kubiaks became part of the great American melting pot.

"Eventually; my grandmother got homesick, so they moved back to Poland after World War I in 1922. My father was 6 at the time; he was an immigrant in his 'native land'– an unusual twist."

What about you?

"I was born in Poland during World War II."

A hostile environment at that time.

"The Nazis had about 50 camps in Poland. There were two kinds of concentration camps. Many Gentiles went to the labor camps; Polish Jews were sent to the death camps."

I can't even imagine the horror.

"In the rural areas, the Nazis would march to the farms and tell people they had an hour to pack their bags, 'We don't care where you go; if you don't leave, we will shoot you.' People would grab a horse, pack a wagon, and go to who knows where. German farmers took over our farms and sometimes used the Poles as slave labor.

"My mother's brother was sent to a concentration camp on an island in the Baltic (Sea). The camp was not yet built; the inmates had to build it. He survived there for six years. With the war almost over, the Nazis wanted to liquidate the camp. They told the prisoners they were going to put them on boats and send them to Sweden."

Sweden was neutral.

"Yes, but they were leaky boats; the Germans were well aware of that – the Poles were supposed to drown. Through spies, or however, Sweden got wind of this and sent the Red Cross with a ship to rescue the Polish inmates from the leaky boats. My uncle was hospitalized when he reached Sweden.

"Sweden has always been an altruistic nation. My uncle was given the choice of going back to Poland, at no cost, or becoming a Swedish citizen."

And?

"He became a Swedish citizen and married a Swedish woman."

What happened after the war?

"Once the allies chased the Germans out, the Soviets came in. My mother considered Joseph Stalin as bad or worse than (Adolf) Hitler. My mother's younger brother, Chester, became a communist in Poland. He knew if he wanted a job on the railroad he'd have to join the Communist Party. Poland had puppet governments until 1989."

Your father?

"He returned to the United States in 1947. Dad lived with his American cousins in Gary for more than a year before my mother, two younger siblings and I came to America. I was 5 years old."

Did your father get a job at U.S. Steel as his father did?

"Yes, his cousin, Henry Wilski, who was in the union, got him a job. We lived with my father's aunt on Massachusetts Street. That area was the St. Hedwig's Polish Parish on the east side of Gary in Midtown."

From rural Poland to Gary, Ind.

"What's strange is the neighborhood was integrated, but the churches and schools were segregated. It was in the days of separate but equal."

Grade school?

"It was tough for me. Even though the nuns spoke Polish, they refused to give me remedial (English); I should have been held back. The parochial schools were terrible in that regard. I feel the (Gary) Diocese and St. Hedwig's owed us something.

"I didn't feel comfortable with English until I was 10 years old. I was always translating inside my head. I would go to the washroom and cry because I was such a slow learner."

High school?

"Lew Wallace; we moved to Glen Park in 1955. The Gary schools had a wonderful program for immigrants called TESOL (Teachers of English to Speakers of Other Languages). There also was the International Institute which was like a settlement house for immigrants across the street from Froebel High School. My dad praised Elizabeth Wilson, who used to run it.

"To supplement his income, my dad started a Polish radio program in 1949. It was an hourlong variety program for the immigrants on WWCA, WGRY and WLTH; he did that until he died in 1978."

That's interesting.

"The life of immigrants is hard. I'm very sympathetic to not only the legal immigrants, but the illegals as well; they are the most desperate. When economic times are tough in the United States the feeling against immigrants grows. Then, in good times, it ebbs. The life of a migrant hasn't improved since 'The Grapes of Wrath.'"

One of my favorite novels, and one of the most frequently banned books in the United States. What a powerful ending "The Grapes of Wrath" has.

"Yes, when Rose of Sharon, who has just lost her baby, breastfeeds a starving old man who is a complete stranger. I think 'The

Grapes of Wrath' is the equivalent of Pearl Buck's 'The Good Earth.' Rather than Chinese peasants, it dealt with American peasants who also survived many hardships. (John) Steinbeck should have won the Nobel Prize much earlier than he did (1962)."

His politics weren't mainstream.

"My Swedish relatives say the most humane government is that hybrid combination of socialism and capitalism."

Where did you go to college?

"I attended IUN for two years and then IU in Bloomington for two years. Then, I got a job teaching at Bailly Junior High School. After three years, I transferred to Lew Wallace and taught ninth grade for 10 years. I was at Lew Wallace 15 years... ."

Then what?

"I earned my second masters (degree) at Purdue (University) Calumet. After 18 years of teaching, I decided I wanted to be a librarian. In 1983, I got a job at Hanover Central High School and retired in 2006."

You didn't stay retired for long.

"I've been here at IUN since '07. I love it. This is the best job I've ever had. Hey, I worked with teenagers for 41 years."

Have you ever been back to Poland?

"Yes, in 1969 and 1971."

You're probably a minority in your neighborhood.

"There's one other white family on our block. Most of my neighbors are senior citizens. We have about five or six abandoned houses. I was told by a Realtor that the west side of Glen Park was considered the wealthy side back in the day. The east side, where I live, was for the poor newcomers."

* * *

Barb Kubiak was a poor newcomer who became an English teacher.

Slow learner? I think not.

Moanes Khawalid *(Feb. 2009)*

*"Oh I've been smiling lately,
dreaming about the world as one
And I believe it could be,
some day it's going to come."*
– Yusuf Islam (Cat Stevens)

Although we'd never met, Moanes Khawalid shouted my name as I stood dazed and confused before a large-scale map of the Indiana University Northwest Campus in Gary.

Like a lemming, I followed Khawalid, 25, from the cafeteria to the library. Picture Dustin Hoffman (Manes) walking beside Tom Cruise (Moanes) in "Rain Man."

* * *

Moanes, forgive my borderline dyslexia; it knows no bounds. Did I look that lost? How did you know it was me?

"Your photograph appears with your column," Khawalid said.

Oh, yeah. Kid, if I was ever to write under a pseudonym, it would be Senam Moanes.

"Senam Moanes?"

My surname spelled backwards for a first name and your first name for a surname. I know a Methodist from Hegewisch named Zaki Zaki.

"That is very common in the Middle East, to have the same first and last name."

The Rev. Zaki was originally from Cairo – the one in Egypt. You?

"Israel."

Funny, you don't look Jewish.

"I'm not; I'm a Muslim. I've been living in Pine Island Apartments in Crown Point with my psychology professor, Terry Harman. He is Jewish."

Moanes, this is getting interesting. It's time to break out the power tools.

"Power tools in the library?"

My tape recorder. How long have you lived in America?

"Since May of '06; I spent a year in Montreal before that."

Your English is very good. Parlez-vous francais?

"Oui; I speak Arabic, Hebrew, English and French."

What other countries have you visited?

"Greece and Turkey. Was the Manes family originally from Greece?"

No, Albania. The Turks were slaughtering them about 500 years ago so they fled to Italy.

"Terry's wife is of Italian descent, she's a Christian. The Harmans treat me as if I am family. We celebrate Jewish, Muslim and Christian holidays all year long. I've attended Temple Beth-El in Munster; mosque in Merrillville and Living Grace Nazarene Church on Taft Street, also in Merrillville."

I hear you're a fine student at IUN and have recently made the dean's list. What's your favorite subjects?

"Math and physics; I can do the problems in my head without a calculator."

Impressive.

"There are times when I spend hours just doing math problems; I love it."

Very impressive.

"I graduated high school by the time I was 16; my IQ is about 160."

Yikes!

"I should have my bachelor's degree in psychology sometime in 2010; I plan to attend medical school in Chicago. It has always been my dream to be a doctor. I like to help people however old or young, whatever color skin, no matter where they're from."

What kind of doctor?

"A plastic surgeon."

Hobbies?

"I like fast cars and motorcycles; I want to own a Ferrari some day. I also like to stay in shape; I work out at least an hour a day.

"I used to run three miles to school everyday in Israel. I was on the track and basketball teams in high school. We played soccer almost every day. I took karate lessons for about six years. Living 10 minutes away from the Mediterranean, I swam a lot."

You didn't frequent hookah bars?

"No hookah; it's very unhealthy – way worse that smoking cigarettes."

That's good, Moanes. Save your money for that Ferrari.

"I do pay three times more for my undergraduate credits than other students here because I'm not from this country."

Tell me more about Israel.

"I'm from Shaab Village, a town of about 6,000 people. It's near Haifa City, in northern Israel. It is a mixture of Muslims, Jews and Christians."

My buddy, Sam Ahmad, told me he has more Jewish friends in the United States than when he lived in Palestine.

"It depends on what part of Israel you live in; north is more diverse. I went to school with Jewish kids, played with them, and shopped in the same stores with them. My dad's business partner is Jewish.

"My grandparents were living in Palestine before 1948; they stayed after Israel became a state. It is similar to American Indians who stayed here."

Moanes, American Indians who once lived here in Lake County were forced to walk more miles than Israel is long to "stay" on reservations. And there are a lot of killings on these mean streets of America, but I can't imagine what it must have been like for you and your two brothers growing up.

"During the first Gulf War, we could see the rockets going over us and hitting Haifa City. You get used to it."

Really?

"Well, sort of get used to it. My older brother worked as a paramedic. He had to go to a site where a suicide bombing had taken place on a bus. He couldn't sleep for long time afterwards; he said body parts were scattered for incredible distances.

"There was a time, I had just left a gas station, my car was idling nearby at a stoplight. A Muslim woman who lost her fiance and two brothers in the war entered the gas station with bombs strapped to her body. Four or five of the people killed were Arabs; the station was owned by an Arab.

"I still have hope that one day the war will end. That people from both sides will just say: 'You know what guys, this is it, we have to meet each other halfway – no more killing.'

"In war, there are no winners; both sides are losers. The only solution is peace."

* * *

Khawalid told me that his favorite movie is the 1997 Italian-made film "La Vita e Bella" ("Life is Beautiful"). The main character is an Italian Jew.

For those who haven't seen it, the first half of the movie is comedic, bordering on slapstick. The ending is dark and very sad – similar to the chat between Moanes and Manes. Funny and sad.

But there's something about young Khawalid's heartfelt words and smile that gives an aging boomer hope.

Ken Eng *(Feb. 2011)*

"Enable every woman who can work to take her place on the labor front, under the principle of equal pay for equal work."
– Mao Zedong

Today is New Year's Day in China – the Year of the Rabbit.

At first, I couldn't understand Ken Eng when he pronounced Chiang Kai-shek's name. That's because I pronounce Chinese words with an American accent and he pronounced the late President of the Republic of China's name correctly. Eng, 72, is a widower, who lives in Highland and practices Chinese calligraphy.

* * *

Ken, I born under the sign of the Cock. What are you?
"A Tiger," he began. "Last year was (the) Tiger."
What kind of people are Rabbits?
"I have no idea; I don't believe in astrology."
Chinese New Year?
"It is taken very seriously. All of the factories will close down for an entire week."
Where were you born?
"In Hong Kong."
How long have you lived in the United States?
"More than 30 years; I used to live in LA. I moved here about six years ago after I retired."
What letters of the alphabet are the toughest for you?
"The letters 'V' and 'R.' I have a very difficult time saying the word that means an area out in the country where farms are located."

"Rural" is kind of tricky.

"I speak the Cantonese dialect of Chinese. Most popular language in Chinese is the Mandarin. I can speak that, too. There are thousands of dialect in China."

Growing up in Hong Kong?

"Hong Kong was all right; it was British Colony. After July 1, 1997, Hong Kong belong to China; they took over. Hong Kong has changed; they are influenced politically by Beijing. One (political) party."

Why did you leave Hong Kong for America?

"Because I hate communists."

Why 1997?

"Hong Kong is a little island smaller than Manhattan. To survive, Hong Kong needed some of the mainland in China. The British rented the peninsula for 100 years in 1897. The Chinese government had the right to take over the peninsula in 1997."

The Nationalist, Chiang Kai-shek?

"After Chiang Kai-shek was defeated by Mao (Zedong), he moved to Taiwan. Chiang's son became a very good leader. He was the president of Taiwan."

The Communist, Mao Zedong?

"Mao was a great man. He was very smart, actually. But the bad part of him is that he loves power too much. When he sees his power grow weak, he use every way he could to get the power back. He killed all his comrades.

"Have you ever heard of the (Great Proletarian) Cultural Revolution? That was the period between 1967 and 1977. Millions of Chinese people died. And that was peaceful time – not wartime."

Let's talk a little more about your childhood. Your father?

"He died when I was 4. He was a cameraman."

A cameraman?

"He took portraits in a studio; the old-fashioned way."

Siblings?

"What's a sibling?"

Brothers and sisters.

"I have one sister who lives in Beijing and one brother who lives in Canada."

Did your mother remarry?

"No, she had a hard time to raise three of us. The old-tradition Chinese society would look down on her if she remarried."

The former practice of binding women's feet?

"No more; that was stopped in the early part of the 20th Century. If my grandmother was still alive she would be about 120. Her feet were bound until she was 7 or 8 and then the practice ceased. Still, her feet were smaller than average. "

Chinese food?

"When I was little, during World War II, my mom mixed sweet potatoes with rice because there was a shortage of rice. Every day for more than a year, she fed us sweet potatoes and rice. I hate sweet potatoes to this day."

As a kid, were you too poor to own a pet?

"Chinese have dogs as a pet, but they eat them. They eat cat, too."

What about crickets for pets?

"The Chinese people eat that, too. But to answer your question, yes I played with crickets like a toy. Crickets fight together, like in Spain, the cow."

Like bullfighting?

"Yes, you own one; I own one. We put those two together in a jar and they fight. We just do it for fun; adults would do it for money."

They'd gamble on crickets like they were at a cockfight?

"Yes."

What's another popular sport in China?

"Ping-pong."

Favorite Chinese food and favorite American food?

"Peking Duck is my favorite Chinese dish. I still can't get used to hamburgers. I like American cookies and chocolates."

Ken, there are a lot of Americans who complain everything is made in China these days. Your thoughts?

"To me, the Chinese people are getting paid very low. The Chinese government is very rich and the people are very poor. A small percentage of the people are rich. There are poor Americans, too. But the middle class in America is much larger than in China.

"For past 15 years or so, China has the policy of one child. Many Chinese people still don't like girls; they want sons."

Liu Xiaobo, the 2010 Nobel Peace Prize recipient?

"That young man sacrificed himself by becoming imprisoned. He did a great job. The Beijing government had a hard time because of that news. That's very good. I like it."

I saw a program on TV the other day claiming the Chinese government warned the United States not to get too chummy with Japan.

"There will not be a war between China and United States. A war is no good for both countries. It would destroy everybody."

* * *

Ken Eng is one of the most humble and good-natured folks I've met in a long time. He couldn't help but laugh at my pitiful attempt to maintain a poker face when he talked of the Chinese eating crickets, cats and dogs.

But on my way home from Highland, it occurred to me how Americans have been known to eat the legs of frogs and the testicles of hogs. Not to mention the most disgusting of all, Marshmallow Peeps.

The main difference between Eng and me?

He can speak Chinese and I can't.

Jack Gross *(Aug. 2008)*

*"God, I know that we are the chosen people,
but couldn't you choose someone else for a change?"*
– From 'Tevye The Dairyman' by Sholem Aleichem

It was the second day of August when I interviewed Jack Gross – his 75th birthday. He and his wife, Sondra, live in a beautiful home on Lake Michigan in Miller. The couple has raised two daughters, Melissa and Amy, who graduated from Andrean High School. Both of them played varsity tennis for the 59ers' boys team during the '80s.

Seventy-five years ago, Gross' surroundings weren't so plush. He was born in Czechoslovakia. The family surname was originally spelled Grosz; it was Americanized when his father came to Ellis Island.

I found Gross both pensive and witty. He has sold groceries, shoes, real estate, and, like Tevye, in "Fiddler on the Roof," peddled milk – for Bowman Dairy Co. in Gary. He also bears a remarkable resemblance to the late newspaper columnist Mike Royko.

* * *

"My father came to this country first," began Gross. "My mother, siblings and I eventually came to the United States in 1940; I was 6 1/2 years old. I don't really remember much about Europe except that we were on the last ship from Genoa, Italy, to New York before the Holocaust."

Your father found employment in Gary.

"Yes. He worked his ass off, managed to save a few dollars, and would send money to my mother while we were living in Czechoslovakia.

"He eventually saved up enough money to open up a small neighborhood grocery store near 16th and Delaware. We all lived in one bedroom behind the grocery store. What are you going to do?

"Then we moved a block or so east to 1750 Maryland Street – that one had two bedrooms behind the grocery store! I went to Pulaski Grade School.

"When Pearl Harbor was attacked my older brothers instantly became U.S. citizens and were drafted. We eventually moved to 4th and Cleveland when I was 12 or 13 years old. We were moving up in the neighborhood."

What high school did you attend?

"Horace Mann, Class of '52. I played basketball for Coach Crown and was a hurdler on the track team for Coach Kaminsky. I tried out for the football team as a freshman but came home from practice all bloody one day. My mother called the coach and told him in her broken English that my football career was kaput. I was a skinny kid. What are you going to do?"

Gary during the 1940s?

"When I was growing up most people bought their groceries on credit. They worked in the mill or a place that supported the mills. After a couple of weeks, when they got paid, they'd pay their grocery bill – same thing with clothes. Everything was credit. There was a mutual trust. But sometimes people would up and move – you lost money. If a person is working they can pay; if they're not working, they can't pay. What are you going to do?

"After Horace Mann, I attended Indiana University down in Bloomington. I graduated in '56, a marketing major."

You learned the business working for your father; eventually you started your own grocery store.

"Yes. In '57, Sondra and I were married and I opened up a store. It was located at 21st and Ohio. By 1980, I got out of the grocery business and got into real estate – still am.

"I've joked, saying that I'm in the recycling business. I buy property: HUD homes, sheriff's sales, tax sales – whatever. Then I rehab the properties and put them up for sale on contract.

"My lawyer always told me I'm too lenient. If I had the money people owe me, I wouldn't be here talking to you – I'd be living on a tropical island somewhere. What are you going to do?"

You appear to be in good shape.

"I was in great health until March of this year. I had just finished working out on the tread mill, took a shower, and then made myself a bowl of lentil soup. All of sudden, I couldn't breathe. Sondra was in Florida; I stayed home to pay the bills.

"At first I thought it was gas from the bean soup. Luckily, Sondra called from Florida; she told me to take some Tums. I promised her I'd call my brother Bernie down the street. He's 87, by the way – he's getting married this month.

"Over the phone, Bernie said if I could lift my hands over my head and I didn't feel like an elephant was standing on my chest, I wasn't having a heart attack. When Bernie arrived all I could do was open the door for him and lie down on the floor. Bernie called 911. What was happening, unbeknownst to me, was that I was bleeding internally. I had a cancerous tumor on my liver that ruptured – a rarity. I lost six pints of blood and ended up at the University of Chicago.

"They put me in a semi-private room. A nice young Rabbi brought me a little care package Friday evening – our Sabbath begins on Friday night. I was in bad shape. He asked when was the last time I wore a prayer shawl. Jokingly, I told him, 'Probably my bar mitzvah.' We prayed. He gave me what was almost like last rites. Next to us was another patient and his family. They're watching what the Rabbi is doing. I'm thinking that they're thinking, 'What kind of voodoo is he performing on this guy?' The next day I felt great. It was miraculous. I got up and walked around the hall. It was like a transformation."

The gentile next door to you was probably ready to convert.

"It was the power of prayer, I guess. I don't know what the hell it was. I owe it to God."

What was the prognosis; are you going to live to be 120?

"From your mouth to God's ear – I hope so. I take a lot of Chinese herbs. Amy found me an oncologist by the name of Guo who had practiced western medicine until the 1980s. Dr. Guo saw the effects our methods of treatment do to people. He's strictly concentrating on treating cancer with Chinese Herbs. I also get acupuncture once a week."

Your faith.

"I'm not a real religious person, but I've always believed in God. I belong to Temple Israel in Miller, which is Reformed, and I belong to a Conservative temple in Munster – Beth Israel. I also support Chabad House of Northwest Indiana which is Orthodox. I'm a 'conservadox' Jew who's covering his ass."

Was Sondra of the Jewish faith when you met her?

"Oh, yes. Her maternal grandfather, Abe Rosen, was one of the founders of Temple Beth-El back in 1908, which was located at 8th and Connecticut in Gary.

"My parents were orthodox; they kept kosher. They followed Judaism almost to a T. They would walk to temple. My parents spoke Czech, Slovak, Hungarian, German, Polish, and at home – Yiddish. We came here with zilch. We worked hard."

Hobbies?

"Making a living. I'm not a golfer; I used to play tennis.

Gary in 2008?

"I hate to see what has happened. It's terrible. Gary looks like a bombed-out city except for the Miller area and a few other sections. There is nothing viable downtown.

"Who to blame? Hatcher? White flight? The economy? It's always good to blame somebody else. What happened to all the money that used to come into Gary?"

Can Gary make a comeback?

"I doubt it, unless the school system changes. Would you send your kid to the Gary school system? The most important thing is education. Kids are trying to get out of Gary. It's not the building. You can build all the schools you want. You need good teachers and students who are willing to learn. Horace Mann was a great school. Froebel was a great school...

"Jeff, I try to live by the Ten Commandments. I try to help others who are less fortunate – in a quiet way. And I believe in sacrificing for family."

* * *

I've read a short story entitled 'Zelig' a time or two. It was written in 1915 by Benjamin Rosenblatt. 'Zelig' is comprised of about 1,800 brutal but brilliant words describing the living conditions of a Jewish family that emigrated from Europe to New York City. It is a story of sacrifice similar to that of the Grosz family.

Slavery, potato famine and flight from ethnic cleansing helped populate these United States of America. And the struggle to enter this country will continue for human beings desperately seeking a better life for their families.

What are you going to do?

Larbi Kharchaf *(Jan 2012)*

Ilsa (Ingrid Bergman): " ...Let's see, the last time we met... ."
Rick (Humphrey Bogart): "Was La Belle Aurore.
Ilsa: "How nice, you remembered. But of course, that was the day the Germans marched into Paris."
Rick: "Not an easy day to forget."
Ilsa: "No."
Rick: "I remember every detail. The Germans wore gray, you wore blue."
– From the 1942 movie "Casablanca"

I recently interviewed Paul Montemeyer of Morocco. Larbi Kharchaf also has lived in Morocco – Africa, that is.

He's a debonair chap who speaks with a slight accent and reminds me of actor John Cassavetes who always reminded me of actor Martin Landau.

Kharchaf, 65, lives in a studio apartment in Crown Point, is a former soccer player and coach, and an artist who currently cooks at Bronko's Kitchen Delite in Lowell.

* * *

Please tell me about the exotic, mysterious country of Morocco.

"Morocco is located in the foremost northwest corner of Africa, across from Spain and the Rock of Gibraltar," he said. "We had a lot of Spanish people living with us."

But you're not a Spaniard.

"No, I'm a Berber. Berbers in northern Africa are like American Indians in this country. My surname is the Berber word for artichoke. The different tribes of the area often had skirmishes over land. My ancestors would hide behind the artichoke plants."

Is the Berber language Arabic?

"Yes; actually we're tri-lingual. We speak Arabic, French and Spanish. In grammar school, I took Arabic in the morning and French in the afternoon. I ended up being a French teacher in Morocco."

Impressive.

"Before and during World War II, we were occupied by the French ... not occupied. What is the word? Protectorate. The French protected the king and our people from the Nazis.

"A lot of Jewish people came to Morocco because of (Adolf) Hitler. The same with the Spanish people, who were fleeing their (fascist) dictator, (Gen. Francisco) Franco."

Tourism in Morocco?

"There is much tourism in Morocco. The boats and ferries come in every day. It takes about two hours to cross the Strait of Gibraltar."

Larbi, there's a small town in Newton County named Morocco.

"I've been there; it's south on U.S. 41. I asked the older people of the town how Morocco got its name; the stories I was told differed."

Newton County Historical Society member Beth Bassett once told me that several men were working on what would become the west boundary of the town during the mid-1800s, when a stranger rode up on horseback. He dismounted and asked for directions to Kankakee, Ill.

The stranger happened to be wearing a pair of boots trimmed in red Moroccan leather. The workmen were so impressed by the boots they decided to call their town Morocco. Beth also told me Morocco is the only town of that name in the world.

"Interesting. Moroccan leather is very popular around the world; it's tanned in the ancient southern town of Marrakesh. It's a very beautiful part of Morocco with many palm trees, dates and oranges.

"All the buildings are mauve. If you go to the country of Morocco, you must visit Marrakesh. Another tannery is in the town of Fez."

Like the Turkish hat.

"Correct."

Casablanca?

"Casablanca is in Morocco, about 350 kilometers south of Tangier. The hotel where they filmed the movie with Humphrey Bogart is still there. The lounge is still there, too."

Rick's Cafe.

"The American tourists follow that. The owners keep the place looking just like it did in the movie. The pianist has to be a black man."

When did you come to this country?

"In 1971; I married a Polish girl from the south side of Chicago. We met on the beach in Morocco. We were married in Morocco in 1969. I spoke very little English and she spoke very little French. She got homesick after a few years.

"We're divorced now, but she is a good lady."

Did you and your wife have children?

"Yes, two sons."

"We lived in Park Forest, Ill. so one of our sons graduated from Rich East High School; the younger son attended Crown Point High School."

Are you a religious man?

"I'm a Muslim, but I don't really practice. Are you Greek?"

No, my grandfather's family emigrated from Italy when he was 10.

"I'm learning Italian with the CDs. If you know French or Spanish you can learn Italian very quick."

How long did it take you to become fluent in English?

"About two years. I learned from my wife and in-laws."

Your working career in America?

"I started out a Barnaby's restaurant in Park Forest, then I got a job at General Electric in Chicago Heights, Ill. I worked there about 14 years until it shut down in 1987.

"After my divorce in 1980, I moved to Chicago Heights. I used to hang around with the Italian people at places like Savoia's Restaurant. I would come to Dyer to buy cigarettes because they were cheaper."

When I lived in Schererville, I would come to Lynwood to buy beer on Sundays because they were open.

"I went to bartending school in River Oaks after GE closed down. I tended bar at Idlewild Country Club in Homewood, Ill. It was a private Jewish club. Bartending started getting boring after awhile."

Then what?

"I got homesick and went back to Morocco for six years. My friend opened up a little coffee shop. Music was played there; my friend was a very good lute player.

"I worked for him and slept at the coffee shop. Then, I started painting post cards. Some of my paintings are hanging in the Main Street Cafe in Crown Point."

When did you return to the United States?

"About '93, I moved to Lowell. I've been in Crown Point since '95. You come next time and I'll prepare couscous for us. It's like a grain pasta. It's all wheat – very healthy for you.

"You put it in hot water first, a little bit of butter, a little bit of salt. Then you cover it and let it stand for five minutes like rice. You eat it with a spoon."

You eat pasta with a spoon?

"We serve it shaped like a volcano with a hole on top. In the crater, you put the chicken or beef. We place the vegetables around the base of the pyramid. You wet the volcano with a bowl of sauce and a ladle on the side."

Like marinara?

"No tomatoes. Spices like olive oil, parsley, cumin, garlic... ."

No tomatoes?

* * *

I learned a lot from the likeable Larbi Kharchaf.

Roger Brewin *(June 2011)*

"My dear, I don't care what they do, so long as they don't do it in the street and frighten the horses."
– Beatrice Campbell

The above quotation has several variants and its source has been attributed to everyone from Henry VIII to Mr. Rogers, but I'm going with British actress Beatrice Campbell.

I think the quote is a good fit for the Rev. Roger Brewin, pastor at the First Unitarian Church of Hobart, and his congregation. Brewin lives in the Beverly neighborhood of Chicago. He has been married to Katherine for 42 years; they've raised one son.

* * *

Age?

"I'm 63," he said.

Were you born in Chicago?

"I grew up in Nottingham, England. My parents emigrated when I was 9. My dad was part of what they called the 'brain drain' – engineers and scientists coming to America from Europe. I spent five years in English public schools and then came into the public school system in upstate New York."

College?

"I started out at the University of Akron; my last two years were at St. John Fisher College in New York. I was a physics major at Akron, but ended up becoming a philosophy major.

"St. John Fisher had a strong philosophical tradition whereas Akron did not. My administrator at the time, Robert West, went on to be the president of the Unitarian Universalist Association. He said, 'You would like to do what I do for a living.' And that was my call... ."

What time frame was that?

"That was 1968; I was 21."

You're an old hippie.

"Pretty much. When I went to college in Akron, I found a group called Student Religious Liberals which explored religious questions from almost every culture. I became that group's president and I discovered there was a church behind it – the First Unitarian Universalist Church of Akron. It had been a Universalist Church prior to the merger. What convinced me to join it was that Sojourner Truth gave her 'Ain't I a Woman?' speech from the pulpit of that church."

I knew Sojourner gave that speech in Akron; I didn't realize it was it was at a Universalist Church.

"A longstanding part of the UU tradition is that it's not enough to hold ethical positions; you have to witness for them. For example, I went to both Indianapolis and Madison for the pro-union rallies. To me, that's part of my ministry and I'm backed by the congregation."

First church you served?

"The First Unitarian Church of Rochester, N.Y., which is distinguished by the fact that Susan B. Anthony used to be a member of it. There's a portrait of her about 6 feet tall that hangs right outside the front door.

"Louis Kahn designed the church. It has massive front doors that are pivoted at the two-thirds point; they look like they'd be very hard to open. Stepping into a free church aught to be a deliberate act, but the doors pivot so beautifully you can open them with one finger."

After Rochester?

"I spent two years at a little Universalist church in Pataskala, Ohio; it's a 150-year old church with less than 50 members. Half the members are the great-grandchildren of the people who founded it.

"They are liberal Christians from the countryside, basically. They are the people who told me I didn't have to limit my sermons to 20 minutes. They said: 'We drive an hour-and-a-half to get here; we bring our lunches and we stay most of the day – you can talk as long as you like.' So I did."

Are you a Christian?

"No, I'm a Humanist."

The history of the Unitarians?

"Unitarianism began during the Protestant Reformation period, so that puts it more than 450 years ago. When (Martin) Luther and the rest of the Protestants broke from Catholicism, the people who became Unitarians were on the far left wing of the breakaway Protestant church."

The merger between the Unitarian and Universalist churches?

"We merged almost exactly 50 years ago. This church was founded as a Unitarian Church in 1874."

Tell me more.

"We are a non-creedal church; we don't have any required beliefs for membership. As a member of the UUA, there are 1,000 other congregations like us across the U.S., there is a set of common principals. We tell people, 'You're free to come here, whatever your religious beliefs, as long as your practice of religion is likely to fit within a congregation that adheres to these principles."

Principles?

"I'll make a copy of them for you; they're very broad. Most people would consider them socially and politically liberal; they're certainly very religiously liberal.

"Somebody who is an orthodox believer, in say, Judaism, Christianity or Islam, is welcome to come here, but they would have a very hard time finding worship that met their needs. If you need to believe that there is one set of truths and one way, this is not the place for you.

"What we believe, as a congregation, is that when the person sitting next to you in the pew believes differently than you do, that's an opportunity for both of you to learn something and grow spiritually."

Amen, brother.

"We have Buddhists, Christians, agnostics, atheists, pagans and general theists in our congregation. I'd say the majority of people here would call themselves humanists. They have their doubts, at least, certainly questions, about anything supernatural. And they believe that all religious and ethical truths come from human experience and not from revelation or divine books.

"In other words, no prophet, no bishop, no piece of scripture, no parting of the clouds... . "

Do you occasionally read from the Bible during your sermons.

"I might. One of my favorite passages is the Good Samaritan. To me, it embodies the spiritual virtue of surprise. He's the last person anyone expected to do the right thing. All the others were religious officials who were on their way to services. The Samaritan didn't have those obligations, so he was free to act purely as a human being."

How many members in this congregation?

"We have 104 and we're taking in 11 new members in two weeks."

How long have you served here?

"Since 1999."

Plan on retiring in the near future?

"I retire in three months, three weeks and six days. But who's counting?"

* * *

The roots of the First Unitarian Church of Hobart run deep in the history of Northwest Indiana. It was built in 1874. The sanctuary is listed on the National Register of Historic Places. The original pews are used to this day.

The diverse congregation hails from all over NWI and draws from many different spiritual sources to form a community that cherishes religious pluralism and promotes the inherit dignity of every person.

Brewin has performed 3,000 weddings since becoming a reverend and has been editing "Religious Humanism" biannually for 10 years. He will continue to do so in retirement, maybe as a quarterly.

Wolfgang Rubsam *(Feb. 2011)*

"I worked hard. Anyone who works as hard as I did can achieve the same results."
– Johann Sebastian Bach

Wolfgang Rubsam's beautiful farmhouse is located on the LaPorte County side of County Line Road – look for the 120-foot wind turbine and barber pole.

Rubsam, 64, is a barber with a pilot's license, he's also a world renowned organist and a retired professor. Rubsam taught music at Northwestern University for 23 years, at the University of Music, Saar in Saarbrucken, Germany, and at Lawrence University in Appleton, Wis. He has more than 100 recordings.

Due to my lack of knowledge regarding classical music and the fact I didn't have a set of prepared questions and I use a stone-age reel-to-reel tape recorder, Wolf hesitated with our interview. But, at my urging, he was kind enough to stick it out and eventually warmed up to my quirky self.

* * *

Where were you born?

"In central Germany, near Frankfurt. Fulda is a very baroque town – lots of churches including a very beautiful cathedral.

"We lived a couple blocks from the cathedral; I was an altar boy. There was a huge, wonderful pipe organ and that certainly was the motivation for me. Looking up at it was like, 'Wow, this must be heaven on earth.'"

At what age did you begin playing music?

"At about 3 1/2 or 4 years of age, I started playing the piano. As a child, my toy was my piano. My parents had to drag me from the piano to do my homework.

"You can't play the organ unless you're very well-educated on the piano. Anyone who has made some headlines internationally usually has started at a very, very early age. When I say organ, I don't mean an organ with speakers; I mean an organ that has pipes."

Were your parents musical?

"Yes, they were both music educators."

Europe?

"Europe has incredible culture and history. This country is really a baby by comparison. It is a very small amount of time that has influenced this country. The cultural issue in Europe is very deep-rooted. Our younger generation is not really aware and need to rediscover this. There is so much to be learned from the riches of Europe.

"Unfortunately, in terms of schooling, Americans are not inclined to learn foreign languages. In Germany, most high schools require three foreign languages to be learned."

What languages did you learn?

"English, Latin and Greek. I also learned French, but I'm not really fluent in French any more.

"I believe it is extremely important that the childhood of an individual is guided in a very structured and a very involved way. Children should not sit in front of the television or computer all the time. They should rather read a book or learn something in terms of a language or be involved in learning an instrument rather than doing all these manipulations with their fingers. I don't know what these things are called – video games.

"It has been proven when you learn to play an instrument it improves your academic excellence in school. You learn discipline."

How old were you when you emigrated to the United States?

"About 27."

Is your wife, Jan, American-born?

"Yes, she's a native Texan; you don't mess with Texas."

Playing the organ?

"The organ is one of the most complicated instruments you could ever play. It is like learning to fly a 747; you have to start learning the roots of flying a little Cessna first and work up to this incredible machine.

"It doesn't happen overnight; it is an unbelievable amount of work. Unfortunately, you'll never be paid very well. The organ is definitely church-related. It is not a concert hall instrument."

Talk about varieties of organs.

"When I go to Italy this September for an organ recital, those organs are completely different. Every organ is different. It takes several days to prepare a recital.

"It's completely different than pulling your flute or violin out of its case and being a prima donna in front of a huge audience and getting paid unbelievable amounts of money when you're famous. You can be as famous as you want to be being an organist, but you'll never get super-rich. That's fine; the organ is what I love."

Is there a particular make of pipe organ you like best?

"I cannot answer that question because there are too many wonderful instruments. It is the same with composers, with the exception of Johann Sebastian Bach. He is certainly on the very top of my list."

Tell me about Bach.

"As a composer, I don't believe he has ever been matched. He's been the model for many composers after him. His is like Godly music; it's not normal. The amount of music the man wrote is hard to believe. There were no computers or copy machines... . I think there was something very powerful from above.

"J.S. Bach influenced music, including the Beatles. They structured their compositional strategy of creating songs in the Classical music, not in the Pop music. You have to think of a tree that starts somewhere and suddenly all these branches come out of the tree. It is definitely true that one of the branches was the Beatles."

Music?

"Music is an unusual language in itself. It is internationally understood. You don't have to learn grammar, you just have to listen. Music really touches the heart and the soul of people.

"There was research done in Africa on tribes from very remote areas. They didn't know what Bach or Mozart sounded like. The researchers played them examples of sad, happy and meditative music and they had pictures that were parallel to the musical moods. These people, who heard for the first time, Western music, were able to put their fingers on the picture that reflected that kind of music."

Very interesting.

"Again, everything has to start with some kind of root formation. For me, it snowballed into some kind of international tree that has a lot of leaves. My students are worldwide in leading positions today. Two of them are now professors at Indiana University in Bloomington; others are in Europe. I started from a little seed and became some kind of tree; now, I see the fruit going further."

Wolf, let's switch gears. You probably own and operate the only wind-powered barber shop in the world. When did you open?

"About 12 years ago. ... We have four acres that have to be mowed, but we have another 10 acres we have leased out to the farmer."

Barbering?

"Barbering is a second career upon retirement from the music field. It also is a profession where you try to make a very good, artistic outcome in the haircut; you make people happy with that. It is more than simply going over the head with the clippers. It is really an artistic endeavor that needs attention to detail. ... I also have a barber instructor's license and teach part time at Merrillville Beauty College."

You're certainly not an idler.

"The word 'retirement' is really a dirty word. You should always be on the move rather than sitting around, watching the wall move."

How long will you cut hair?

"Barbers usually don't retire. They just keep cutting until it's time to bite the grass. Ha ha!"

Wolf, do all Germans have such a zany sense of humor?

* * *

Like "hero," Americans use the word "genius" quite liberally. That said, I believe the talented Wolfgang Rubsam probably is a genius.

Panida Girddonfag *(June 2010)*

"For the first time in my life, I know what I wanna do! And for the first time, I'm gonna do it!"
–From the 1989 film "Dead Poets Society"

Panida Girddonfag, 23, has gone to school in this country for more than six years. She has attended Indiana University Northwest for the past four years. Girddonfag lives in Lake Station with her fiance, Max Jackson-Boyd.

The first 17 years of her life were spent in Bangkok. She has a 10-year-old brother living in Thailand with her parents. Girddonfag's mother is a pharmacist; her father is an electrical engineer.

* * *

I've interviewed four people for this column with the surname of Spencer – Tom, Kathy, Mark and Dave. You're my first Panida Girddonfag.

"Think of the word panda with an 'i' in the middle," she said. "My last name is kind of long and sounds weird. I came here as a foreign-exchange student at Carrier Mills High School in Illinois. It was a very small town."

Then what?

"I went to Southeastern Illinois for two years where I received an associate's degree in science. I'm a class away from earning a bachelor of arts degree in biology here at IUN."

Life in Carrier Mills, Ill., and Lake Station, for that matter, has to be a far cry from the big city of Bangkok. Tell this Midwesterner about your native land.

"Bangkok, the capital city, is really crowded. Of the 60 million people living in Thailand, 12 million of them live in Bangkok."

Give me an interesting fact about Thailand.

"It's the only country in the surrounding area that wasn't colonized by another country."

I know Thailand is about the size of California, tell me more.

"Thailand is a wonderful place, but it's very hot and humid. April is the hottest month. There are many cultural things like Buddhist temples."

Are you a Buddhist?

"Yes."

Popular sports in Thailand?

"Soccer."

What about our national pastime, baseball?

"No baseball. I went to a RailCats game a couple of weeks ago, and we had to leave early. I was sooo bored."

You speak English well.

"We are taught English from the kindergarten on. But I didn't actually use it until high school."

Visually, is the Thai written language similar to Chinese characters?

"No, it looks more like Indian or Hebrew. But my family is Chinese-Thai. My great-great-grandparents came to Thailand from China."

An example of a national holiday?

"Wan Wisakah Bucha."

Yeah, well, Pannie, that's easy for you to say.

"It's a Buddhist observance commemorating the birth, enlightenment and death of Budda."

One of your favorite Thai meals?

"Steamed egg. You mix it with milk and water, steam it, and season the egg with soy sauce or oyster sauce. Sometime we put ground pork or shrimp in it."

Is that considered breakfast fare?

"Dinner, mostly. At my parents' house, we have rice soup and maybe some fried vegetables for breakfast. Have you ever heard of salty egg? You can buy them in the stores. It's like a boiled egg that's often eaten with the rice soup. We don't like sweets too much."

Me either. As a kid, I remember munching on stalks of rhubarb

I'd pulled from my grandmother's garden.

"Rhubarb? Is it like a fruit?"

Well, it's sort of like red celery that's sour like a lemon. In America, we make rhubarb pie. Lemon, too.

"I like sour. There is a restaurant in Crown Point called Five Star Thai that is good."

Is it authentic?

"For the most part. But some of the ingredients are Americanized, which is understandable."

Example?

"They use broccoli instead of certain vegetables that we would use such as kanar."

Kanar?

"I thought I bought kanar at the grocery store the other day, but it was something called mustard greens."

How did you like that soul food?

"I found mustard greens more bitter than kanar."

Are there McDonald's in Thailand?

"Yes, but there is no breakfast menu at our McDonald's. Most McDonald's in Thailand are usually located in malls that don't open until like 11 a.m."

"I prefer Thai food over American food. Thai is healthier, there's more vegetables and less grease. At breakfast, we don't do too much sugar."

Yeah, nothing like four of five tablespoons of white sugar over a heaping bowl of Frosted Mini-wheats. Let's switch gears.

I know a guy who received a degree in biology back in the '60s; he said for their final exam, they had to identify 80 different types of flora or fauna. He only was stumped on one – a catfish whisker. Are you familiar with the catfish?

"Oh, yeah. We eat those."

So do we!

"They're awesome! We put catfish on a stick and roast it."

How did we get back on food? Our mutual friend, Patty Wisniewski, says you're a very talented artist.

"When I want to draw, I guess I do good. I like drawing and crafting."

You're modest.

"My parents kind of support me with my finances here; they want me to go back to Thailand to medical school. The school that I talked to said some of my credits could be transferred."

Would you rather be a doctor than a biologist?

"I would rather not be both. My passion is to be a costume designer. I remember when I was 5 or 6 years old, my father bought me a Madonna video cassette. It showed one of her concerts where she was all dressed up in Victorian costumes. I always thought she looked wonderful.

"What I find different between my Asian culture and American culture is that you teach your kids to be whatever they have a passion for. In Thai culture, they don't teach you that way; they expect you to be the best – to get a good job that pays good money."

Kid, you know why I write this column for a living? For the bennies and big bucks. Passion is overrated.

"I'm struggling with myself. I was taught to obey my parents, but I also would like to express myself. I like craft. I want to be an artist."

Panida, are your eyes welling up?

"I'm sorry. Max bought the house in Lake Station so we could be together. But, I'll probably go back to Thailand in August to apply for medical school."

How's that going to affect your and Max's relationship?

"I don't know."

* * *

Panida Girddonfag is a sincere, kind person. She wants me to interview one of her classmates who is a Vietnam vet confined to a wheelchair and who also suffers from post-traumatic stress disorder.

Soon after surgery, our mutual friend, Patty, took a set design class at IUN with Panida. Pat's my age and was told by her doctor not to lift anything. Panida was the only student in the class who offered to help Patty, who was walking with an obvious limp. For Panida, it was an easy decision to help someone who was struggling.

Who knows what her decision will be come August?

I hope she goes with her passion.

Ed van Wijk *(June 2005)*

"Sometimes you have to give up the life you have chosen to find the life that is waiting for you."
-Author Unknown

Last week Norwich, England; this week we take the ferry for a short jaunt across the channel and narrows of the North Sea to Holland.

I always wanted to travel.

Today, we visit the home of Cornelis Eduard van Wijk. Ed and his lovely wife Mary have three children, Cecilia, Johan, and Michael.

Ed grew up in the city of Dordrecht – The Kingdom of The Netherlands. He is a soccer coach for the Lowell Parks Department and always one of the top finishers in the two-mile race-walk that coincides with The Buckley 5 Miler.

His grandfather's smoker's cabinet and pipe rack hang on one wall. A wedding picture of Ed and Mary on another. In the portrait, the American bride is seen inching up her white wedding gown. She sports a gigantic pair of wooden clogs.

* * *

You know, Mary, I vaguely remember you getting up in front of the church years ago and telling the sweetest story about when you first laid eyes on this dashingly handsome seafaring man, how it was love at first – what's so funny, Mary?

"Yes, yes that's exactly how it was," Ed recalls. "You have excellent memory, Jeff!"

Talk to me, you dashing, seafaring Dutchman.

"My first career was in the Dutch Merchant Marines; I worked on cargo ships. All kinds of them. In 1985, I got assigned as a radio officer to cruise ships on the Holland-America line. They make journeys out of Vancouver, British Columbia up to Alaska in the summer; during the fall and winter, they make trips through the Panama Canal and the Carribean. It was Sept.1, 1987; I was minding my own business in the radio room and the lady says, 'I've come to get my life jacket but the door says,'No Entry.' I asked her, 'Who are you?' Mary replied, 'I'm one of the new nurses.' Being as she was not a tourist, I allowed her in. She thanked me. We had a little conversation. She left. I thought, 'This is a nice young lady, I'd like to get to know her.' And the rest is history."

I saw that episode on The Love Boat. Seems like Kate Jackson played the stunningly beautiful youthful nurse. See Mary, this version ain't so bad.

Tell me about Holland, Ed.

"Right now, we don't have a king. We have a queen – Beatrix. The Netherlands hasn't had a king since William III back in the late 1800's. Dordrecht is the oldest city of Holland, there are about 115,000 people. Although it's in the middle of the country, it is like a triangular island surrounded by three rivers. Holland is about a third the size of Indiana, but has four times as many people. Nearby Rotterdam is the largest seaport in world."

What about the daily life of a school boy growing up in Dordrecht?

"I played a lot of soccer, and I'm a pretty good ice skater. By the time I was in the fourth or fifth grade, I worked at a strawberry operation as a picker. I picked beans, too. In Holland you must learn three other languages. I was taught English, German and French."

Probably came in handy working on cargo and cruise ships. Why did you get out of the Merchant Marines?

"Mary and I decided it was too difficult to start a family while working on the cruise ship. We decided to move to the United States. I was 35. Being married to an American citizen, I'm a permanent resident. I have my green card, renewable every 10 years."

What did you and Mary do then?

"Mary went back to working as a nurse in a hospital and I decided to get a degree in computer science. Computers were replacing the job of radio officer. While going to Purdue Cal, I worked different jobs. I knew nothing of how the American tax system worked so I took a tax preparation class, too. H &R Block hired me as tax preparer. I did that for three years. I got my bachelor's degree in computer analysis and design. I continued my studies while working various computer programming jobs. Eventually, I was recruited by a consulting company for the implementation of Oracle Human Resources software. The company would find a client that wanted the system implemented. My company would fly me to wherever.

"The first year, I worked in San Francisco. I'd fly out of O'Hare on Sunday evening to San Francisco. I'd stay at an apartment, work until Thursday, sometimes Friday, and then fly back to see my family here in Lowell on the weekend. Fifty weeks out the year I'd do that. When I finished up the San Francisco job, they sent me to Reading, Pa. for a year. Same thing. Work five days a week away from my family and come home on the weekends. Then a year in Griffin, Ga., Washington D.C., Texas,..."

Might as well been a trucker making long hauls. Tough gig for a family man.

"Yes, it was. Two-and-a-half years ago, Mary and I decided that God was calling us to become pastors in the United Methodist Church. We applied with the Garrett Evangelical seminary and that's where we've been going for the last two- and-a-half years. I've been very involved with church all my life, mostly as a volunteer. But to give up your life as you know it, and pursue it as a full time thing, that did not happen until two-and-a-half years ago.

"Mary no longer works as a nurse. We both work 20 hours per week each at the Methodist Church here in town. I'm in Christian education, organizing Bible studies and Sunday school classes. Mary helps the pastor take care of people when they are in hospital or shut in."

Surely, growing up in The Netherlands you were Christian Reformed.

"Yes, I was. Christian Reformed is based on the teachings of John Calvin. We attended Church twice on Sundays. We rode our bike or walked to church. You didn't drive your car. No sports or TV. We didn't buy or sell things on Sunday. When I go back to Holland to visit my parents and siblings, I still enjoy attending church with them."

Why did you and Mary convert? She was baptized Catholic.

"As Methodists, we believe people have a choice. Calvinistic beliefs are more rigid, they believe everything has already been set in stone. I think whether it is Sunday or Saturday or any day of the week, you need to take time out, which in Hebrew would be Sabbath. We need to rest and focus on God."

A little meditation throughout the day probably wouldn't do any of us any harm, Ed. Ever venture over and visit our neighbors to the southeast in Demotte?

"Yes, my brother-in-law went to church in Demotte – The Church of the Dutch Corners. It started out more than 100 years ago as a Dutch-speaking congregation. Most of the Dutch-Americans from Demotte and Highland are from northern Holland originally – farm area."

You and Mary will finish the seminary in two years?

"Yes, and once we graduate, we will become commissioned. After a three- year probationary period, we will be ordained."

It will probably be a bit of a struggle – financially – for you the next couple of years.

"As a consultant, I made six times what I make now. Scholarships and student loans will help. And living frugally.

"Jeff, do you know how the copper wire was invented?"

No, not really.

"Two Dutchman fighting over a penny."

Ed, you're a real cut-up.

"We are following a call. Mary and I are doing what we want to do. It's not about money. I, as a Dutch person worry about money. Do I have enough? Can I afford this? I always worried whether I would make enough money to provide for my family. Since I've followed this calling, I haven't worried about that."

* * *

Ed van Wijk. An intelligent, hard working man. A family man. A man in the midst of changing professions at age 50. Following his passion. Answering a call.

Some things money can't buy.

Millie Rytel *(May 2011)*

"Poland is an ally of the United States of America. It was our duty to show that we are a reliable, loyal and predictable ally. America needed our help, and we had to give it."
 – Adam Michnik, journalist, essayist, former dissident

By some miracle, Steve Rytel didn't die on the battlefield in Italy during World War II.

After the war, he eventually emigrated from his native Poland to the United States where he found work at Inland Steel as a pipe fitter.

Like her husband, Millie Rytel, 84, was born in Poland; she is a petite lady who has a delightful accent.

Millie lives in a duplex in Highland. The Rytels had two daughters, Chris and Elizabeth. In 1973, when the girls were 14 and 11, their father died from burns received at Inland's No. 2 Coke Plant.

* * *

Tell me about the old country. Let's start with your father.

"He was a World War I veteran and a farmer. He grew the wheat and the potatoes, but the main thing he raised is the pigs – special for the bacon. They had to be a certain age and weight. He always get highest price for his pigs. He win awards for his pigs."

When you were growing up, Europe was in turmoil.

"My family was abducted by the Russians in February 1939. They came into our house at 2 a.m. with guns and ammunition and said, 'You have a half-hour to pack your belongings.

"My younger sister was very sick. The Russians told my mother that she could stay at the house with my sister, but the rest of the family had to go. My mother said she would go with the rest of the family; she wrapped the baby in blankets."

Then what?

"In a cattle wagon, they took us to the railroad station about seven miles away. They didn't tell us where they were taking us; the Russians just said that we were going to change residency for a while."

Where did they relocate your family?

"Siberia; it took a month to get there.

How old were you at the time?

"I was 13. I made fun of the Russian soldiers' uniforms when they came into our house in Poland. They told my father to tell me to shut up or they would shoot me.

"My sister, who was sick, they put her on a sled. It was in the middle of the winter. We walked all night with the snow almost up to my waist. I had just regular shoes; my feet froze. We slept on hay when we finally get to barracks."

How long were you in Siberia?

"We were fortunate; after 18 months they let us go. Poland made an agreement with (Joseph) Stalin; they fight against Germany if (Russia would) release the prisoners."

Your late husband fought against the Germans while in the Polish Army.

"Yes, he had to lie about his age; he was only 15. His family also was abducted by the Russians. That is why he joined the army, so he could get out of Russia.

"He was wounded the night before they put the Polish flag atop Monte Cassino in Italy. He was covered with rubble. In the morning, the dew came and it was refreshing; he awakened. He heard somebody walking by, so he threw pebbles at the men who were piling up the dead bodies."

Had your husband been shot?

"The shrapnel. He lay out on the battlefield for 24 hours, holding his guts in his hands. They never thought has was going to survive.

"A Polish surgeon and an English specialist told Steve, 'We did what human hands can do. If you are going to survive it will be because of God.' Steve was two years critical condition in England. He recovered so well. He never was sick and never take off work at Inland Steel in 24 years."

What year did you emigrate to the United States?

"In 1948; I was 21. I meet Steve at a dance in the (Indiana) Harbor (section of East Chicago) in 1952.

"He built our house in Woodmar (neighborhood of Hammond) by himself, the bricklaying and everything. We had been living in North Hammond; I didn't want to move so far away."

Millie, you traveled from southeast Poland to the United States. Moving from North Hammond to Woodmar isn't that long a trek. Would you care to talk about the coke plant explosion of 1973?

"Steve was 60 percent third-degree burns. He didn't have a skin. They isolated him. I talk to him with intercom and look at him from the hole for the key. ...He was very strong."

Millie, how long did Steve live?

"He was burned on March 9 and died ... on March 22. Charlie Rankin lasted a week; he was like a father to Steve. I didn't tell Steve when Charlie died.

"The night before Steve died; they let me in. I wear the gown and the mask. I said: 'Stefan, you've got to drink; I'll give you a cup. You are losing all the moisture from your body.' That was almost midnight. He collapsed. They make me leave room.

"My daughters don't go to the cemetery. They would tell me, 'We want to remember what a good daddy we had.' My youngest, she was 11 and Steve would carry her to bed yet. He would read her stories. She would sit on his lap.

"It seem like yesterday."

* * *

There is a memorial at the United Steelworkers Local 1010 union hall in East Chicago with 389 names on it. It's a list of bargaining-unit employees killed at ArcelorMittal East (formerly Inland Steel Co.).

The first name to appear is Joseph St. Clair who was killed at the open hearth on Feb. 21, 1903. The last name is Jason Ham of Union Township who was killed at No. 3 Cold Strip on Oct. 21, 2010.

Steve Rytel, the man who cheated death during World War II, also is on the list.

Millie Rytel had a book published about three years ago entitled "Four Continents to Freedom." It's her biography.

It's on my list.

History Books

Steve McShane *(July 2012)*

"...And I said good-bye to the Mayor of Gary and I went out from the city hall and turned the corner into Broadway.
And I saw workmen wearing leather shoes scruffed with fire and cinders, and pitted with little holes from running molten steel.
And some had bunches of specialized muscles around their shoulder blades hard as pig iron, muscles of their forearms were sheet steel and they looked like men who had been somewhere."
– Carl Sandburg, 1915

Steve McShane is a native of Joliet, Ill., but he knows a whole lot about Northwest Indiana. He's a history professor and archivist at Indiana University Northwest.

McShane, 53, and his wife, Cindy, have lived in Valparaiso since 1982 and have raised two daughters.

* * *

Do you have a long history of having an interest in history?

"Yes, I always liked history; probably because my parents took me on trips to see historic sites.

"But I wasn't sure what to do with a bachelor's degree in history; it's not exactly the most marketable degree. Then, I took an archives class my last semester, and I thought, 'I like this; it's pretty cool. You get to preserve stuff.'"

What kind of education is needed to become an archivist?

"A master's degree in history, for starters, and you also need some internships for practical experience. It so happened, while I was attending Northern Illinois University in Dekalb, they had a regional history archives. So I enrolled in the grad school at Northern Illinois. During my two-year program, I served two internships in their Regional History Center. I also have a master's in library science from Indiana University Bloomington."

Then what?

"As soon as I got my degree, these regional archives opened up here at IUN. I interviewed in 1982; Professors Ron Cohen and Jim Lane, said, 'Yeah, great, come on in.'"

Do you teach any classes?

"One; it's called 'Survey of Indiana History.' We do some state history at the beginning, and then shift our focus to Northwest Indiana history. I do that because I figure history helps you answer two main questions: Why is the region the way it is today and how did it get that way? We use the archives here; the students do research here. It's a fun class, really."

How does the class unfold?

"We start with the glaciers and their impact on the terrain. We progress to the organization of Lake and Porter Counties in the 1830s, then the railroads, post-Civil War, Hammond comes along, the big heavy industrial development in Whiting and Indiana Harbor... .

"The interesting thing about the class is it's a requirement for education majors whether elementary or secondary. The rationale is, if you're going to be teaching around here, it's good to know the background of the region."

How did the archives come to be at IUN?

"Cohen and Lane's research interest was Northwest Indiana, specifically Gary, to start out. They found that a lot of original Gary residents were still around because Gary was so young.

"These folks had boxes of old photographs, publications and documents in their garages and attics. Cohen and Lane obtained some of this material, and said, 'This is important stuff – it's local history.' They started bringing things back to campus."

They sound like a couple of hoarders to me. What year are we talking?

"Around 1973. They just kind of self-declared themselves as the co-directors of something they called the Calumet Regional Archives.

"In 1980, this library building opened; Lane and Cohen were able to secure two rooms here on the third floor to store the material.

But they didn't know how to organize it or preserve it."

And along came a young archivist to save the day back in '82. Tell me about your latest book.

"'Steel Giants' came out in May of '09. I collaborated with Gary Wilk. ArcelorMittal and U.S. Steel donated all the photographs.

"The book focuses on workers, but not necessarily organized labor. We do mention the 1919 and 1937 strikes. It's a steelmaking by 'steel people' kind of thing."

I resemble that remark.

"'Steel Giants' is a tribute to the workers who took on those jobs under dangerous conditions. It was amazing what they did, just building the mills in the first place, with nothing but horsepower and steam power. And then, making the steel in such a labor-intensive way.

"Chapter 1 describes how the mills were made. Chapter 2 delves into how the steel was made. Chapter 3 goes into the two communities: Gary and Indiana Harbor. Chapter 4 is strictly worker shots. The book goes from the turn of 20th century to about 1950. We still have a ton of photos from 1950 to the present."

What about a "Steel Giants II"?

"Not a bad idea."

How much is "Steel Giants"?

"You can buy it for $26 on Amazon. It's also available at the IUN bookstore in the Savannah Center, Barnes & Noble and Borders.

"Let me take you for a tour; we have a great collection of local history books."

Prof, I thought you'd never ask. What's in all these gray containers about the size of shoe boxes?

"Old Pullman-Standard cards. They tell the employees' marital status, date of birth, whether they're a citizen or an alien, ethnicity, white, black... ."

Could we take a look at a few?

"Sure; this guy was an assembler. Says he's been disciplined for habitual absenteeism. He was born in 1851 and was hired December of 1918 at the age of 67."

That's before the merger with Pullman Palace Car Co., back when the place was known as Standard Steel Car Manufacturing Co.

"This guy, a Charles Crable, came from Pennsylvania to 2184 Broadway in Gary. He's black, married, two dependents... . Didn't learn a trade, it says. He finished his first year of high school. The last place he worked, before Pullman-Standard hired him in 1942, was Carnegie Illinois Steel in Gary. He was born in 1919."

Prof, I can feel the history in this place.

* * *

Professor McShane also showed me some very cool original Southshore posters from the Roaring '20s. They came from a private collection. Rather than storing them away in his basement, the previous owner felt more people could enjoy the posters if he donated them to the Calumet Regional Archives.

I'm sure McShane feels that way.

John Hodson *(May, 2008)*

"Never in all my world travels, have I found a more perfect spot, not a more tantalizing river."
-Lew Wallace

After traveling east on 900 South, I turn south on Baum's Bridge Road, eventually entering Pleasant Township and the home of John Hodson.

Pleasant Township is, well, pleasant. Hodson, 57, and his wife, Mary, live in a cream-colored house nestled in a patch of woods. There also is a cream-colored barn.

The Hodsons have a Kouts mailing address and a 150-acre back yard. He doesn't mow much grass; he has been known to burn it.

* * *

"I've planted native grasses," Hodson begins. "Periodically, you need to do prescribed burns to eliminate invasive species and restart the native grasses.

"Besides my involvement with Kankakee Valley Historical Society, I'm working toward developing a wildlife area on the property east of the Collier Lodge. Two years ago, I entered into the wetland reserve program and placed 100 acres into the WRP. Previous to that, I entered 10 acres in the conservation reserve program. Native grasses were planted in both programs."

Were you born and raised down here in Kouts along the Kankakee River?

"No, I was raised in Munster. I also lived in St. John Township for 30 years. Mary and I moved here in 2002."

You attended Munster High School.

"I started there. My dad was killed in a car accident. I was getting into trouble, so my mom shipped me off to Howe Military School. Howe turned me around; it was a great thing for me. I send them donations every year."

Did you buy this spread with all these projects and programs in mind?

"Initially, I bought the property so I could have a place to hunt. We didn't buy the land with ideas of restoring the lodge. The historical aspect of it all just sort of developed."

Tell me more about Collier Lodge. I realize that it is near where the archaeological digs have taken place the past several years.

"The lodge was in bad shape in 2002, and it's still a wreck. I started reading about the history of it. The lodge was located on one of the river's oxbows (bend in the river) but they straightened the river and now it cuts through here (shows me a map). The creek next to the lodge is actually a segment of the original Kankakee River.

"We have a claim on the Grand Kankakee Marsh No. 2 bridge; they want to get rid of it. I think it would be appropriate for the GKM bridge to be moved to a historic site on an original segment of the Kankakee."

The area around Baum's Bridge has quite a history.

"It was a spot along the marsh that was relatively narrow and it held its banks, so it was a reliable crossing place. After the last ice age, the Native Americans used it.

"In the 1700s, an Indian battle was fought there for control of the ford. Baum's Bridge was formerly known as Potawatomi Ford.

"In 1838, there was ferry there. The sportsmen also built there because they knew they weren't going to get their buildings washed out."

There were lodges or hunt clubs other than Collier?

"There were four main lodges by the 1880s near Baum's Bridge. Businessmen from outside the area frequented the Louisville; the Rockville, Terre Haute and Indianapolis; and the Pittsburgh. The Valley Gun Club, which was also known as the White House Gun Club, was used by locals. Collier Lodge was a private business; it included rooms, a restaurant and general store."

You're the president of the KVHS.

"Yes, we started the Historical Society by searching and writing letters to any organization that might help us with restoring Collier Lodge. I received a response from the Historic Landmark Foundation; we're an affiliate now. Out of all 50 states, Indiana is probably the strongest regarding historic preservation."

How much will it cost to restore Collier Lodge?

"At least $250,000; the building is in the holding stage right now. We've received loans and have applied for grants.

"The KVHS only has been around six years, yet we have more than 100 members. Anybody can be a member, no matter where you live – Kouts, Kankakee, Ill...."

Some very famous people came to this neck of the woods to hunt and fish.

"Yes, (former president) Benjamin Harrison, the Studebaker Brothers, Lew Wallace; Gen. Lew Wallace owned property on the Kankakee River. He was really a fascinating man.

"What we are trying to accomplish is an educational tool to tell children the history – what it was like before the dredging – and also explain how man came along, straightened the river, and destroyed the marsh. We have tours for Valparaiso University's Geography Department."

What sort of outside help have you received?

"After I bought the property, I started noticing all the wildlife. I realized that I could really make a difference by starting a conservation program. There are state and federal programs and private organizations, like Ducks Unlimited, that have helped us. All our grass seed ($7,000) was donated by Pheasants Forever.

"We have 2- and 5-acre shallow water areas. The native grasses are really nice for upland game. We actually have a nice population of quail; 90 percent of the quail population was decimated. I have food plots (grain sorghum). We picked up 200 white pine seedlings from Jasper-Pulaski Game Preserve; Mary and I have planted them."

How do you maintain such a high energy level?

"When I first undertook these projects, everybody told me, 'You can't do this.' I started out by painting a sign: 'Help me save this building.'

"If somebody would have told me this is where I'd be 10 years ago, I would have told them they were crazy. Circumstances developed and opportunities arose. And that's where partnerships develop with people like Jim Sweeney, Dick Blythe and Jim Hitz."

"Howe Military taught me organizational skills; I can see the path I want to take with this project."

* * *

Hodson, a former field engineer, started out on the wrong path while in his teens. Today, Hodson walks the straight and narrow with perseverance.

He worked for two years on his wetland restoration plan. The Natural Resource and Conservation Service told Hodson it was the best wetland reserve program they had ever seen.

Hodson hopes to restore part of the ford the Potowatomi used until forced to take what is known as The Trail of Death in 1838. Like Enos Baum, he has visions of a bridge.

And he'll see to it that a grand old dame gets nipped and tucked – all the while keeping her who she is. Collier Lodge deserves a little pampering; she had her uncivilized and rough-hewn lover, the serpentine Kankakee River, stolen from her.

For some, straight and narrow just ain't natural.

Stanley Swanson *(Nov. 2012)*

"There isn't any finer folks living than a Republican that votes the Democratic ticket."
– Will Rogers

Stanley Swanson has been married to his beloved wife, Laverne, for 68 years.

They raised five children and moved from Riverdale, Ill., to Lowell 24 years ago.

Swanson wears a hearing aid in his right ear and is missing part of his left ear due to bouts with cancer. After 14 surgeries, he ordered the doctor to remove it.

At nearly 90, Swanson, a World War II veteran, still is sharp as a tack.

* * *

You must be of Scandinavian descent.
"My parents were born in Malmo, Sweden," he said.
What about you?
"The Highland-Beverly area of South Chicago. We had the gaslight streetlights. Our Democratic precinct captain, who was a hunchback, also served as the lamp lighter. Every afternoon he'd climb a ladder and open up the glass top and light them. In the morning, he'd go around and snuff them all out."
Another era, Stanley.
"Yeah, it was all horses and wagons back then. The iceman would come around every other day, and you'd put a sign in your win-

dow for 25, 50, 75 or 100 pounds of ice. Everybody had an icebox on their back porch. The iceman had a key to open the iceboxes."

High school?

"There were two technical high schools in Chicago at that time. Tilden Technical High School was on the South Side in back of the Yards, and Lane Technical High School was on the North Side. It was male students only for both schools. I had a wonderful four years with a wonderful education at Tilden Tech.

"Everything was strict at Tilden Tech; nobody stepped out of line and nobody talked back. You greeted your teacher at the door of each class, 'Good morning Mr. Arbuckle' or 'Good afternoon Miss Mahan.' Female teachers weren't allowed to be married in those days."

Life after high school?

"I went to work for Goodman Manufacturing Co. We made electrical mining machinery. The Congress had stipulated that aircraft building, ship building and mining machinery workers had automatic deferments from the military.

"My brother joined the armed forces when he was 17; less than a year later, Bert's ship was torpedoed by the Nazis in the North Atlantic off of Greenland."

Did he survive?

"No; he went down with the USS Dorchester on Feb.3,. 1943. The German U-boats picked off those guys like sitting ducks. When we got the word Bert had been killed, I got mad."

Although you had a deferment, you enlisted anyway.

"Within two weeks I got a letter stating: 'Greetings, you have hereby been nominated to represent the neighbors of your community in the Armed Forces of the United States – Franklin Delano Roosevelt.'"

Like your brother, you also were in the Navy.

"Yes, I started out at the U.S. Naval Torpedo Testing Range on Long Island, N.Y."

How did you get transported from the East Coast to the West Coast, by train or boat?

"By Pullman coaches which were loaded with sailors and soldiers. I was the only person to be in a room by himself. I noticed that the porter was sleeping on the stool of the men's washroom next to my quarters.

"There were two berths in my quarters. I asked the porter, 'This was your sleeping area, wasn't it?'

"Then I told him, 'There's an empty berth in this room, you come in here and sleep; I don't want you sitting in the shit house all night. Come in here and we can talk; we can read."

The porter's reply?

"All the porters were black; they were very polite. He said, 'Well, I shouldn't be in there.' I told him he had my permission to share the room with me, and he did."

Good for you, Stanley.

"He tried to make my bunk every morning, but I wouldn't allow it. I told that man I was taught to make my own bed."

What ship did you end up on?

"The USS LST-270. We called them a large stationary target because our maximum speed was 8 knots."

Were you in the thick of things?

"Our ship went through six invasions; we saw a lot. We went right up on the beach at full speed, where we would deliver all the troops and their equipment."

Many of those poor guys didn't make it very far once the plow doors opened.

"You got that right; it was something else. Our B-29s were bombing the Japs around the clock. We were getting ready to invade Japan."

Then what?

"My buddy (President) Harry Truman, ordered the first atomic bomb on Hiroshima on Aug. 6 by the Enola Gay. On Aug. 9, Harry ordered the second one dropped on Nagasaki.

"By the way, Lt. Col. (Paul) Tibbets (the pilot of the Enola Gay) spoke to us a few years ago at the Lowell Public Library. We had a nice talk. I told him, 'You saved our asses.'"

American casualties would have been unprecedented if Truman hadn't ordered the bombings.

"We were loaded for bear; they estimated we were going to lose a million men when we hit the beach."

Are you a Democrat?

"No way, Jose. I'm a Republican, but I did vote for Truman – Jack Kennedy, too."

* * *

The LST-270 earned four battle stars during World War II in the Pacific Theater, where she participated in several operations, including: the occupation of Kwajalein and Majuro Atolls, a campaign on Guam and the Battle of Leyte Landing.

Today at 11:00 a.m. and 11 p.m., Lakeshore Televison (WYIN), will air its version of Ken Burns' "The War," featuring World War II veterans from Northwest Indiana. Several have appeared in this column.

Hats off to all the men and women who have served in any of our armed forces, including Petty Officer 2nd Class Stanley Swanson who made it home from World War II... .

And to men like Bert Swanson, who did not.

Betty Balanoff *(Sept. 2007)*

"...We have been enjoined by the courts, assaulted by thugs, charged by the militia, traduced by the press, frowned upon in public opinion, and deceived by politicians. Still, labor is the most vital and potential power this planet has ever known..."
– Eugene V. Debs

In the early 90s, when I was a griever steward at Inland Steel in East Chicago, union reps received quite a series of lectures on American labor history when a special guest showed up and spoke for three or four hours each visit.

She covered everything from silversmiths at the time of the American Revolution to nurses' aides of the 1990s. The students were men and women of various ages and colors. Most could probably be deemed a little rough around the edges. Some were downright militant. They were all street smart.

When that white-haired dame held court she commanded our respect. "Mrs. Balanoff" knew her stuff. For some of us, it was the closet thing to college we'd ever know. Actually, it *was* college.

Elizabeth "Betty" Balanoff is the widow of Jim Balanoff, former President of Steelworkers Local 1010, and the mother-in-law of Jim Robinson, United Steelworkers District Director of Area 7. The Balanoffs raised four children: a lawyer, union representative, CPA and a nurse. Betty is 81 and lives in Hammond.

* * *

"I was born in a small town in Missouri," Balanoff began. "It was surrounded by farms."

Are you a farmer's daughter?

"No, I'm a dentist's daughter."

How did you meet your husband?

"Through his brother while I was attending the University of Chicago. We married and eventually moved from Chicago to Gary in 1955. We moved to Hammond 17 years later."

You're a retired college professor.

"Yes, I retired from Roosevelt University in '91. I taught Labor History."

Talk to me.

"As far back as you want to go in this country, whether it was in the North or South, they had their ways of exploiting the worker – whether it was black slaves, white indentured servants, or free factory workers. These people would work until they dropped dead, and sometimes they died pretty young.

"During the 1800s, children were often working before their fathers could get a job. You could get 10 kids for the price of one man. You could probably hire three women for the price of one man."

I remember you telling us at the union hall about the Drayers (early Teamsters), the Sons of Vulcan (Ironworkers), and a mysterious organization that evolved around 1870 known as the Knights of Labor that fought for equal pay for women and fought against child labor. They excluded bankers and lawyers, deeming them unproductive members of society.

"The Knights of Labor took in almost everybody – including housewives, blacks, and even employers. They were very religiously oriented so they also excluded liquor dealers. The reason the Knights were a secret society for so long was because they always got fired if they were found out. They were big on cooperative employer-employee ownership."

Which labor leaders from long ago do you really admire?

"Eugene Debs from Terre Haute. He was so solid. Debs received a million votes when he ran for president of the United States – while in prison. Another one was A. Philip Randolph who was trying to organize during the '20s – the worst possible time. It was a miracle what Randolph accomplished – such courage. During the 30s, came the birth of the CIO."

John L. Lewis.

"Yes. Some say if Lewis would have died right after he organized the CIO, he would be deemed the greatest labor leader of all time. But he lived too long and became reactionary.

"If people knew the truth about the past, it would be a lot easier to organize workers. A lot of younger workers think the companies gave them all the benefits they do have. Did you see that movie 'Sicko'? Great film.

"When I started teaching labor history, I asked the students, 'Why did you happen to pick this course?' A lot of them said that their parents or grandparents were immigrants who had worked in the mills. I started teaching a course in immigration history.

"There was such an overlap between immigration and labor because new immigrants always get the worst in everything. Often, they would be used as scabs, but later, they would be the union organizers. Then, I decided there was one more course I really wanted to teach – Indian-white relations. It spanned from the time of colonization up until now.

"Every time I wanted to teach one of those three courses, they didn't want me to. They'd say, 'Well, we need you to teach this.' And I'd say, 'Well, if I agree to teach that, will you let me teach this one, too?'

"I ended up teaching twice as many courses as the professor who had the second-highest amount of courses at Roosevelt. I had to stagger them over a two-year period, but I did what I wanted to do and it made the job fun instead of drudgery."

You're also an environmentalist.

"That was fairly late. I always liked nature, being outside in general. But that's not what got me into environmentalism; it was pollution!"

"When we lived on Michigan Street, we were three blocks north of the Calumet River. There was a sulphuric recycling plant to the east of us and a whole bunch of chemical plants to the west of us. We were in a nest of pollution. What got me active about it all was the river. At that time, during the '80s, Hammond, Gary and East Chicago were all dumping raw sewage illegally into the river.

"In Hammond, the beds where they treated the sediments were old and they hadn't been cleaned out regularly. Their solution, instead of putting city money into the infrastructure of the sanitary district, was to go the cheap way and dump it in the river. People were complaining that by 2 a.m., they would wake up choking, as if they were drowning in sewage.

"I hooked up with a woman from East Chicago. We had a public meeting at Spohn School. The teachers couldn't even let the kids out for recess; they'd get nauseated. There was also a great increase in liver disease. It ended up that the EPA sued all three cities, forcing them to clean up their sanitary districts. That was the one time we worked with the EPA."

"This was one of the naturally wonderful spots of the United States, but it was convenient for transportation, so industry settled here. If we had better regulations, people could still have good paying industrial jobs and also a clean environment."

Betty, I heard a story about how Cowboy Mezo, Joe Gyurko, and your husband walked into a board meeting at Inland Steel's main office in Chicago. Gyurko held up a vial of dirty water while explaining in no uncertain terms that it was an example of what workers were forced to wash up in after a day or night in the mill.

"I was there, too. Those guys had all kinds of eye infections and skin problems from that water – it came straight out of Lake Michigan. Joe testified; he was one of the best.

"You know who else was great? A couple of elderly women who owned a few shares of stock each. The big shots who owned tons of stock could care less about the men who made the steel.

"You should have heard those little old ladies tear into those 'suits,' 'You need to treat these people better!' The water situation was resolved.

"Right now, we're working on a confined disposal facility in East Chicago. They're going to dredge the ship canal. The old Sinclair refinery site is where they're going to put the stuff. I'm with a small group called the Coalition for a Clean Environment. We need more young people.

"I'm from the past, but I do sense a resurgence in the labor movement. Even now, in Congress, you have people talking openly about changing the labor laws."

Pat Tilton *(March 2010)*

"If you come down to the river
I bet you gonna find some people who live
You don't have to worry if you got no money
People on the river are happy to give"
-John Fogerty

Pat Tilton compiled and published a book about the history of Shelby the year Chevrolet came out with a red, white and blue Vega – 1976.

Her labor of love ranged from 1886, when William R. Shelby laid the town out at the junction of the Monon and Three I railroads, to the day the American Freedom Train came through town in July 1975.

Tilton, 74, was one of seven children; her maiden name is Hickey. She married Dean Tilton in November 1954 and they raised six children. Dean passed away in 2007.

Pat lives less than a half-mile north of the Kankakee River in Shelby on a stretch of Ind. 55 that's as serpentine as the river used to be before the meanders were taken out it nearly a century ago.

* * *

"When we moved to this house in '57, Shelby was all sand roads and muddy driveways; we'd get stuck every spring," Tilton began. "I wouldn't want to live any place else; I have wonderful neighbors. At one time, I thought I knew everybody in Shelby, but it's changed as years go by. People move in, people die."

Where did you grow up?

"On the east side of Cedar Lake, in a neighborhood called Cedar Point Park. I graduated from Crown Point High School; we were referred to as Lake Rats. Just like the Shelby kids were referred to as River Rats at Lowell High School."

Who you talkin' to? I grew up a Swamp Rat along the south side of this river and eventually became a mill rat like your brothers. Pat, you're my people.

"We spent a lot of time swimming in and skating on Cedar Lake, and at Crescent Roller Rink, too; that's where I met my husband."

Your parents?

"They were originally from Chicago. Dad was a truck driver; he was of Irish-Polish descent. Mother was of Ukrainian ancestry.

"My maternal grandfather used to sell tools on Maxwell Street in Chicago. While many Chicagoans would spend their summer vacations in Cedar Lake,
I used to spend mine in Chicago with relatives."

From Cedar Lake to the big city.

"My Aunt Violet was married to my mom's brother, but he got killed in World War II and was buried in France. They never had any kids, so she would borrow me.

"I'd ride the Greyhound bus all by myself and then take a taxi to her house. Aunt Violet would take me to places like the Palmer House (a plush downtown hotel) and Riverview (amusement park, at Western and Belmont avenues). I was scared to death of the bobs. She also played the piano and the accordion.

"When I was in eighth grade, there was an essay contest that I was all excited about; the topic was conservation. My mother's other brother, Uncle Johnny, said, 'If you win that contest, I'll buy you a typewriter.'"

And?

"I won the contest and got my typewriter. I've always loved English and journalism. During my junior year, I wanted to be the editor of the school paper, but one of the senior girls got the position."

Seniority rules.

"She ran away from home; I ended up getting the job. We used mimeograph paper at that time. Then, my senior year, I was editor of the first printed paper. It was printed at the Lake County Star.

"The people at the Star were very good to me; I did all the high school news. Right before I graduated, I got called to the office. I thought, 'Am I in trouble for something?'"

You must've written something unflattering about one of your teachers.

"It was the Lake County Star wanting to offer me a job. So, I never did go to college for journalism."

How long did you work there?

"About 40 years. Bert and Charlotte Verplank were my bosses. The Verplanks taught me a lot of things I didn't learn in school."

What were your duties at the paper?

"I wrote headlines, took pictures, covered news stories and had the police beat at one time. I also wrote a couple of my own columns."

Tough gig at times.

"'At Our House' was about my family and the neighborhood. I wrote that column for many years; it was very popular.

"Today, I take three newspapers. It's no fun reading the newspaper online; my father was a great newspaper reader. He'd read every single line."

Pat, what did Dean do for a living?

"Construction, lumberyards, milk man, insurance man, for the last 22 years of his working career, he was the superintendent of the grounds at Chapel Lawn Memorial Gardens in Schererville.

"I was his bookkeeper and secretary for 10 years. I started out writing obits for the paper and ended up doing cemetery work when I retired."

* * *

As a girl, she lost her brother, Jimmy. Many years later, she lost her grandson, Jedidiah. Both were riding bicycles when struck by vehicles; both drivers were drunk.

"Little Jed" was a classmate of my twin daughters. Although only 6 or 7 years old, Nic and Nat asked me to take them to Sheets Funeral Home so they could say goodbye to their friend.

Tilton also lost her daughter, Nadine, to Friedreich's ataxia in 2004; she was 41. Pat's daughter, Tricia, also has the disease; she's in a wheelchair a lot, but doing reasonably well.

Tilton belonged to St. Theresa Catholic Church in Shelby until it closed; she now belongs to St. Augusta in Lake Village. She is the secretary and treasurer of the Lafayette Diocese National Council of Catholic Women and belongs to the Shelby Senior Citizens.

These folks who volunteer, worship, work, mourn and sometimes struggle are the people you'll read about in this column.

The Pat Tiltons, not the Paris Hiltons.

Fern Eddy Schultz *(April 2009)*

*"Virgil Caine is the name,
and I served on the Danville train...
...In the winter of '65
We were hungry, just barely alive..."*
-Robbie Robertson

While meandering along Indiana 2 from Lowell to LaPorte, I felt like a 21st century voyageur paddling against the current of the Kankakee River in a canoe made by Ford Motor Co.

I passed by tiny Pinhook. Methodists can baptize 'em and bury 'em in Pinhook; the church sits a pew's length from the cemetery. A little further down the road, I said "Hola" to Pinola. Blink. "Adios, Pinola."

My rendezvous was with Fern Eddy Schultz, 80, at the LaPorte County Historical Museum. She is a widow who resides in the same house she grew up in. Said house was built the year the Civil War began – 1861. Her only child, Lannette, lives with her. Lannette has never married and is a retired Chesterton postmaster.

Because Eddy Schultz has spent her entire life in LaPorte County, those who have grown up with her or know her best refer to the LaPorte County historian by her delightful first and maiden names.

It was St. Patrick's Day when we chatted; Fern Eddy wore a Kelly green sweater.

* * *

"My father's parents were from Ireland," she began. "My mother's folks came to LaPorte just two years after LaPorte became a county."

What year was that?

"The McIntyres arrived in LaPorte County in 1834. In tracing them, I haven't got out of the United States. They moved from Pennsylvania to Ohio and then Indiana."

Fern Eddy, let's back up a couple centuries. LaPorte was probably named by French Canadians who bartered for fur with American Indians as early as the 1660s.

"Yes, LaPorte means 'the door" in French. The area was originally referred to as 'the door to the prairie.'

Tell more me about antebellum LaPorte County – before the Civil War.

"It's a lot different now. The Kankakee River was much wider before it was dredged and straightened. We have lots of information regarding the swamp lands and how they eventually were drained. There were many islands. Of course, those islands no longer exist; they are history.

"The bottom four townships in our county initially were part of Starke County. Early settlers had to cross the Kankakee so they could pay their taxes, etc, which posed a problem in those days. So, back in 1842, that area became part of LaPorte County.

What are some of the cities and towns in LaPorte County this museum represents?

"LaPorte is the county seat, although Michigan City has a larger population. We also have several small towns located in LaPorte County such as Union Mills, Rolling Prairie, Hanna and Otis.

"Door Village, in Scipio Township, initially was quite a little village. There were hotels and other businesses. It looked to be the hub of the county, but the railroad bypassed it and came through LaPorte instead. That pretty much ended Door Village. We don't even have a train that stops in LaPorte anymore."

Fern Eddy, the railroad created and destroyed a few towns in southern Lake County, too.

"Back in 1865, the Lincoln train came through here on it's way to Michigan City. There are markers at both Wanatah and Westville commemorating stops made in both towns."

Fern Eddy, two score and a few years after John Wilkes Booth assassinated Abraham Lincoln, LaPorte's Belle Gunness allegedly did some killing herself – I noticed your exhibit.

"I've never been fond of promoting Belle, but she certainly has brought people to LaPorte County."

Somebody certainly made sure a couple dozen would never leave.

"Last year was the 100th anniversary of the fire at Belle's place – where she disappeared. Heaven only knows where she went or what happened to her. We didn't want to honor her, but we did do some things to commemorate the anniversary of the big fire. We were able obtain funds to purchase headstones for victims who didn't have stones on their graves."

Our mutual friends, Merle and Suzanne Miller, live in a section of LaPorte that was referred to as Pole Town.

"Yes, that's the northeast side of town; it was also known as the Warsaw District. Sacred Heart Catholic Church is located in that part of town. The owners of local factories would go to Poland and bring back employees to work in the woolen mills, for example.

"The city of LaPorte also had a lot of Italians who worked on the railroad. We still have a number of Italian families living here. On the west side of LaPorte was a large German population."

What did your father do for a living?

"He was a farmer. Originally, there were forests on the edge of the prairie, but the early settlers cut many of the trees down because they needed timber to build log cabins. Timber also was cleared to create farmland. Of course, you don't have the farmland you used to either; much of it has been subdivided in LaPorte County."

Other changes to LaPorte County since your childhood?

"We were just talking the other day about different birds that have disappeared. We used to have so many quail. I remember hearing their call, 'Bob-white, Bob-white!' I remember when wild asparagus was abundant. All that's gone now. I don't know what's happened to it."

Where is your home in La Porte County?

"I live halfway between LaPorte and Michigan City on Johnson Road, so I've had the benefit of learning about both towns. The lake has made Michigan City what it is; that started early on. Today, Michigan City draws a lot of tourism."

Fern Eddy, I'm very impressed by this amazing three-floor museum. There is so much to see and read about.

"The LaPorte County Historical Society has been around since 1906."

Charter member?

"Ahem. I've served as the official LaPorte County historian for 19 years. I'm also the founding president of the LaPorte County Genealogical Society which is celebrating its 25th year."

What are the hours of the museum?

"Tuesday through Saturday from 10 a.m. to 4:30 p.m. Everything has been donated to us; we don't buy anything. We're really fortunate people have considered us rather than throwing things away. We have wonderful collections of just about any category you can think of.

"Since the 1930s, we've showcased a tremendous gun collection which was willed to the city of LaPorte by a gentleman named W.A. Jones. Another huge attraction is a portion of Dr. Kesling's automobile collection. And there's our collection of LaPorte County memorabilia and artifacts. So, it's like a three-fold museum. We have something for everybody."

You mentioned Dr. Kesling; wasn't he the orthodontist from La Porte County who invented braces?

"Dr. Peter Kesling and his father invented many things. This building was formerly Kesling's Door Prairie Auto Museum. Our historical society was looking for a new location because the county wanted our space downtown; we were able to move here in August of '06. Dr. Kesling is a philanthropist who always has been interested in history; he also paid for an addition to the building."

Do you get an occasional straggler from across the state line or maybe a visitor or two from south of Lafayette?

"People visit this museum from Europe; they come from all over the world."

* * *

Last summer, I covered an event called the Living Cemetery Tour; it's part of the Door Village Festival. The tour was Fern Eddy's brainchild; it's been well-received since debuting in '96.

While meandering through the Door Village cemetery, I noticed a gravestone with the surname Pattee etched into it.

Lewis Pattee was born in Montreal in 1802. He and his wife, Susan, settled in LaPorte County circa 1830. The couple moved to West Creek Township (Lowell) in 1851.

The Pattees parented eight children; Constantine, was born near Michigan City in 1841. At the age of 19, he enlisted in Company B, 20th Indiana Volunteer Infantry. Although wounded, Constantine survived the battle of Richmond only to be killed by a train in Lowell in 1917. The old Yank didn't hear the whistle.

Two of Constantine Pattee's brothers were captured at the battle of Gettysburg. Like the once common quail of Fern Eddy's childhood or the withering islands within drained wetlands, the young Hoosiers became history.

Casimer and J.E. Pattee died of starvation in Confederate prison camps.

Dr. Ruth Needleman *(Aug. 2008)*

"It is the responsibility of intellectuals to speak the truth and expose lies."
– Noam Chomsky

Labor Studies is posted on the front door of Professor Ruth Needleman's third-floor office at Indiana University Northwest's Lindenwood Hall in Gary. I received a hands-on lesson in just that – labor. Rather than start off our interview with an oral history or dissertation regarding the working class, 'Dr. Ruth' put me to work.

After moving 60 to 80 large cardboard boxes of books and binders from her office to the hallway, we wiped the sweat from our brows, rolled up our sleeves, and got down to it.

* * *

"I graduated from an all-girls public high school in Philadelphia in 1962," Needleman began. "I attended college in the Boston area, and got my first job in 1969 at the University of California, Santa Cruz, teaching Spanish and Latin American Literature.

"When I got there it was a very chaotic period of the '60s. The anti-war movement was very strong, the women's movement was emerging, the farm workers' movement was very strong."

You live on the east side of Gary – Miller. Tell me more about your family on the east side of the United States.

"My father was a union man. He was a typesetter. His father was a typesetter – they were all typesetters. I don't come from middle class.

"My great-aunt came over on the boat from Russia. Halfway across the ocean she took her wig off. Orthodox Jewish women had to shave their heads when they got married so they wouldn't be attractive to anybody else. My aunt threw her wig into the Atlantic. She became an organizer for the garment workers."

How long have you been teaching at IUN?

"Since 1981; I got the job by arguing that I knew how to transfer Don Quixote's windmills into steel workers' steel mills.

"I love teaching; I love learning. A good education is always an education where the teacher is a student and the students are also teachers. It's the only thing that creates a dynamic. I'm selfish – I usually learn more than they do.

"Students often say, 'I want to learn labor law' as if somehow knowing that would help them. I've taught labor law many times. But I always teach people that it's not what's legal that matters – it's what works. And sometimes what works is legal, sometimes it's not legal, but unions were illegal for much of our country's history."

Speaking of legal and illegal, would you care to touch upon the anti-immigration sentiment amongst much of the hoi polloi in this country.

"That is an issue which has haunted labor forever. I just wrote an article on the 1919 steel strike in Gary. At that time the news media and the steel industry were able to turn the country against the strike by calling everybody aliens, foreigners, and reds. The first people to cross the line were the white skilled tradesmen. It's an example of how we get snookered.

"The media? It doesn't even call them immigrants; it calls them aliens. Excuse me, but to me an alien is someone from another planet. This is a human being like my grandparents who came to this country because they had no choice. Nobody leaves their own homeland because they want to. They have family, roots, their own language – they do it out of desperation.

"You also have to remember that a third of the United States belonged to Mexico. There are lot of Mexicans who were here infinitely longer than anybody else – certainly more than these third generation white workers who think immigrants are stealing their jobs."

Strong words, indeed.

"Unfortunately, politicians and the corporate elite in this country have always pitted men against women, white against black, and native-born against the foreign-born. And it worked time after time.

"First of all, the U.S. fought to make that an open border for trade. You cannot have an open border for trade and a closed border for people. The trade we've done through NAFTA destroyed the Mexican economy. It opened the door for U.S. agribusiness to go in and buy up the farmers' land. We now have destroyed corn in Mexico. Mexican people cannot buy a corn tortilla on the street that they can afford.

"The border industries destroyed the domestic factories because they undercut the labor. So all these people who lost their land, who lost their jobs in the domestic industries, have gone to the border for border jobs – but those jobs are dangerous. They pay nothing and a lot of those factories are now moving to China. Some of those factories have moved back into Texas, into the federal prisons."

Into prisons?

"Prison jobs in rural areas are sometimes the only jobs available. They live off of arresting everybody. Eighty-five percent of the so-called criminals in the jails are young people who couldn't find jobs. They are locked up for drug use or petty theft.

"Where is Mr. Enron? Where are the people in the current administration who lied to the American people and killed 4,000 sons and daughters? They're not in jail."

And where does all this leave America?

"We have a situation where, first of all, the highest growth of capital investment in the United States is not domestic corporations; it's foreign corporations. Who owns our water system here in Gary? It's an Austrian/British company. Who owns the highways? They sell the Toll Road telling us nothing is going to change. The 15-cent toll is now 50 cents. The 50-cent toll is $2. That's within a year of the privatization."

How can this situation be resolved?

"The only way we'll be able to deal with the current trend as a labor movement is to globalize solidarity. The district director of the Steelworkers, Jim Robinson, says that very clearly, 'Either we raise their wages (Mexican workers) or we'll be working for what they're working for.'

"You can't have one big trade area (NAFTA) with closed borders. Inevitably, the poor people will move to the rich countries.

"Global capital has no nationality. And it will go wherever it can get the best deal on labor. China is now outsourcing to Thailand and Cambodia. It's one vicious circle moving the jobs to the lowest possible place and pulling the living standards of the entire world down with it."

Except for the prosperous few.

"No company should be able to earn the kind of profits that the oil companies are earning right now – 8.6 billion dollars in one quarter!"

What are some of the courses you teach?

"I teach all the basics – arbitration, collective bargaining, grievance handling... I also do a lot of labor history. I've taught courses on African-American working class history, on working women's history, on the labor movement's history. I teach law courses, organizing, leadership development. I've taught a lot on building unity and solidarity.

"This fall, I'll be teaching a course on labor and social movements. What kind of work should we be doing right now that would help to build a movement? We're going to study the CIO (Congress of Industrial Organizations) in the '30s and the civil rights movement in the '60s."

Unions are only as good as the members.

"Labor has endorsed (Barack) Obama; I think that was the right thing to do. But now they must fight Obama to get their issues into his agenda. We have numbers. The only way to make that count is not to wait until he's in the presidency, but to fight every day for policies that will help working people – no president has ever given labor anything. Not even FDR. During the Great Depression, labor was in the streets in the millions – the unemployed, the homeless, the industrial workers were out there demanding justice. Roosevelt had no choice, if he wanted to get elected the second time around, then he had to implement a new New Deal that gave workers the protected rights to organize.

"It's all about pressure; we get what we fight for!"

* * *

Like IUN professor emeritus James Lane and the late Charles Tinkham of Purdue University Calumet, Needleman could have taught on more prestigious campuses.

In 27 years, she has learned a lot from her students. And there is no place she'd rather be than Gary – speaking truths and exposing lies.

Dave Howkinson *(Feb. 2011)*

"I had a little bird,
Its name was Enza
I opened the window
And in-flu-enza."
– Author unknown

Dave Howkinson, 94, lives southwest of Cedar Lake. He is a retired dairy farmer and his wife of 68 years, Harriet, is deceased. They raised two children, Mary Alice and Charles. The latter runs the farm. Dave was the oldest of four children, but is the only one still living.

* * *

"I was born and raised in this house," Howkinson began. "I've lived here 94 years."

Where did you go to high school?

"Lowell."

Did you know Lowell's town historian, the late Richard Schmal?

"I graduated high school with Dick. See that house across the street? Dick's wife, Georgene, was born there. The Rev. Timothy Ball lived there at one time."

Rev. Ball was quite a historian, too. Dave, I often hear folks refer to Howkinson Marsh in Cedar Lake, but I've never been there. Where is it?

"Right below the hill next to the lake. It's named after my family; we used to own a good portion of the marsh. The marsh is quite an interesting thing, there's a sink hole down there.

"My grandfather sold some the land to the Monon Railroad. The tracks ran right through the middle of the marsh. I inherited the land west of the tracks and Bob (a brother) inherited the land east of the tracks."

Who was the first Howkinson to settle around here?

"My grandfather, Peter Howkinson. He came to the United States from Sweden; he lived in Chicago for a while. He got in the ice business down here about the time of the Great Chicago Fire. He had one of the original ice houses in Cedar Lake and would have the ice delivered via the Monon Railroad to Chicago's South Side. I've lived in this house for 94 years."

Dave, your long term memory is splendid. Tell me more about Pete Howkinson.

"He settled near the Conference Grounds in Cedar Lake. He was a fella who traveled around by horse and buggy; he never owned a car. But he ended up with three farms because of the ice business. Grandfather owned the farm my Uncle Harry was on, he owned this 'un, and he owned one that his daughter, Ada, lived on. She was a widow at a young age; Aunt Ada had two boys."

What was your father's name?

"Martin. After he retired from farming, he became vice president of the Commercial Bank in Crown Point. I've lived in this house for 94 years."

How many acres is this particular farm?

"It's 173 acres now; we used to own 240 acres. This is the aerial map. Here's our farmhouse. This is the marsh road; it comes out right by the south end of Cedar Lake.

"I used to trap muskrats in the marsh. We tried to farm part of the marsh, but we didn't have very good luck. My brother got out of farming and got in Real Estate. When his health began to falter, he decided to sell his portion of the land, which was the swampiest, to some kind of conservation group. The Lake County Parks Department manages it using the objectives set forth by the North American Wetlands Conservation Act."

My friend Barb Dodge told me there have been 145 species of birds, including 19 species of ducks, sighted in Howkinson Marsh. Plus, eight species of frogs and toads, several rare types of snakes and countless species of dragonflies. Not to mention the most humongous white oaks she's ever seen. Impressive, don't you think?

"I remember when the mail carrier used a horse and buggy on his route. He'd get out there in the swamp and throw all the junk mail in the sink hole so he didn't have to deliver the damn stuff."

Let's switch gears. What breed of cattle do you have on the farm?

"Holsteins. Before you leave take a look at the milking parlor. We have 150 head."

Do you have any bulls?

"No, we have artificial insemination. Bulls are dangerous."

How often do the cows get milked?

"Twice a day; 4 a.m. and 4 p.m."

Does your son milk them by hand?

"No, we have milking machines."

You've probably milked a few cows by hand.

"Oh, yeah, before and after school."

How much milk do your Holsteins produce in a day?

"We fill a tanker every other day."

How many gallons does a tanker truck hold?

"About 18,000 pounds; they go by pounds."

Tell me more about your childhood.

"We farmed with horses. I think we got rid of the horses in 1940. I went to Lincoln Elementary School in a horse-drawn school bus. We were the first class at Lowell High School to have a regular school bus. My cousin lived on the south end of the lake; he walked down the railroad tracks every day to Lowell High School."

Wow, that has to be seven or eight miles each way.

"He was one of Aunt Ada's sons. His dad went to New York for business and caught the flu while he was out there. He came back to Cedar Lake and died the next day. It killed him that fast. It was towards the end of World War I."

Dave, Dick Schmal told me there's a graveyard out in the woods and east of South Shore Golf Course that is comprised of nothing but people who died from that outbreak of influenza.

"Parrish Avenue was a dirt road when I was a boy. If you look through the picture window out across Parrish, that used to be all woodland. They came in and cut all the trees down to make a subdivision. They haven't built any houses, though. I really miss looking out at the trees."

* * *

I consider Dave Howkinson a living history book. He told me he paid $600 for a new 2-door Ford back in '41.

Howkinson also told me to go down to his basement before I left to check out his incredible arrowhead collection. When I returned upstairs to say goodbye, he had his wheelchair turned around toward a bulletin board.

He was leaned forward reading a newspaper article that ran the day one of his high school classmates was laid to rest last November. Howkinson turned and said: "That was nice what that Jeff 'Mainze' wrote about Dick Schmal. Do you know him?"

Sure do. I knew Schmal, too.

"You know what one of my goals is?"

What's that, Dave?

"To live in this house for 100 years."

You take care, old-timer.

Up to the Challenge

Super Fan *(March 2006)*

"In thy face I see the map of honor, truth, and loyalty."
– William Shakespeare

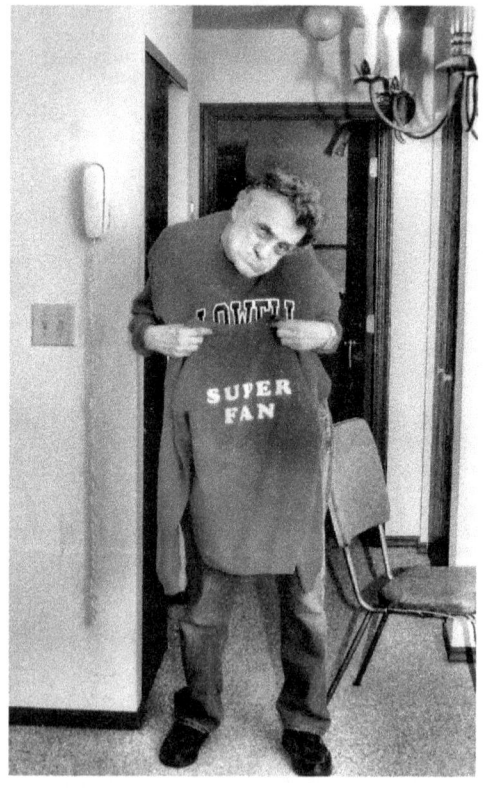

On June 24, 1935, a doctor on Chicago's South Side delivered an infant into this world who was born with cerebral palsy. That child was named Edward L. Regnier. A dozen or so years later, it was a doctor who delivered a near killing blow to Edward L. Regnier while he walked Chicago's streets during a blizzard.

Ed Regnier has never driven. That doctor who hit him shouldn't have been – he was drunk.

Regnier didn't ask for cerebral palsy nor did he ask to be blind sided by 3,000 pounds of steel and glass. Those were the cards dealt him. He has never folded his hand. The bones in his body might be somewhat contorted, but not a one of them knows resentment.

Because of his penchant for Lowell High School athletics, Regnier is known as Super Fan. He's a diehard.

* * *

Nice digs, Ed. Well, let's get down to brass tacks – sports. You have attended most of the sporting events at Lowell High School for nearly 30 years. There is no fan more loyal. Who have been some of your favorite Red Devil athletes down through the years? I know, Ed, that's a tough one.

"Cash, Lampa, Langen," he said."

You've got quite a collection of high school sports mementos here.

"I really like this football; it's from the 2000 season. It's signed."

Let me read some of the names of the players: Sam Voss, Keith Powers, French, Wragg, Sewell, Sidell, Kimbrell, Kersey...

What's your favorite sport to watch?

"All of 'em."

What do you think of football coaches Kennedy and Carlson?

"They are my friends. Jeff, can you put Coach Carlson's name in this newspaper story? Please?"

Sure. Ed, can you tell me about your early years? Your friend Leon told me a little bit about when you were struck by the automobile in Illinois. You've mentioned it to me as well. How did it happen? What do you remember?

"It was snowing that day."

Yeah, I'd probably rather not recall such an event either. You have one sibling. A sister, correct?

"Does this help you?" *(Ed unfurled his billfold and showed me a picture of his sister, brother-in-law, and mother.)*

You live alone, Ed?

"Yes."

Leon told me you've had a girlfriend for years. You met her at your workshop. Talk to me, Fast Eddy.

"Yes, Marie. We went to Leon and Vanessa's wedding together."

Are your parents deceased?

"My mother died five years ago. She is buried in Cedar Lake. My father is at Holy Sepulcher in Roseland, (Ill.). I came to Lowell in 1971."

You eat at George's Restaurant everyday I'm told. It wasn't always that way, was it Ed?

"Leon and George pay for my meals. I ate Lunchables every day for years before that. I was very thin back then."

They tell me you're big on spaghetti, liver and onions, and shrimp on Saturdays. What's your favorite meal?

"All of 'em."

You said you work at Bridges in Crown Point? What do you do, there?

"I make puzzles. I go on the mail runs on Tuesdays. I don't get home until almost 5 p.m. sometimes. I missed the bus this morning. My sister took me to work. I also work at St. Edward's carnival in July."

* * *

Ed Regnier is an institution in Lowell. His was not an easy interview. We got through it.

I've been told the sudden impact was so traumatic when Ed was hit by the car as a youngster, that every bottom tooth in his head left his body. And because he only possesses half the teeth the good Lord gave him, twice, Leon Bland has had to perform Heimlich maneuvers on Super Fan after he'd attempted to gum concession stand hot dogs. Lodged hot dogs can be deadly. So can out of control Buicks.

Ed wanted to take in "Of Mice and Men" staged at the 4th Street Theater in Chesterton a few weeks ago. I couldn't take him or get him a ride on such short notice. He *will* watch the play in Lowell – on DVD at my apartment in the near future.

In the story "Of Mice and Men," George needs Lennie as much as Lennie needs George. I believe Lowell needs Super Fan. He helps us to be a better community.

And like many of us, Ed is a creature of habit. Whenever he leaves me a message on my answering machine, he always signs off the same way...

"This is Edward Regnier, please – that's all."

That's all?

That's plenty, Super Fan.

Rich Zmuda *(Nov. 2007)*

"Once you've spent two years trying to wiggle one toe, everything is in proportion."
– Franklin D. Roosevelt

November – a month of gratitude, when many gather together to give thanks for all their blessings.

I wasn't sure what to expect when I visited Rich Zmuda at his Crown Point home.

* * *

"As a kid, I went to St. Mary School, right next door," Zmuda began. "It's weird; I remember looking out the window of my classroom in sixth-grade and seeing this yard. Now, I look out the window and see St. Mary's."

Rich, you worked at Inland Steel's (now ArcelorMittal) No. 3 Open Hearth, No. 7 Blast Furnace, and the bull gang (Mobile Maintenance). Anyone who ever worked alongside of you in the mill will attest to what a hard worker you always were.

"I didn't mind working. If I was out there, I worked. I had a perfect record when I worked in the mill.

"After the accident, they cleaned up the hydraulic room and tagged all the stuff that was supposed to be tagged just in case – but they didn't do it before the accident."

How many years has it been since your accident?

"It happened May 16, 1999. I was 48 years old. One foreman told another foreman to push a button to see if a hydraulic arm worked, before we put back a piece of equipment that lifts the coils so they can be compressed. A platform was jolted. I fell 26 feet into the hydraulic room of the basement.

"When all was said and done, I was just shy 29 years in the mill. They wouldn't give me the 30. That kind of sticks in my craw – that's a big difference in pay.

"The main bean counter for the company – she fights everything tooth and nail. I had to go to court to get them to pay for my prescriptions. Everything is a battle... I'm still fighting to get the lift fixed out in front of the house."

While you were in the hospital, no money was coming in?

"One of my union reps had a fund-raiser for me and got enough money together so I could buy a van because all my stuff was repossessed by the time I got home."

I remember.

"I'm grateful I'm alive. It took eight months of therapy before I could stand with crutches. I'm an incomplete paraplegic. My spinal cord isn't completely severed. It's just like an electric cord with the insulation peeled away – and it's arcing.

"For years, I wouldn't take anything for the pain. Some of that stuff is like heroin. They have medicine now that isn't addictive, thank God, because sometimes the pain can be almost unbearable. They shoot me up with epidurals twice a year.

"I'm blessed that I have minimal control of my bowel and bladder. If I start feeling sorry for myself, I can always go to the Rehabilitation Institute of Chicago and see somebody who has it worse. It is a constant struggle to stay positive. There are many paraplegics and quads who kill themselves. They just get tired of it."

You look like your staying in pretty good shape – your arms.

"I still have to watch what I eat because I'm not as active as I used to be. I sold a lot of my tools. I did all this tile work myself. I can't do ceiling work anymore, but I can still drag my body around on the floor and do this kind of work.

"I'm like the poster child for my workman's comp lawyer because of my attitude. A lot of it is my faith in God. If I didn't have faith, I don't know. I've been clean and sober for 28 years. Sharon is my third wife; I finally got it right. We've been married for almost 20 years.

"I'm 55 now; I couldn't ask for a more wonderful woman. I have two sons – Eric and Ryan. Richelle is my youngest at 15. I like to tease her by calling her 'Junior.'

"I guess it's the luck of the draw. I remember when I worked in the open hearth, they were going to change a door on the furnace. It was my turn to shut off the water. I was just coming from doing another job, so my workmate, Lee, said, 'I'll get it for you, Rich.' He suffered burns over 70 percent of his body because he decided to do me a favor. Blew my mind."

Rich, I realize you are a devout Christian. How do you feel about embryonic stem cell research?

"First of all, the way it is now, you reach a certain plateau of what your level of injury is, and what you can get back, and that's it. Nerves don't regenerate. Most of those stem cells, they were going to throw away in the garbage.

"To me it makes perfect sense if they can inject certain stem cells that regenerate the nerves that can reconnect – it's a no-brainer! I'm all for it."

Christopher Reeve.

"He gave a lot of us false hope. 'Look, I'm walking.' People don't realize how much health care he was getting per day because he was rich and famous.

"I try to concentrate on things I can do. The things I can't do – I gotta let it go. I asked God what he wanted me to do. I went into prison ministry for awhile.

"I was a worship leader at another church. I started playing the guitar again. It gets you out of yourself. You have to have a passion for something otherwise you're dead."

"I look at it this way; my condition is temporary compared to eternity – some day, I'll have a new body."

* * *

After our interview, Zmuda stood; we shook hands. Then, he released his crutches. Instantly, his body crumpled to the couch, like a 100-pound sack of Idahos.

I walked away.

It's interesting to me that it takes a bullet to the skull before a man like James Brady changes his tune on gun control, or Ronald Reagan's mind has to deteriorate before Nancy champions the crusade to cure Alzheimer's disease.

I can't help but wonder if our current president would continue to veto the funding of stem cell research if his spine was severed.

As far as the honchos of the steel industry and their efforts to ensure a safe workplace for their "beloved" employees?

Well, I figure the bottom line is simply that – the bottom line. It costs a lot of money when a man or woman gets maimed in the mill.

Ask Rich Zmuda.

He's paid dearly.

Jason Delgado *(Nov. 2009)*

*"But Oz never did give nothing to the Tin Man
That he didn't, didn't already have."
– Dewey Bunnell (America)*

Since writing this column, I'm like 12 of 13 when guessing that an interviewee is left-handed. Somehow, I can tell. Weird.

Southpaw Jason Delgado and his wife, Jessi, have lived in Crown Point for 11 years. They have an 11-year-old daughter named Skylar and a 7-year-old son, Miles, named after jazzman Miles Davis.

The walls of the Delgado living room are decorated with an eclectic assortment of album covers featuring artists such as Frank Sinatra, Frank Zappa, The Chipmunks, Bob Dylan and a very young Dustin Hoffman.

* * *

"I was born a blue baby," Delgado began. "I had congenital heart disease. They put a balloon in me to get my blood flowing when I was just a few hours old."

Did you continue to have medical problems as a child?

"Yes, I had my first pacemaker by the time I was 2.. I've had three change outs – one lasted 16 years."

Crown Point High School?

"No, I attended Whiting High School. I worked at Wayne's

Trick Shop in Hammond my senior year; I also was a magician.

"I grew up above Jake's Tavern on New York Avenue. Ten years after moving out of there, I still had to go to bed with a radio on because I'd grown accustomed to having to fall asleep that way – the radio drowned out the sound of clinking glasses, juke box music and bar fights."

Well, Jace, it wasn't me. I was across the street in the New Yorker. A buddy of mine named Scott Pollack grew up in Whiting; we'd stop there for a cold one after 3 to 11s on occasion. Pollack was one of 12 or 14 kids; he told me he was a "slow hungry crow" referring to the fact that he was of Slovak, Hungarian and Croatian ancestries.

"Although I have an Hispanic surname, my mother is Slovak. My maternal grandfather owned Lovasko Studios."

What did your father do for a living?

"Not too much. That's why my mother divorced him. He's deceased now."

Life after high school?

"A month after I graduated, I enrolled into the Art Institute of Pittsburgh to pursue film and video production. After about a year-and-a-half, I decided to go to Point Park College which is an affiliate of the University of Pittsburgh."

Also film and video production?

"No, instead of dealing with make-up, it was more film studies. It covered film theory, film criticism and making film. We'd break down movies like 'The Bicycle Thief.' I stayed there for a year, but never did get a degree and ended up coming back to Northwest Indiana."

As a kid, did you have an interest in becoming a Hollywood make-up artist?

"Yeah, I always was freaking out my family. I'd put on prosthetics and chop off one of my 'limbs' with a fake knife and fake blood."

Slasher movies were the genre you really grooved in on?

"Yeah, Bob Savini was a big influence. He was the make-up artist for 'Friday the 13th.'"

I see you have a huge collection of movies. Personal favorites?

"'Aguirre, Wrath of God,' 'Pulp Fiction,' 'Silence of the Lambs' and 'Bad Taste.'"

What did you do when you got back to NWI?

"Met my wife, got married, and got a job as a supervisor for Aramark."

Jason, it sounds like you said adios to your hockey mask-wearing namesake and Freddy Krueger and became a member of the establishment. Sorry to hear that.

"After about five years at Aramark, I noticed I was getting short of breath and it was getting progressively worse. They did a biopsy."

What did they find?

"That I'd need a heart transplant within three to five years. I was told to stop working, enjoy life, and get on the transplant list. After two years of getting progressively worse, I got put on the list; you have to be in real bad shape to get on the list."

What happened next?

"After four months, I went from being pretty bad to much worse. I had an I.V. to keep my heart pumping."

Yeah?

"I got the call on Thanksgiving weekend, Nov. 27, 2005. It was pretty amazing. It's been almost four years now.

"The mother of the young man who's heart I have has written me and I have written back. She said her son died tragically, but didn't go into any details."

Organ donation is a great thing, Jason.

"Obviously, I'm proponent of it."

Still, it has to be a heckuva thing, knowing that a surgical team is going to remove your heart from your chest and replace it with someone else's.

"It beats the alternative, but you're right, it is a heckuva thing. That's why I volunteer my services with New Beginnings Transplant Support Group. We help support pre- and post-transplant patients deal with things like their upcoming operations, emotions, anxiety, the drugs they have to take, insurance issues...

"When I was getting ready for my transplant there was nothing like New Beginnings in the area."

The last four years?

"On the way to Indianapolis, to get my transplant, my wife and I made an agreement."

What was that?

"If everything went OK, I wanted to go back to school. College didn't work out the first time; I wanted a second shot at it.

"I decided I wanted to do something I would enjoy for the rest of my life instead of something just for the money. I made good money at Aramark, but I was a boss and the guys didn't like me and I didn't really like going to work."

What did you decide to do?

"I'd grown quite a passion for cooking over the years because of being home so much. I went to school for three years at Ivy Tech's East Chicago De La Garza campus and graduated from the Culinary Arts department this spring. I was named Distinguished Student of the Year."

Did you get a job?

"Yes, at Giovanni's in Munster; it's an upscale Italian restaurant. I handle the grill station right now and I'm also being trained on desserts."

* * *

Jason Delgado; a guy who got a second shot – at life.

Dan Reynolds *(Dec. 2011)*

"...Most everybody's got seed to sow
It ain't always easy for a weed to grow, oh no
So he don't hoe the row for no one
Oh for sure he's always missing
And something is never quite right
Ah, but who would care to listen to you
Kissing his existence good night..."
– James Taylor

When Dan Reynolds was in Little League baseball, he prayed the opposing pitcher would walk him because he almost always swung and missed when batting.

Reynolds knew back then that something wasn't quite right, but who would care to listen? About a year-and-a-half ago, at the age of 60, Reynolds was diagnosed with attention deficit hyperactivity disorder. He's had ADHD all his life.

Reynolds lives in Ogden Dunes about a beach ball's toss from Lake Michigan with his wife, Jeanne. They have raised a son who is a Chicago firefighter.

* * *

Lived in Ogden Dunes all your life?

"No, my wife and I were raised in Chicago," he said.

What neighborhood?

"Beverly; on the South Side. I went to Quigley South High School; it was a preparatory seminary. You went there because you intended to be a priest."

Dan, give me an insider's point of view regarding ADHD.

"When I was 11, I joined Little League and spent most of my time in the outfield chasing the ball and praying to God that I'd get a walk rather than suffering the humiliation of striking out yet again.

"Also, at 11, I joined the Boy Scouts and 3 1/2 years later became an Eagle Scout. Those two events point to one of the many paradoxes surrounding ADHD. We have incredible strengths and, at the same time, incredible weaknesses."

Kids can be vicious.

"I was the kid who was ridiculed and made fun of. I was never part of the group in the neighborhood."

How did you do in school?

"I was in the slow reading group, slow to do my work and slow to answer the teacher's questions. Not only was I slow, I also was sloppy and careless. My desk was a disaster area. I had trouble paying attention. Parent-teacher conferences come along and we learn that we don't apply ourselves, aren't motivated and don't meet our potential."

You probably start getting the reputation of being lazy.

"Yes, we do. When in fact, people with ADHD work much harder to accomplish the same things normal people do. We know there is something wrong, but we don't know what."

What are other symptoms of ADHD?

"We lack attention to details, make careless mistakes and are forgetful. People with ADHD lose things like their keys or wallet or purse a lot and are unable to sustain focus. We appear not to listen and are easily distracted. We're also restless and can't sit still. We talk excessively and blurt things out and can't wait our turn."

Dan, I have some of those traits. Ma blamed it on chemical imbalances, left-handedness and too much pasta as a child, but that was back in the early '60s.

"We all exhibit some of those symptoms at times. To actually have the disorder, it has to be pervasive and you have to have a majority of the symptoms, not just one or two."

Dan, you're obviously intelligent.

"ADHD has nothing to do with intelligence. I've been assessed several times and my IQ always has been higher than normal.

"My son had the highest IQ in the school district. I have two grandchildren; both have been assessed and both have been accepted into gifted programs in Chicago public schools. All four of us have ADHD."

It's a genetic thing?

"Yes, ADHD is a neurobiological or neurochemical disorder. If you have ADHD, the odds are 77 percent that you got it from a parent. If you are an identical twin, the chances are 92 percent that your twin sibling also has the disorder."

From whom did you get it, your mother or father?

"I don't know, I'm adopted."

Is ADHD curable?

"No, it's a chronic disorder. It is, however, one of the most treatable neurological disorders that exist."

Myths about the disorder?

"Some people blame poor parenting, diet or our fast-moving culture. Some people claim that it doesn't exist and some claim that it's a conspiracy among the pharmaceutical industry and doctors to sell more drugs. Science doesn't support any of those notions and all the conspiracy claims have been dismissed by the courts as frivolous."

High school?

"More of the same; I finished in the bottom third of my class."

College?

"I flunked out my first semester. My dad stopped paying my tuition, and I returned to enroll in a local community college. I spent a lot of time studying in the cafeteria while smoking cigarettes and drinking coffee."

And?

"All of a sudden, I could focus in class. In three semesters, I completed two years of college with a 3.5 (grade point average). I was instrumental in forming the first student government and was elected president. I felt vibrant and alive; I was learning. Not only was I part of a group, I was a leader. By accident, I had discovered the primary treatment for ADHD."

What's that?

"Stimulants. That was the hippie generation. While most kids were seeking illegal drugs to enhance their experience of normal, I was using legal stimulants to feel normal."

Tobacco and caffeine.

"You got it. Effective treatment for ADHD is a multi-modal approach consisting of medication, education, psychotherapy and coaching. Stimulants are the most effective treatment and work well for about 85 percent of the ADHD population."

Your working career?

"After earning a bachelor's degree in psychology with a 3.91 GPA, I went on to have an extremely successful career in developing software."

Amazing turn-around.

"Then, 13 years ago, almost overnight, my life began to fall apart."

You quit smoking and drinking coffee.

"When I quit, I was smoking three-and-a-half packs and drinking six pots of coffee a day. Three years ago, I closed my business down. I lost over $400,000 in out-of-pocket business expenses. A year ago, I came to the realization I had ADHD. My wife had suggested the possibility for years. I started reading a book entitled 'You Mean I'm Not Lazy, Stupid or Crazy?!' Before I finished the first chapter, I knew what was wrong.

"As I sat in bed that night with tears in my eyes, I understood why I always felt insecure and lacked confidence. Within two months, I was officially diagnosed and started taking medication. Almost overnight, I could sustain focus again."

What are you doing today?

"Since last year, I've trained to be an ADHD coach and I've formed a support group for adults with ADHD. I'm also in the process of forming a not-for-profit organization called the Northwest Indiana ADHD Network; its mission is to improve the quality of life for people with ADHD and their families "

* * *

Dan Reynolds showed me some staggering statistics regarding adults with ADHD as far as divorce rates, job termination, traffic tickets, accidents and the percentage of our prison population that has ADHD.

Reynolds also told me Thomas Edison and Albert Einstein were both thought to have had ADHD, and that discount broker Charles Schwab, actors Bill Cosby, Jim Carey, Whoopie Goldberg and Robin Williams, and former Chicago Bulls superstar Michael Jordan have all acknowledged their ADHD.

Cathy Wunderink *(Dec. 2007)*

"What we have once enjoyed, we can never lose. All that we love becomes part of us."
– Helen Keller

Cathy Wunderink was raised on a farm outside of Shelby near the Kankakee River. She lives in a modest 100-year-old house with Brownie, her trusty chocolate lab. Her brother, Mark, and her parents live nearby in farmhouses where she grew up.

Cathy graduated from Lowell High School when this country was celebrating its bicentennial. At Purdue University Calumet she majored in safety, leadership, and personnel. She has earned two associate's degrees and three bachelor's degrees with distinction.

We first communicated via e-mail. When I received a phone call from Cathy, it was actually the operator who initially spoke. It was my first relay message. Cathy Wunderink is deaf. She doesn't sign, but reads lips and speaks well.

* * *

"The Wunderinks came from the Netherlands through Canada and into the United States," Wunderink began. "They were vegetable farmers. My mother's maiden name was Mital. I'm one of five children."

Tell me about your childhood.

"I went to Elim Christian School in Palos Heights (Ill.) even before preschool. I learned with the great big earphones because you pronounce words the way that you hear them. For one year, I'd stay there all week and come home on the weekends. I was about 4 or 5."

How did you feel about that?

"I can still remember it to this day, when they'd drop me off on Monday morning. I'd cry and cry. I had to leave all my animals and everything. But I can also remember Fridays, waiting for them to pick me up.

"Last spring me and my older sister talked about all that. She told me, 'Cathy, after mom and dad dropped you off they would cry all the way home.'

"I give my parents a lot of credit because they encouraged and pushed me to make my way in the hearing world. People are amazed how well I can talk with the amount of hearing loss I have."

After a year in Palos Heights?

"I went to a private school for the first four years – DeMotte Christian. They didn't have the teachers for my hearing disability. I wasn't very good in English, so they transferred me to a public school. There was a teacher who would travel around to different schools and work with the children who needed help. I did that from fourth grade all the way until 10th grade. I went to summer school every year. I did a lot of lip reading and learned speech."

Life on the farm.

"I was like a tomboy growing up. I love all animals, but horses and dogs are my favorites. I had a horse from the time she was 4 months old until I had to put her down; she was almost 25 years old. Now I have a chocolate lab. She's an outside dog when she stays at my parents while I'm at work, but she's an inside dog when I get home from work. I haven't named my cat yet. I think I'll call him Lonesome.

"Me and Mark's job was to pick up sticks so Dad could farm the ground. My dad bought this ground cheaper than dirt because it was all trees; it wasn't farm ground. We didn't watch TV; we were always outside. Mom would save old coffee cans. We were told to go out and pick wild blackberries – and not to come back until our cans were filled. We always had a big garden. We'd grow muskmelons and watermelons and sell them at the Vandercarr log cabin on Indiana 2. We saved the money we made and that's how we bought our bicycles. I remember mom and dad taking us to pick out our bikes.

"I have a lot of fond memories growing up here. You take that with you in everyday life. I learned my values on this farm."

The workplace.

"After I graduated from Lowell High School, I got my first job here in Shelby at White Advertising (eventually Avery Graphics). I worked in Shelby for 18 years and then transferred to the Lowell plant. They let me go. Here's some of my certificates of recognition when I worked at Avery.

"It wasn't until 1989 that I went to college – I loved it. I received an Eli Lily grant. I was the first one hired out of Purdue Cal's internship. I did a lot of safety programs and grant writing.

"What started me going to college was when I was working at Avery down here in Shelby. They had the professors come to the plant and give all the supervisors safety training. I said to myself, 'I can do this. Maybe I should go to college.' I took some off-campus classes at Crown Point High School. I worked toward my certificate. Then I went for my associate's.

"Growing up on a farm is what got me interested in safety. You hear a lot about the auger accidents, people getting crushed or smothered... My dad lost his right hand in a corn picker before I was ever born. My older sister lost her right hand at a factory in Lowell – she has an artificial hand now.

"People are your most important asset in the workplace. If you can provide a safe workplace for them, you can save money in the long run. We all take short cuts. Sometimes doing something the safe way may take a little bit longer but you have to think of the outcome if you didn't. You can't take that time back. Once you lose it – you lose it."

Who do you work for now?

"I'm one of three safety managers in the United States for Dawn Foods. I make sure the planning and programs are in place. I travel all around. There are more than 20 plants nationwide. There are close to 300 people working at the facility in Crown Point. I love my job – but I'm very busy."

When you're not managing safety programs across the Midwest and helping your brother get the crops in, what do you do in your spare time?

"I volunteer with the Shelby Fire Department and I still help the

Lions Club. I work with the senior citizens, too. I love their stories – their history and experiences.

"My father is retired now. He suffers from Alzheimer's disease. We all take turns watching him. I stop by every morning and check on him. My dad had a disability and never let anything stop him. He taught me a lot.

"I have accepted my hearing disability. You make the best of what you have. I've had so many people help me. My family, friends... I appreciate that. This was originally a one-room house similar to the old Sears and Roebuck homes – very economical. It was built by a man who sawed lumber out of river bottom – rock hard cottonwood mostly. It didn't have a kitchen or bathroom. My brother and his friends remodeled it for me. Those guys did excellent; I wouldn't change a thing.

"By going to college it has given me more exposure outside of my comfort zone. There are a lot of good people in the world. You watch the news and read some of the newspaper articles and they seem to concentrate on the negative. I do enjoy reading about people overcoming their struggles and the sacrifices they've made to get where they're at.

"I worked in Chicago for a while at Allied Tube. It was good to get home after work. I'd invite some of the people I met up north to my home. Most of the city folks said they could never get used to living out here in the middle of nowhere."

Why's that, Cathy?

"They said it was too quiet."

Characters

Carl Matury *(June 2010)*

"...Baseball cards, rusty tools
Trinkets, baubles, costume jewels
Playboy mag with pages stuck
Barbie car and Tonka truck
Nostalgic junque, generic goods
Suckers, geezers, fences, hoods
Betty Boop and Billy Beer
Furniture with ruin'd veneer
Hold your ground, make 'em squirm
Sorry bub, my price is firm
Picaresque chicanery
Caveat Emptor, at the flea"
– Jeff Manes

I first met Carl Matury, 79, a year ago when he showed up at my front door. He gave me the name of a close friend he said I should interview. It was an offer I couldn't refuse.

Matury's family moved from East Chicago to Lowell when he was 10. His parents were born and raised in Sicily.

Matury and his wife, Diana, have raised four children who all graduated from Lowell High School.

* * *

I've never met a Sicilian whose surname ended with a "y."

"When my father said his last name was 'Maturi,' some Irishman at Ellis Island probably wrote it down as Matury," he said.

The man in that old photograph is wearing something similar to the regalia Knights of Columbus members wear.

"That's my father. During World War I, they came to his parents' home while he was very ill, dragged him out of bed, threw him in an ambulance and took him to a military training base; he was 17."

"Dad served in a light brigade; they pulled their cannons with horses and mules. His unit got caught in a pass – the Germans in front and the Austrians behind. He said they fought in there for eight days."

Then what?

"They ran out of ammo and were taken prisoner for 13 months. My father weighed 200 pounds, when he was released, he weighed less than 100."

Your childhood.

"I was born in East Chicago on Jan. 9, 1931, the oldest of six kids. I learned to speak English when I went to grade school.

"I remember my mother studying to get her citizenship papers. That was a big thing. You had to know English, who the president was, what the three branches of government were... .

"We lived in an apartment on Tod Avenue. I don't want the landlord's name mentioned, but he was a well-known banker, and he was Italian, too. Anyway, we got thrown out because Dad couldn't pay the rent. Hey, it was the Depression; he'd lost his job."

Did your famiglia attend Immaculate Conception?

"Yeah, would you believe I went to church every day for a year? Father Campagna gave me a prize for that. I got to go to a camping place in Michigan for a week. Anthony Radice went, too. Anthony got killed crossing Indianapolis Boulevard when he was 13 – hit and run."

Lowell during the 1940s.

"We had a garden and chickens. My job was to run the egg route in a '37 Dodge on Saturday mornings up in East Chicago."

You drove from Lowell to East Chicago to sell eggs? How old were you?

"Almost 14. I'd usually be done by 11 a.m."

Then what?

"After purchasing groceries for the family with the egg money, I'd go to Hot Dog John's and buy a hot dog and a pop for about 20 cents. Then, I'd spend another dime to see a show at the Vogue Theater."

Your working career after high school?

"I ended up a union carpenter for Chicago Heights Construction for 32 years. We worked on industrial jobs, mostly.

"An architect once wanted me to build plank sidewalks because he didn't want to get muddy. Hey, I've worked in the mud lots of times. I told him, 'Those planks are $20 apiece; (you can) buy another pair of shoes for 15 bucks.'"

His reply?

"He wrote a nasty letter to my boss. My bosses didn't like me, either, because I didn't take no shit. But I ran their jobs and made them big money.

"My daughter made big money for the federal government, but she quit. I didn't speak to her for a year."

Because she quit?

"No, because she became an architect; I have an utter disdain for architects; I met one who I really liked. He never swore until he got around me."

Why's that?

"Because I cuss. I got him started cussing. It was funny to hear him swear; he wore $1,000 suits."

Since retiring 15 years ago, you've frequented flea markets while searching for old tools to resell.

"Yeah, I do five festivals per year."

An example of a unique transaction.

"I paid 50 cents for a tiny monkey wrench."

And?

"My kid was with me at a festival soon thereafter. I told him I was gonna take a look around. We had everything all set up. As I was walking away, he asked me how much to charge for the wrench I paid a half a buck for. I told him to put $65 on it."

Yeah?

"Yeah, he told me I was crazy. Well, I came back an hour later and asked if he'd sold anything. He said, 'Yeah, the monkey wrench sold for $55.'"

Nice profit margin.

"Months later, I spotted that same wrench at a show in Hoopeston, Il.; the guy wanted $275."

Carl, you're a Democratic precinct committeeman for West

Creek Township; do you prefer present-day Lowell over those hardscrabble times during the early 1940s?

"I prefer 1940s Lowell; it was a pleasant place to live. We didn't have the dope; we've had a few murders... ."

That's everywhere.

"These are hard times for honest, hard-working people – especially people who are retired and trying to make ends meet. Taxes are a big problem. There are two things that worry me."

What's that?

"That I'll outlive the money I've saved, and that I'll become a burden to society or my kids.

"I was in Rockville yesterday, looking for tools. I didn't buy nothin'. But it was peaceful, like Lowell used to be. And, Jeff, you wouldn't believe the characters you meet at flea markets."

Carl, I believe you.

* * *

Carl Matury is a good egg.

And, because of characters like him, I'll never run out of work.

Linda Kiechle *(June 2009)*

"Si fractus fortis"
- Official motto of the Foster family.

Paris Hilton, Donald Trump and the late Princess Di never will appear in this column. I write about the guy who tosses your garbage into a big truck every Friday morning or the lady who rings up your frozen pizza on Friday night."

When Carl Matury, 78, recently rang my doorbell, I figured his intent was to offer me a free copy of the Watchtower. I'd never met the man, nor had I spoken to him on the phone.

But the mysterious Sicilian let himself into my modest apartment where he proceeded to tell me quite a bit about myself, himself and a woman named Linda from Lowell. Matury said I had to interview her because she is of royal descent and her story needed to be told.

I could have shot the bull with the likeable cuss for hours, and I'm sure I will, but I was about to take my fiancee to see "Drag Me to Hell" and I wanted to get there before 6 p.m. so I could get the deal.

Linda Kiechle didn't grow up in a palace, but it was a nice Sears home built in 1940. For the past 27 years, she and her husband, Fred, have lived in a house well-known for it's royal purple front door.

In the 1980s, Fred adopted Linda's only child, Ryan, when the young man was 18 years of age. She, too, is an only child.

There was a day when Kiechle, 62, had flaming red hair; she has let nature take its course. When I said something that tickled her, she'd bust out in laughter like Ethel Merman could belt out a song.

The redhead still has spark.

* * *

"They call me the Purple Lady," Kiechle began. "Do you have your sunglasses with you?"

Huh?

"Check this out."

Whoa – the bathtub, bathroom scale, magazine rack and Felix the Cat wall clock are very purple. The lavender hamper is nice. I believe that's the first purple pooper I've ever seen.

Linda, I noticed you've also decorated the house with some non-purple pieces, those old radios and clocks are cool.

"I like antiques. This is my parents' ice box with the original drip pan. Here's an old pump organ that works."

What kind of glassware is in that beautiful walnut china cabinet?

"Fostoria – I have more than 400 pieces. I inherited most of the collection from my father's side of the family.

"I also collect dice, salt-and-pepper shakers, trolls and Barbie dolls. My two oldest Barbies were made in 1961. Mother bought them for me at Sears in downtown Gary for $1.99 each. They've been taken out of the box, but not played with.

"One is a blonde bubble, she's getting green ears which is a common characteristic. The other is a redhead with a ponytail; I was a natural redhead – all this white is mother nature. My grandfather and father were redheads."

What's your maiden name?

"Foster."

Your friend, Carl, told me you have royal blood flowing through your veins.

"I suppose that's true, but like I told Carl at 'Snoops,' 'Who cares?'"

Snoops?

"Schoops restaurant here in Lowell. I call it 'Snoops.' That's where a lot of townsfolk go to catch up on the latest. I have breakfast with five men every morning.

Scandalous.

"Your dad's cousin, Mike Manes, is one of them."

Yikes. Linda, is it because of your heritage that you like the color purple?

"No, I loved royal purple before I ever knew about my lineage."

That's my point; it could be an inherited thing. Tell me about the Fosters. "Well, Anacher, the Great Forester of Flanders, died A.D. 837. He is believed to be the ancestor of all the Fosters in the world – except for those who adopted the name."

Slaves, for example?

"Yes. About six generations of noble Foresters later, Sir Richard Forester, called by his Latinized name 'Forestarious,' traveled into England with his sister's husband, William the Conqueror."

You're related to William the Conqueror?

"Yes; and, if we fast-forward yet another 150 years, there was Sir John Forster who accompanied Richard the Lionhearted to Palestine, where he received the honor of knighthood for his valor. He was among those who compelled King John to sign the Magna Carta in 1215."

You're pulling my leg.

"Why would I do that? In 1314, Sir Reginald Forster fought at Banockburn. His descendants, many being knighted, were great chieftains and were closely allied to the royalty of Scotland, England, Ireland and Wales."

Which family member was the first to arrive in America?

"I believe that would be Reginald Foster who was born in Brunton, England about 1595. He came to America in 1638 and settled in Ipswich, Mass. Reggie was one of the first of the brood to go by Foster."

It does sound like many of these fightin' Foresters, Forsters and Fosters were warriors.

"Some of them married the daughters of warriors, too. Jedediah Foster of Andover, Mass., married Dorothy Dwight in 1749; her father was Brig. Gen. Joseph Dwight."

Who was the first member of your family to settle in this area?

"Probably my great-great grandfather George Lyman Foster who was born in Athens, Pa. He had 10 children, the third of which is my great-grandfather, Volney Orlando Foster.

Great-grandpa Volney traveled around a bit, including a stint as a miner in Colorado, but eventually came back to farm the old homestead in West Creek Township. Volney and Florence Foster had seven children; Grandpa DeWayne was the third born; he went by D.W.

"My dad was born Leon Austin Foster; folks around Lowell called him Pat."

* * *

In 1834, George Lyman Foster, Alfred D. Foster and two other hardy pioneers survived the winter of 1834-35 by holing up in a crude dug-out shelter north of what is now the intersection of Indiana 2 and Calumet Avenue. The area was known as West Creek Settlement.

In 1842, native New Yorker Melvin Halsted married Martha Foster in Dayton, Ohio. The newlyweds visited Martha's father's family, who lived south of Indianapolis, that fall. Halsted didn't set foot in Lake County until 1844. He platted out the town of Lowell in 1852.

Linda Foster Kiechle recalled that in the early 1950s, her mother drove west of Cedar Lake to a feed store near Reickert's Tavern and the Hudson dealership, where she obtained discarded feed sacks. The area is known as Brunswick, not too far from where Linda's great-great-grandfather stayed almost 120 years before. The cotton feed sacks were used to make Linda's clothing.

And the English translation of the Foster family's ancient motto?

"Although broken, strong."

Chris Christian *(Sept. 2010)*

"...Mama, put my guns in the ground
I can't shoot them anymore.
That long black cloud is comin' down
I feel I'm knockin' on heaven's door..."
– Bob Dylan

While waiting for Chris Christian to get off work, I enjoyed a bowl of his pizza soup.

Filled with Italian sausage, pepperoni, green peppers, onions, mostaccioli and shredded mozzarella on top, it was to die for. I wondered if a Lenten version, replacing sausage and pepperoni with anchovies, also would be a hit.

Christian, 56, is a cook at Pav's restaurant in Hebron. He was born in the Indiana Harbor neighborhood of East Chicago, but has hung his hat in many places. Christian currently lives in Lowell with his ex-wife and daughter.

He also has the most unique speech pattern and voice I've ever heard. His sentences start out like runaway trains, taper; and then conclude with a crescendo almost in the form of a question. Think Al Pacino imitating Popeye while reciting Edgar Allen Poe's poem "The Raven." I don't always know what Chris is saying, but I can listen to him all day.

* * *

Talk to me.
"My father was born Chris Hristodoulou in Greece," he said.

"His family came to the United States in 1904; our surname was changed to Christian. Hristodoulou means "worker for Christ" in Greek, man. Dad was a World War I veteran."

Chris, you're only three years older than me. Your father easily could have served in Korea or World War II, but a World War I vet?

"He was born in 1896, man."

How old was he when you were born?

"Sixty; he died when I was 11. I remember him taking me into some of the gambling houses in the Harbor. He hated the Chicago White Sox because he lost a lot of money when they threw the World Series in 1919."

Your mother?

"My ma never remarried; she was an old-fashioned Greek lady. She came to this country in 1954."

Fifty years after your father.

"I can speak, read and write Greek. My mother spoke no English. I didn't speak English until I started school.

"When I was like 4 or 5, my best friend was a Puerto Rican kid; he was a year older than me. I spoke only Greek; he spoke only Spanish, but we communicated."

Example?

"I'm left-handed and my ma wanted to break me of that; she wouldn't teach me how to tie my shoes. While playing outside together, I'd point to my feet and then look my Hispanic friend in the eyes. He'd nod that he understood and then tie my shoes for me."

Best buds; I like that story. You've been around the restaurant business nearly all your life.

"I was baptized in a restaurant, man."

How's that?

"When I was real little, I was running around in the kitchen of the Olympia restaurant and one of the cooks didn't see me while he was walking with a pot of soup, man. He dumped the entire container on my head."

Gazpacho, maybe?

"Minestrone; burned the shit out of me, man."

When did your family move to Gary?

"When I was 6, but I started working in the Harbor at John's Eat Shop when I was 11; my cousin had just bought it. Today, he owns

Harry-O's in Cedar Lake."

Let me guess; his name is Harry Onassis.

"Jim Xerrogiannis."

I was close. Life in Gary?

"Gary was real bad when I was growing up, man. (Richard) Hatcher was running for mayor; there were a lot of riots – teachers were getting beat up. We got chased home from school almost everyday. It was a real crazy time, man.

"When I was in seventh-grade, we were the first school to be one-third white, one-third black and one-third Latin. By '72, there were only about five white kids left at Horace Mann, man. I've seen a lot of changes in Gary."

Did you play sports at Horace Mann?

"Yeah, man; I played football, baseball and wrestled until my senior year; then, I transferred to Andrean and became a hippie."

You worked at Inland Steel Co. for five years.

"Until 1980."

Permanent layoff?

"Yeah, man; I got caught playing poker, man."

Chris, sometimes you gotta know when to hold 'em and know when to fold 'em.

"You got that right, man. But, if I wouldn't have gotten fired, I would've never moved to Seattle for a year or lived in Alaska for five years. I was climbing Mt. Si when Mt. St. Helen's blew; I watched the Northern Lights, man.

"And I got to do stuff like that when I was young and could really enjoy it, man, not as a tired out, hunched-over retiree. I could've had a good mill pension right now, but it's better to be happy. Besides, I've known a lot of people who died a year after they retired."

Greece?

"I was in Greece for almost four months in 1969. I went to see my only living grandparent – she was 104 and died like three days later."

Pav's?

"We've been open for a month. Chris Pavlou is the owner. We specialize in gyros, pizza, ribs and Italian beefs; the patties for our Hawks Burgers are made fresh – never frozen. I enjoy the customers who dine at Pav's; they've been very receptive."

Have you ever owned your own restaurant?

"Yeah, man, Conela's in Lowell for 10 years. I named it after my daughter – Anastasia Conela Christian."

You're also a musician.

"Yeah, man; I play guitar, harmonica and sing. And I just joined a band called Pegasus; they've been around a long time, but I'm the first new member they've hired in like 20 years."

A few of your favorite performers?

"Carlos Santana, Buddy Guy and the Allman Brothers. One of my all-time favorite songs is 'Knockin' on Heaven's Door.'"

Mine, too. Regrets?

"I went to Indiana University Bloomington because I wanted to be a writer, but I quit college in '73 to join a band. I wish I would've stayed in school, man. I didn't even tell my ma I quit. A private eye located me about six months later."

* * *

Life's left hooks have knocked Chris Christian to the kitchen floor on more than one occasion. But, like an ancient Greek firebird, he has risen from the ashes each time.

Heaven can wait.

Mary Kay Emmrich *(Oct. 2011)*

"They're my people; I could never write down to them."
– Raymond Carver.

Ray Carver, dubbed the American Chekov, was referring to the laborers and service workers about whom he so often wrote.

If Carver had condescended to his characters, he would've condemned the first 40 years of his life. Carver grew up on a small river town of 700 souls.

Mary Kay Emmrich is library director in Lake Village. She lives in Morocco with her husband, Roger; they've been married 12 years.

Emmrich, 56, is the daughter of the late Harold and Hallie Martin, the former owners of the Hilltop Tavern in Morocco.

Emmrich is a southpaw who has a razor-sharp sense of humor that I adore. Her niece, who has hazmat training, refers to Mary Kay as "Auntthrax."

Mary Kay Emmrich is not your mother's librarian.

* * *

"My parents moved from Raub to Morocco when they bought the Hilltop in 1966," Emmrich began.

High school?

"North Newton, class of '73."

Did you participate in extracurriculars at North Newton?

"I filled beer coolers. My parents were strict because their biggest fear was that people would say, 'Yeah, Mary Kay is a wild thing, but what do you expect? Her parents own a bar.' I was kept on a short chain. I rebelled later on, but we won't go there."

What did your dad like to call the Hilltop?

"The Bucket of Blood; it was a farmer's bar. Papa always said if there was dirt under the bar stools, there was money in the register because the farmers had been in."

I recall "Mustard" Hanger bringing some homemade head cheese to the bar; he bartered it for beer.

"You can see pieces of eyeballs and other body parts in that stuff."

The Hilltop served nice meals.

"We always had sandwiches, but on Friday and Saturday nights, we served fish and a variety of steaks. I probably made more potato salad by the age of 21 than most women make in a lifetime.

"Jeff, everybody thinks the world is divided between Democrats and Republicans or men and women, but the division is between Miracle Whip and Hellman's (mayonnaise)"

I know you're a Democrat; do you prefer Miracle Whip?

"I'm a Hellman's woman."

We were raised on the cheap stuff – Miracle Whip, oleo, Karo corn syrup... .

"Nothin' better than French toast and Karo white syrup – holy moly!"

Your maiden name, Martin, is the most common surname in France.

"Yes, my father's father came here from Quebec; Dad's mother's family came from Sweden."

College?

"I went to Indiana Central College, which is now the University of Indianapolis. Then, I came home and worked at People's Drug Store in Morocco for about a year and a half, and then attended Ball State where I earned my degree in English and minored in geography.

"I had a teaching license so I taught for four years to pay for the first four years of college, so I could borrow for the next round."

Next round?

"I went back to Ball State for its American Library Association accredited MLS program; that's where I got my masters of library science degree. They don't have that program any more, so I'm one of about 40 people who graduated from Ball State with an ALA-MLS. We belong to a little group called Great Defunct Library School Graduates.

"I borrowed money from Kentland Bank to go to college. Remember, this was the '70s; interest rates were outlandish – 15 percent. I'd mess with the banker, 'What if I don't pay?' He'd say, 'You can't do that; we'll put you in jail.' I'd say, 'OK, but there is no car or house you can repossess.' He'd say, 'Don't talk like that.' What was he gonna do, perform a frontal lobotomy on me?"

Mary Kay, when did you become library director here?

"In '94, after Mary Rybarski passed."

This little town had some great librarians when I was a kid: Mary Rybarski, Rhoda Kuster, Dorothy Arbuckle... .

"I've had job offers elsewhere, but it's the patrons who keep me here. Lake Village is a comfortable fit. I love Lake Village."

This new building is really nice. Do you know when the old library was built?

"In 1962; Angelus and Helen Kocoshis donated the land for the library."

Good family. A lot of Lake Village boys worked in the cut-flower fields for Angelus. Didn't he also donate the black granite stone that graced the front of the old library? The one that had "Lake Village Memorial Township Library" etched into it?

"Yes, the granite stone was moved to the lobby of this building; I'll show it to you."

Plans for retirement?

"When I do, I'm moving to 'The Village.' This northern portion of Newton county is more diverse. Once you get south of Indiana 114, it becomes Wonder Bread out there."

A few of your favorite authors?

"Kurt Vonnegut, Tom Robbins, Raymond Carver... ."

* * *

Kids from Lake Village and Sumava Resorts who are my age and older didn't have kindergarten, but some of us did have story hour at the Lake Village Memorial Township Library. A lady named Mrs. Louden served as raconteur.

Mrs. Louden wasn't a librarian; she was simply the old woman – in her 90s – who lived in a dilapidated chicken coop near the library. Mrs. Louden had been part of Buffalo Bill's Wild West Show; I believe she was American Indian.

After our interview, Emmrich took me across the street so we could pay a visit to a woman I've known all my life. Doris Hendryx used to clean the library and was a good friend of my mother who worked as an assistant librarian in Lake Village. It was nice to get a hug from Doris.

Worn memories of a wonderful library in a small river town.

And the new library in "The Village" is just as wondrous, thanks to Mary Kay Emmrich and her excellent staff.

Some things never change.

Glenn Novak *(March, 2007)*

*"Radio is the theater of the mind;
television is the theater of the mindless."*
-Steve Allen

Glenn Novak is a throwback. When I toiled with him at Inland Steel he was a grunt in the field – a bullworker. Novak's interests are also nostalgic. He's a fan of The Three Stooges and a collector of old radios. He is an authority on both subjects.

I head east on U.S. 30 for that intriguingly named burg, Union Mills. The 48-year-old lifelong bachelor has resided there for 10 years. Novak is a Hammond native with North Dakotan roots. He graduated from Gavit in 1976.

* * *

"Jeff, can you take your shoes off, please," Novak began.

Glenn, I planned on it. I'm not even through the front door yet. In the mill, you were always the greasiest, dirtiest guy on the job, yet you keep this place immaculate. Amazing. Still working at No. 4 BOF (basic oxygen furnace)?

"Yeah, I'll have 28 years pretty soon. They're sending any of us mechanics to welding school – if we want to go."

To become certified welders?

"Oh yeah. Hey, anybody can weld. They teach chimpanzees how to weld."

Glenn, you take advantage of the fact that I'm wielding a reporter's pad and not a chipping hammer (I was a welder in the mill). Let's talk radio. How many have you bought and sold down through the years?

"Thousands."

Your dad was into radios before you, correct?

"Yeah, he worked at Youngstown (Steel). When they had the big strike back in '59 he took a correspondence course. He did a lot of repairs. I remember him showing me an old Zenith tombstone the family had when he was a boy. You could work it on AC or battery. They used a battery because they didn't have electric on the farm in North Dakota. I'd like to move to North Dakota, but I'd never leave the area while my mom is still alive. Still, I feel a draw to North Dakota – my roots are there. Dad left the farm to me."

How did you end up in Union Mills?

"I was laid off at Inland back around '94 and working at Orville Redenbacher's in Valpo. This house was in the process of being built. I figured if I ever did get called back to the mill it wouldn't be that bad a drive. It was definitely close to Orville's. Sad to see that place shut down."

That's a tombstone, right?

"No, that's a cathedral -- Simplex. There are cathedrals, tombstones, tabletop models, consoles – this one here is a Russian Red Star radio – made for the Russian military elite."

Looks like a small juke box.

"I bid on eBay for that one. Came all the way from Australia. Very seldom do I ever buy a radio off of eBay. Too risky. Less than half the time do you get exactly what's described. This Zenith tabletop was picked up in Lansing, Mich. It's Art Deco. I really like the Art Deco stuff – the style, the angles – very impressive. This is an Atwater Kent – very unusual console. It has a clock; it has motorized tuning. A fairly rare set and, at more than four feet tall, it's a massive piece."

What were some other manufacturers?

"Philco, Arvin, Crosley. Arvins were made here in Indiana. I'm always on the lookout for them. Crosleys were made in Ohio."

Crosley Field; the Cincinnati Reds played there when we were kids. What material is this radio made out of? Bakelite? It's beautiful.

"Catalin. Everybody looks for catalin. The polished marbling is really sharp on this particular radio."

What's the most you ever paid for a radio?

"$2,400."

You go to shows all over the country.

"Yeah; I didn't go to New York this year, but I went to Lansing, Mich. That's the biggest show in the United States that I know of. It's like a huge flea market. People meet, trade, talk, buy. They also have an auction."

Strictly radios?

"Mostly. But you'll find other stuff. My buddy Charlie sold an old voting ballot box in Lansing. It's amazing what people will buy."

Glenn, remember that time when I rode to Kankakee, Ill. with you? When you checked out that dilapidated building filled with "treasures?" I hadn't been to Kankakee in 25 years. I got to talking with the property owner, an odd duck named Jeff, while you rummaged in the attic. I said, "Yep. I was born in this city 43 years ago today." He looked at me kind of funny and asked to see my driver's license. I looked back at him kind of funny, but cooperated. Jeff was also born on April 8 of the same year – in Kankakee! What are the odds? Two Jeffs spending their birthday with a pack rat like you. What was that guy's last name?

"Dahmer," states the poker-faced Novak. (Glenn enjoys irritating me.)

Glenn, I'm tryin' to make a livin' here. (Glenn laughs at me.)
The Three Stooges?

"I've got about everything I want now regarding The Stooges – including all three of their autographs. Do you remember Emil Sitka?"

Didn't he work at the blast furnace?

"No; I've got Sitka's autograph as well. 'Join hands, you love birds... '

Oh, that guy! He was in a million stooges episodes.

"A guy I've dealt with through eBay sent me this photo. It's from when he was a kid. Jeff, look, he's standing with Moe! He actually met Moe. He talked to Moe. Had lunch with Moe... ."

Glenn, do you need a tissue? Get ahold of yourself.

"Let me show you the basement."

Geesh, it looks like a very well-kept auto parts store down here.

"To me, restoring radios is like bringing back something, like keeping a piece of history alive."

When did you really get into the restoration of radios?

"Somewhere around 1986. About the time I stopped drinking. Jeff, want a pop for the road?"

Glenn, that sounds almost as good as your catalin Arvin.

Linda Arnold *(Jan. 2005)*

"I want to live, I want to give
I've been a miner for a heart of gold
It's these expressions, I never give
That keep me searching for a heart of gold
And I getting old"
-Neil Young

Linda Arnold lives in Lowell across the railroad tracks from Reiter Corporation, formerly known as Globe Industries. She has rented the same 120- year-old farmhouse for nearly 30 years. Her hobbies are refinishing things and tending to her perennials. She is a 50-year-old, twice-married buxom brunette who when so inclined, possesses a vernacular that could make a sailor blush.

Linda never had children. She does have a black cat and a white dog. The canine, an American Eskimo, barks at me as I enter.

* * *

"Don't mind Reba," says Linda, "her bark is worse than her bite. Take a seat."

Linda, this place looks like something out of the Smithsonian with your olio of antique furniture, fiestaware collection, books, and an assortment of junk ad infinitum.

"Yeah, I'm the yard sale queen of Lowell. This place is decorated in 'Early Rummage.' Ask me questions while cut up these fresh vegetables. I'm making soup. You can stay for dinner."

I have to get going after this interview.

"You can take some home with you then. I have some leftover frozen chili for you, too."

Where were you born?

"St. Vincent's Orphanage in Chicago. My mother was a Canuck – French Canadian-American Indian. She came down to Chicago, gave birth to me and went back to Canada. My biological father was of Irish descent. That's all I know.

"My parents adopted me as an infant. I went to good Catholic schools. Graduated from Mother McAuley High School – all girls. Old Mayor Daley's niece went there."

How did you end up in Lowell?

"My grandfather built a cottage on Lake Dale. I spent every summer of my life in Indiana. After graduating from Mother McAuley my parents moved from Chicago to the cottage for good. It wasn't much of a transition, I made a lot of friends during my 17 summers on the lake. Many of them didn't even realize I'd ever lived in Chicago at all."

Life after Mother McAuley?

"I attended TSI computer programming school in Hammond where I received a certificate.

What does TSI stand for?

"I don't know."

Did you become a computer programmer?

"No, I went to the Porter County Fair that summer."

So?

"I traveled with them for two seasons."

Huh?

"A barker, mostly."

Huh?

"You know, the games."

Like the mouse game?

"No, I never worked that one."

How did your parents feel about you opting for the carnival life over computer programming?

"How would you have felt if one of your twin daughters ran off with the freaking circus?"

(No reply).

"I tried spot welding in Grant Park (Ill.) for a while. That didn't last too long. And I worked at Baker and Taylor, you remember, the book distribution place in Momence (Ill.). Then I learned to bartend at Midway Ballroom in Cedar Lake.   *Pretty rough crowd at times?*

"I dunno know, from ages 15 to 30 every guy I dated had to have a beard *and* a Harley. Anyway, I moved on from there to Clyde's Saloon in Highland and then Dante's here in Lowell. I stayed at Dante's for five years. I've been at the Radisson for the last 21 years now.

"Somehow, I did manage to get an associate's degree in fine arts and a bachelor's degree in continued studies while waiting tables down through the years. And I went for a degree in psychology and nursing too, but at the age of 38, I decided I didn't want to go to school for the rest of my life. Hey, the money's good at the Radisson and it's one of the few places a server has benefits. I have insurance and a 401k plan."

Ever wait on any celebrities?

"Hundreds of 'em."

Who was naughty and who was nice?

"I won't mention the assholes. I did watch them literally carry a famous TV actress out of the hotel."

What happened?

"She was toast. Drunker than seven lords. She found out she had breast cancer."

Are your eyes welling up?

"Onions. I really loved Red Skeleton. What a nice guy. Liberace was nice, too. And what taste he had in men."

Yeah, um, tell me more about Red. He was from Vincennes you know, and he ran away with the circus when he was a boy. Never came back.

"No wonder I liked him. I met him a few years before he died. He got up from his table and told me to leave his food set. After so many years of people asking for his autograph and wanting to shake his hand and whatnot while trying to eat he said he'd grown fond of cold food. No one wanted to intrude on that particular evening, I guess, so he decided to go to them, so his food could get cold.

"Red went from table to table talking to all the other customers, making them laugh, and the entire time he joked with them he drew clown faces on their paper place mats. One of the girls from The Go Go's, they were performing that weekend too, asked him if she could get his autograph for her mother. He laughed and asked her why *she* didn't want his autograph. Then he asked her for *her* autograph. I really liked one of the Oak Ridge Boys. The one with the baritone voice. Very humble. Very serene."

Let me guess. The one with the long beard.
"You got it."
Ever get lonely in this big old place?
"Who's alone? In almost 30 years, I've taken in 31 different people when they needed a place to stay – whether they could help out with rent or not."

* * *

With leftover chili in hand, I get into my truck to leave. I take note of Linda's small station wagon, and her latest pride and joy, an old white pick-up still bearing the insignia of the construction company that used to own it. A valuable tool for the yard sale queen.

I also take note that both vehicles wear ribbons that simply state "Think Pink". Briefly, I think of Ann Jillian. I remember lifting my grandmother's casket – a double mastectomy before she left us. I try to shut out the vision of lifting the bed sheet of my uninsured, semiconscious mother at Wishard Hospital in Indianapolis after her mastectomy.

And as I drive away, I think of Linda Arnold, buxom brunette.

A barker with a heart of gold.

Caregivers & Do-gooders

Val Carr *(Nov. 2008)*

"While there is a lower class I am in it; while there is a criminal element I am of it; while there is a soul in prison, I am not free."
- Eugene V. Debs

It's about 5 p.m. and that evening sun has just gone down on Ivanhoe Gardens near 11th Avenue and Chase Street in Gary.

East of Ivanhoe, Pilgrim Rest Missionary Baptist Church has stood its ground for 84 years.

Whereas razor wire deters trespassers from entering the former public housing project, Pilgrim Rest welcomes all souls – including a wretch like me.

It's Valerie Carr, I've come to see. Carr, 46, is a devout Pilgrim Rest member and the project director of Highly Flavored Inc., an outreach ministry of Pilgrim Rest.

Carr is single and has lived in Gary since 1986. Physically, she vaguely reminds me of Whoopi Goldberg, but better looking. She is a latter-day Angela Davis; she is a modern-day Sojourner Truth.

And she is selfless. It took two years of coaxing for her to be interviewed for this column.

* * *

"I'm from Neptune, N.J., by Asbury Park," Carr begins.

Bruce Springsteen's old stomping grounds.

"That's right, Southside Johnny and the Asbury Jukes territory.

"I'm also an Army brat; I was born at Fort Monmouth in New Jersey. My father was in the military for 30 years. I attended Monmouth College in Long Branch, N.J.; it's called Monmouth University now. I left Jersey when I was 25."

You're quite the social activist here in Gary, but your day job is working for the American Cancer Society in Chicago.

"Yes, that's where I get my money – my paychecks. I left a consulting firm to get closer to a successful not-for-profit organization. The ACS is a very successful conglomerate; working for them gives me good ideas for Highly Flavored."

What's your job title at the ACS?

"I'm an administrative assistant for the vice-president of field operations for the Illinois division; I work on the corporate level."

HFI often works with Gary's youth; it started out as a prison outreach program.

"Correct. Pilgrim Rest has pretty much been the financial foundation in terms of paying for the newsletters we send into the prisons; we do that every quarter.

"Our focus is now more about stopping people from going to prison in the first place, more than it is saving those who are in prison. I think we can cut the wires and stop kids from making bad choices before they get old enough to go in.

"We have very strong mentors in Highly Flavored; people who were originally mentored by me."

When did you become interested in social work?

"Since I was five years old. My sister is 11 years older than me; she was around that whole civil rights movement. I would listen from my bedroom while she planned sit-ins. She attended Howard University as well as Albany State College in Georgia. She was there in the middle of the burning – the fires.

"My mother also was very firm in standing for rights and making sure that the community was empowered. She died when I was 15.

"I think that we need to take back what we had in the civil rights era. We need to mobilize – grassroots it out. We need to teach people how to do what we do.

"I'm 46, but my mentors are under 30. They teach the teenagers. That's what the civil rights era was. But it's gone. It broke off somewhere after (the Rev. Martin Luther) King died, I guess. I don't know where it went, but I'm determined to get it back."

Maybe things will change with our new president.

"I supported electing Barack Obama, but I think that could be yet another excuse for us not to do what we need to do. This is not the time to get lazy; it's the time we need to mobilize.

"If we can all stand in line six hours for Barack, we can stand in line over and over to help clean up our community. The way we cared about the national election is the way we should care about our local elections.

"Yes, Obama is in the White House, but he's not going to come get the drug dealer off the corner of 5th and Madison. We can't sit and wait for him."

Val, I agree with you. He's a man; he's not the Messiah or the anti-Christ.

"Jeff, I'm proud of the moment. It was the coolest thing I've seen since living in Gary. Blacks, Hispanics and whites standing in line to vote. I went to see Obama in Highland – 50,000 people with a common cause.

"If we can do this for one guy, let's do it for the kids, let's do it to change our community, let's do it to get all those people out of prison. There are so many facets killing our society that we can do something about.

"There is no reason why the city of Gary should have a 45 percent high school graduation rate. That's ridiculous. How do we wake up everyday and not be alarmed by that? And there's no reason why there should be 2 million people in prison."

Val, we've known each other for a while, now. We've become good friends. You're one of most altruistic human beings I've ever met. You don't have to answer this question...

"I did two years in a federal prison camp in Lexington, Ky. I got out in '98. I was connected with this church when I went in. This church supported me through that whole process. So, when I came out, I went to the pastor and told him about my vision of having this prison ministry; he embraced it.

Pastor Adams.

"Yes; all the work I do is like a catalyst from when I did my time. When I got out of jail, I became committed to helping that population. There are just too many of us in there. I think that's the biggest problem I have with this society – the fact that nobody seems to care irritates me.

"I met a very special person when I was in prison; she was an actress who worked for Second City Theater. We did time together.

"When we were in prison, I was the choir director and deejay compound. We had empowerment workshops as inmates helping other women. She did shows; I played for her while she did the shows.

"Now that we're out, we've continued working together. At the Sojourner Truth House, we're presenting a series workshops all this month. We do whatever we can do to give back.

"Everything I do in the community is based on being in prison and watching those women turn their lives around while in prison; it was eye-opening. It's like you're reaching a prime population. I dealt with women ranging from drug addicts to murderers.

"I still write some of the women I was in prison with. They're inspired when they hear the stories.

"I also write a lot of guys who are in prison. I tell them, 'You are in prime territory; do your work – especially if you know God. I think that makes a difference, if you're in Christ. When I went in, I was saved and the whole bit. Prison is the best place to preach. Where are they going?"

Val, once again, I concur. To keep this country from collapsing, the government is going to bail out some of these big corporations. But once they've done that dirty deed, there's a bunch of crooked CEOs who should be afforded the opportunity to hear the word of God from a prison cell.

"Jeff, that would only drive up the prison rate."

Are you going to live out your days in Gary?

"Yes, my work is here. I need Gary."

No Val, Gary needs you.

* * *

Late November. For nostalgic folks, that charming Saturday Morning Post cover painted by Norman Rockwell – the one with the family passing around a turkey – might come to mind.

Val Carr also has wistful visions of people eating Thanksgiving dinner.

Behind bars.

Buddy Bell *(April 2006)*

"It is my deepest belief that only by giving life do we find life, that the truest act of courage, the strongest act of manliness is to sacrifice ourselves for others in a totally non-violent struggle for justice. To be a man is to suffer for others, God help us to be men."
– Cesar Chavez

April 11, 2006. That is the date printed on the front page of the Lowell Tribune-Cedar Lake Journal that you hold in your hand. While you read this column, the steel bars of a federal prison cell in Oxford, Wis. will slam shut. Those that have heard that sound will attest that it's one you never forget. It is a sound that will give an exiting visitor an immense feeling of gratitude. For inmates, the slam may trigger an immense feeling of despair. For the next 88 days, Buddy Bell will be an inmate. Why?

Because Buddy Bell heard sabers rattling – a sound he detests.

Buddy attended St. Edward's School through sixth grade and graduated from Lowell High School in 2000. The former Red Devil is now a Blue Demon and a junior at DePaul. Buddy Bell will become a schoolteacher.

March 26, 2006. It is 7:00 p.m. when Buddy arrived at my apartment door. He had driven from Wood Dale, Ill. He is tall and slight of build. His hair is dark and long. He is beginning to grow a beard. In his blue eyes, I detect a trace of sadness but mostly kindness.

Bell looked hungry. I fixed him a plate of spaghetti and a glass of orange juice. Water was the only other choice I had to offer. We talked.

We talked for more than three hours.

* * *

So, Buddy, besides attending DePaul, you are a choir teacher at a Catholic Church.

"Yes, I am," he said. "It's a bilingual congregation in Addison – St. Joseph's Parish. I speak Spanish. I took four years of it at Lowell High School."

You've become quite an activist since the days of treading the hallways of Lowell High. What are some of the causes you've stood for?

"Sat., April 1, we will march from Pilsen to the McDonald's Corp.'s flagship restaurant downtown with the Coalition of Immokalee Workers. Just recently there was a successful boycott of Taco Bell. They (Taco Bell) finally agreed to buy tomatoes from a company that will pay their pickers a better wage. McDonald's is the next target."

Immokalee. That's a Seminole word, isn't it?

"Yes, but the tomato pickers are mostly Guatemalans and Mexicans. I am also part of Peace Pledge, a group that is anti-torture. They address Iraq War issues as well. And I'm a part of DePaul University's branch of Amnesty International. We fight for human rights issues and immigration issues. I do letter writing for people getting deported. I'm against the death penalty and I'm part of an advocacy group that protests for gay rights."

Your stance at Fort Benning got you in some trouble.

"Unfortunately, we have to go to jail before the media pays much attention. Most of the media is owned by big corporations that have some kind of stake in the military industrial complex.

"Eisenhower assured complicity between the media and war issues. For example, GE and their different subsidiaries make so many millions in selling chemicals and weapons – they also own news networks. They are biased.

" Jeff, you work for a small local paper – The Lowell Tribune. Newspapers like yours are the most authentic. They really don't have a bias. They don't make a profit by having the School of the Americas stay open."

No bias? You haven't read some of my Red Devil sports stories. But seriously, about this School of the Americas, I'm told they don't go by that handle anymore. Tell me about it – about your protest at Fort Benning.

"The SOA was closed down for a month. It reopened as the Western Hemisphere Institute for Security Cooperation – only the name changed. The School of the Americas has been around since the 1940s. It started in Panama and moved to Fort Benning, Ga. in 1984."

1984. Sounds Orwellian already. What goes on down there?

"The SOA is basically a school where the US Army trains foreign soldiers from other countries in different psychological warfare techniques for commando operations. The US welcomes certain troops from countries where their people are oppressed and their government is in favor of US government interests. The SOA is very selective in the countries they school. They indoctrinate these soldiers with beliefs that labor unions, environmentalists, and charity workers are communist tools.

"Columbia sends the most soldiers to the SOA at the present time. They are probably the most dangerous and hostile country in Central or South America. Union leaders are assassinated. Their children are kidnaped. Columbia has a superficial democracy – the person in charge was elected, but he has a history of killing anyone opposed to him. The SOA teaches these soldiers how to torture and kill – and to do it in a powerfully psychological way. For example, SOA graduates might leave one of their victims lying dead in a pool of blood on a busy street corner so the peasants can see the corpse – we teach Columbia terrorism."

Since the '40s, huh? Men like Jimmy Carter had no qualms about the goings on at the SOA?

"It goes beyond partisan issues, no matter who's in the White House."

I do know that Panama's Noriega was an SOA graduate. Last I heard, he was in the hoosegow himself, down around Miami way – drug trafficking.

"There have been countless cases of killings throughout Central and South America. Graduates of the SOA killed a nun in the rain forests of the Amazon while she was working with indigenous people. It was allegedly SOA graduates who assassinated Archbishop Oscar Romero in El Salvador. Nine months later they raped and murdered four women of the church."

From what I've read, a former chaplain by the name of Charles Liteky holds a daily vigil at one of Fort Benning's gates in remembrance of the 1989 massacre of six Jesuit priests, their cook, and her daughter in El Salvador. Liteky earned the country's highest decoration for valor – the Congressional Medal of Honor. He returned his medal in protest of the school's existence. November is the anniversary of the massacre.

"I went to Fort Benning in November. Father Jerome Zawada, a Franciscan from Cedar Lake also went. Forty-one people were arrested the entire weekend, 37 for crossing over the line. Four more for protesting our arrest outside the county jail – the town put in an arbitrary random curfew.

"We went to court in January and were convicted of trespassing. I will serve three months in a federal prison in Oxford, Wis. I was given a self-surrender option. Father Jerry received six months in Terre Haute; he has been arrested many times before.

"Even though I am against the war in Iraq, I think that it is fathomable that people *can* believe that the war is really the right thing for human rights in Iraq. They've got themselves convinced and if they're willing to put their lives on the line, that has to be commendable. I'm sort of coming from the same concern.

"Part of our government's mission is to make people believe what they're doing over there is the right thing to do. I would take the approach of trying to peaceably change their minds. I never demonize anyone. That is the first step in becoming what you oppose."

* * *

January, 2006, Buddy Bell before a federal judge...

"Judge Faircloth, thank you for letting me explain why I'm pleading not guilty. I feel I have an obligation to stand for the rights of poor, hungry, and landless peoples. While the SOA-WHINSEC concerns itself with making the hemisphere safe for corporate investment, my concern lies with empowering the powerless and spreading real democracy.

"Just as the structures of racial segregation under the force of law could not have been dismantled except by civil disobedience, the same goes for today's structures of economic segregation. The military and government deference to the rich perpetuates a segregationist mindset. It says that some people's lives are disposable in order to accumulate wealth for a few. My personal responsibility to the human race is to thwart the efforts of those who uphold economic division through the use of torture, killings, and 'disappearances.' Consistent with this responsibility, I intend to take part in civil disobedience whenever the entrenched power of the rich over our culture and democratic systems makes this action a necessity.

"I don't request a specific sentence from this court. I know it isn't my choice. Rather than concern myself with what will happen to me if I get in the government's way, I decide to instead consider what will happen to future victims of SOA-WHINSEC if I fail to stand in its way."

* * *

Then, with a slamming, the gavel sounded.

And he washed his hands of it.

Debra Martinez-Bolanos *(Nov. 2012)*

"They ain't human. A human being wouldn't live like they do. A human being couldn't stand it to be so dirty and miserable."
– John Steinbeck

John Steinbeck was describing white people from Oklahoma when he wrote those words in his classic novel, "The Grapes of Wrath."

When Debra Martinez-Bolanos' father came to this country from Chihuahua, Mexico, he had $1 in his pocket. Did the man enter this country illegally? I didn't ask, nor do I care.

She did tell me her father was educated, went into the U.S. Army, and then became an East Chicago police officer and retired as a lieutenant.

Martinez-Bolanos, 54, has lived in East Chicago all her life and is a graduate of Bishop Noll Institute in Hammond. She is married to Salvador Bolanos; they have three children, ages 15 to 26.

Martinez-Bolanos is the director of a not-for-profit group called Xel-Ha Escuela de Danza, a dance school for young people on Chicago Avenue in East Chicago near the legendary Mexican restaurant, Casablanca. She also is the president and founder of a Mexican cultural group known as Sociedad Cultural Y Civica La Reforma,

* * *

What part of East Chicago were you raised in?
"On Parrish Avenue across from Washington Park," she said.

East Chicago today?

"The city has changed since I was a girl; that is one of the reasons I've stayed. I feel like if you want to make a change, you have to do it. A lot of my friends have moved away."

That's a noble attitude.

"I live here, I have my business here, and I'm a very active community organizer as far as things like the business crime watch on this side of town."

Life after Bishop Noll?

"I went to Mexico City and studied with the Ballet Folklorico School of Dance After finishing my summer courses, I was selected by the Ballet Folklorico De Mexico's scouts and joined them as a professional. We performed at the Palace of Fine Arts. I lived in Mexico City for nearly two years.

"When I came back, that's when I took over the dance school here that my mother started. This will be our 42nd anniversary."

Where did you come up with the name Xel-Ha Esquela de Danza?

"Xel-Ha is in the Yucatan Peninsula; it's an archaeological park where you can go scuba diving and snorkeling. There are many cultural activities in that area, such as swimming with the dolphins. Xel-Ha is a very ancient area that goes back to the Mayans. The Mayan kings and queens used it as a spa."

Tell me about these young people at your dance school.

"We put in at least eight hours of rehearsal per week, year-round with the exception of Christmas. The kids are very dedicated, and they like what they do.

"Most of my students come to me at about age 6 and stay with me until they enter college."

By now, you're probably teaching the children of former students.

"Yes, I'll have people stop me – not just here in East Chicago – I could be shopping at the mall or in Crown Point. They'll say: 'Ms. Balanos, aren't you so and so? I'd just like to tell you that because of your training and the discipline that I learned, I was able to get through a lot of things and now I'm a doctor... .'

"That makes me feel good, and it makes my mom feel good. If you can touch one life and make a change, that's a lot. There are people who sit around and do nothing; all they do is complain. They never touch lives."

The Sociedad Cultural Y Civica La Reforma?

"One of the SCCLR's missions is education; we host an annual golf outing to raise money for scholarships. We also do a Mexican breakfast fundraiser in March; it brings the community together and lets people know how we operate.

"We recently had our Night of Latin Culture ... at Bishop Noll. It's an art gallery featuring Latinos from Chicago and Northwest Indiana who display their work – Equadorians, Bolivians, Puerto Ricans, Mexicans, Columbians – all displaying their art, folklore and history. It's free to the public. That's the kinds of things the SCCLR does."

Women and Hispanics were a major factor in the reelection of President Barack Obama.

"I didn't care about the comments made by some of the Republicans, especially the guy who was running here in Indiana."

Richard Mourdock?

"What he said about women and rape. Why do they feel freely to say these things? I don't like the idea of politicians making rules, regulations and laws concerning a woman's body. I don't like that.

"Another thing that turned me off was the anti-immigration path they were on. I don't like that. I mean, we all came from somewhere. If we want to talk about someone who belongs here, lets talk about the American Indian. Look what they did to them."

In essence, the good old boys club needs to change its way of thinking.

"I feel the Republican party will change real soon. Mitt (Romney) had everything ready – the fireworks. I don't even think he had a concession speech prepared. He really thought he was going to win this one."

A critical miscalculation.

"Hispanics need to stop being a divided group. If we would've been more united in the past, we probably would've had an Hispanic president before Barack Obama was elected the first time."

The sleeping giant.

"That's right. My mom always told me that when I was growing up: 'We're the sleeping giant. When are we going to get up from that long, long nap?'"

East Chicago in the future?

"My fight is in East Chicago. This is why I'm still here. This is why I do what I do.

"I feel like I've been in a fight to help the people of this city to understand this is a good city. But we have to work at it – not only the Hispanics, but everybody – for East Chicago to be a better place.

"Why can't it be like Whiting? Look at downtown Whiting, how nice it is. We can do that. Make it work on Main Street – put the pressure on them. Some Hispanic politicians who get in the council forget; they forget."

* * *

Debra Martinez-Bolanos' parents and Mr. and Mrs. Emilio De La Garza were compadres while she was growing up.

After our interview, I stopped by my old union hall at the intersection of Broadway and Euclid Avenue. There is a large photograph of a De La Garza that hangs on the wall of Local 1010. It is the son of the aforementioned De La Garzas. A Congressional Medal of Honor was given to them.

Their son wasn't able to accept our nation's highest honor. You see, Lance Cpl. Emilio De La Garza, Jr. jumped on a live hand grenade, saving the lives of two Marine comrades near Da Nang, Republic of Vietnam.

Meanwhile, Debra Martinez-Bolanos continues to fight the good fight on the streets of East Chicago. The sleeping giant has awakened and we're a better country for it.

How much more American can you get than Emilio De La Garza and Debra Martinez-Bolanos?

Mary Lou DeLong *(March 2006)*

*"Let brotherly love continue,
for some who have done this have
entertained angels without realizing it."
Hebrews: Chapter 13*

Mary Lou DeLong lives in an apartment complex in Lowell. She is a transplanted Buckeye. The youngest of six children, Mary Lou turned 74 this February.

She is a retired schoolteacher, who taught mostly first-, second-, or third- graders for 33 years. Miss Delong was employed at Lake Prairie Elementary for 28 of those years.

She originally came to the Hoosier State so she could attend Manchester College. She later received her master's from Indiana University in Bloomington. One of her first teaching jobs was in Topeka, Ind. where she schooled first-graders, some of which only spoke an Amish dialect of German.

Mary Lou's mother was Pennsylvania Dutch. Some of her relatives were hidden in wagons and transported from the Quaker State to the Buckeye State during the war – Ohio wasn't drafting.

Mary Lou DeLong remains a pacifist herself and maintains, "Fighting isn't the answer."

Although she has never married, Mary Lou has lived with her friend Rita for nearly 37 years. Rita is a beautiful and brilliant yellow-naped parrot brought home from Costa Rica.

* * *

Mary Lou, to me, you epitomize the quintessential schoolmarm.

You enjoy children, don't you?

"Yes. Children are delightful, so creative. At least they used to be. I think television and video games have cut out a lot of their creativity. I had one little boy who was very sharp, but he was a 'Nintendo boy.' Whenever he'd write a story, he'd have to write about all the killing that was going on in his video game. Finally, I told him you have to write your own story – not about what goes on in your Nintendo world. He struggled with that. And he was very, very intelligent. There were others in the same boat."

I realize that donating your time at The First United Methodist Resale Shop is just one of the many church-related opportunities you participate in. Have you always been a Methodist?

"No, I grew up Church of the Brethren in Ohio. They are one of the three peace churches – along with the Quakers and Mennonites."

Tell me more about that particular denomination.

"The Church of the Brethren didn't believe in ballroom dancing. Folk dancing, yes, but no ballroom dancing. They're not big on going to movies. They used to have closed communion. They baptize three times forward – in the name of the Father, the Son, and the Holy Ghost. Dunk, dunk, dunk in the river or the baptistry. They are conscientious objectors and many of the boys did alternative service instead of going to the war."

Why did you become a Methodist?

"When I moved to Lowell, there was no Church of the Brethren nearby, and I'd always gone to church. I felt that Methodists weren't that different than the Church of the Brethren. Methodists are fairly open in their thinking, so I became a Methodist."

Mary Lou, I realize there are different factions of the Methodist Church across the globe, but I always felt that the First United Methodist Church here in Lowell was a fairly liberal bunch, as far as their overall beliefs.

"I think 'open' is a better word. The word liberal carries such nasty connotations anymore; the Republicans call all Democrats liberals. Actually, I'm much more liberal than conservative, when it comes to voting.

"I think the Democrats are more for social programs. And the Republicans, I feel, are more for the business people. That's just the way I feel personally. I don't know if that's necessarily true. I don't vote a straight ticket either way, but I think I could probably be a socialist rather than a capitalist. And I know that Democrats have been known to bash Republicans, but it seems to me the evangelical churches partake in some bashing themselves. They have such a wonderful message in God's message of forgiveness, loving, and compassion, yet they are so caught up in, 'If you don't believe in the way I believe, you're wrong'. I just know that isn't Jesus' teachings."

You've been known to write a few powerful men in your day.

"I've written to Jerry Falwell. I told him that I listened to his program and never once did I hear him mention Jesus Christ; all he ever mentioned was money. 'You claim to be a Christian and a pastor', I wrote, 'yet you never mentioned Jesus.' I never heard another word from him after that. They took my name off their list.

"I've written to George W. Bush. I said, 'You claim that we have freedom. What about the homeless? What kind of freedom do they have? What about the people who are trying to live on minimum wage? What about the people who can't afford medical insurance?' A few months later, one of his staff members wrote back thanking me for my comments.

I write to (Sen. Dick) Lugar and (Gov. Evan) Bayh, too. I believe Lugar is a good man. Although, I think sometimes you can be in office too long and your tail gets hooked into too many places. But I must say, I've always received good responses from Dick Lugar."

You're quite the globetrotter. Is there anywhere you haven't been?

"South America. My travels began through the Church of the Brethren's Volunteer Service. We received room, board, and $7.50 per month for one year. Many of the conscientious objectors did their work through Volunteer Services. Although opposed to the draft, they helped rebuild the war torn cities of Europe. There were those who helped out at mental institutions as well. I toured Germany, East Germany, Poland, Czechoslovakia, Yugoslavia, Italy, and Greece.

"Later, I joined an International Work Camp and was assigned to the island of Sardinia. They were reclaiming the land by building irrigation ditches. Pick and shovel work, mostly. They took my pick away and told me to pick tomatoes. I'm afraid I wasn't much good with a pick and shovel.

"I'll never forget the time this Sard girl made us dinner. She placed an eel in front of me smothered in oil. I just stared at the plate, thinking, 'I can't do it. I cannot eat that.' I took a bite. It stayed down. Another bite. I got through it. To not have eaten it would have been an insult; eel was considered a delicacy.

"One of the most outstanding experiences I had was when I left Sardinia for Castle, Germany for a three-week peace seminar. I traveled alone. I had to switch trains in Zurich, Switzerland. I went to where I was supposed to go. There was nothing there. No train – nothing. I do not speak a foreign language so I didn't hear the track change. A girl appeared and said, 'You have to go with me. This train is going on another track.' She picked up my suitcases. I followed her. She took me to where I needed to go and then set my suitcases down at my side. I looked away from her for a second."

Yeah...

"When I turned around she had vanished. Today, I believe she was an angel."

You've served through the First United Methodist Missions as well, correct?

"Yes. Africa, Costa Rica, Mexico, Nicaragua, Honduras, Japan, China, Russia, Korea, Hong Kong, Philippines... . What I like about the mission tours is you get into the big cities, but it isn't a big city tour. You go into the smaller places where the people are and you actually see the culture. Through traveling, I've learned a lot about different cultures.

"I'm a firm believer that everyone should be paid a living wage or be supplemented so they can live. I don't know why we can't do that in our country. I don't understand."

You told me that you're a past president of Tri Kappa. Any other clubs or hobbies?

"I was asked if I'd like to become a member of the Red Hats Society. I said, 'No, I don't think so.' I enjoy folk music."

Mary Lou, I've always looked up to you... I mean, I realize we shouldn't put anyone on a pedestal... Well, it's just that you're such a wonderful human being. You make me realize what a sinner I've been. Did you ever, just maybe, stick up a bank or at least cheat on your income taxes? Come on, make me feel better about myself. Lie to me for goodness sakes!

"Jeff, I'm not perfect. I have lied, been unkind, and hurt people.

I am a sinner, too. Whatever I am, it's because God made me that way. It's nothing that I did on my own. God is good to all of us and he's gracious to all of us. He loves us all and forgives us. He loves you, Jeff, just as dearly as he loves me or anyone else."

Mary Lou?

"Yes, Jeff?"

Gospel truth?

"Gospel. Jesus said, 'I come that all may have eternal life... The sinner, the sick, the lonely, the rich, and the downtrodden...'"

* * *

Mary Lou Delong.

Today, I believe she is an angel.

Patty Wisniewski *(May 2007)*

*"Their silent wounds have speech
more eloquent than men;
their tones can deeper reach
than human voice or pen."*
-William Woodman

Patty and Gene Wisniewski live in Union Township; they have a Valpo address. They grew up in Hegewisch where they had a Chicago address. Patty has an adult daughter, Kelly, from a previous marriage. Together, the Wisniewskis have one son, Joe, who is a freshman at Wheeler High School.

* * *

"We bought this house as a kit," Wisniewski began. "They delivered it to the property like Lincoln Logs. We moved here in '95. We have two acres. I didn't like it at first. There was nobody here. I had to get used to it. Somebody told me you have to be here a full four seasons. I was used to living in apartments where if I sneezed, somebody from the other apartment said, 'God bless you,' and I said, 'Thank you.'

"The other day I was talking to my college Spanish professor who grew up in East Chicago. He was reminiscing about how all the mothers on the block would yell to their kids in different languages, but they would all be saying the same thing, 'It's 5 o'clock, time for dinner!' That's what I missed – the melting pot."

"As a teenager, I'd look out the classroom window and see the smokestacks of Republic Steel. The mill recruiters walked across Avenue O into Washington High School. It was 1977; I applied as a typing person – but I couldn't type. They asked me if I wanted to take a job in the labor gang for $6.50 an hour. That was big money for an 18-year-old kid.

"I said, 'Sure, why not.' Then I had to go home and tell my dad who was a bricklayer at U.S. Steel (Southworks) that I was about to become a steelworker.

"They shut my department down in 1986. I had almost 10 years seniority; they gave me $3,000 and said, 'Adios.' Gene worked as a lidman at Acme Steel's coke plant. He's been at U.S. Steel's Gary works since '93."

Everybody should work one summer on a coke battery as a lidman. There would be less complaints about the office water cooler being on the blink. Life after the mill?

"For the next 10 years, I worked finding jobs for laid off steelworkers – the Dislocated Workers Program near the union hall on the East Side. It was federally funded."

What then?

"After my father passed away, and Gene and I had moved to Porter County, I started looking online for ways to get money to go back to school. My dad was a Purple Heart veteran from World War II. The state of Indiana was the only state that would pay for you to go back to school if you were the child of a Purple Heart vet – no matter what your age. Other states do it, but only for younger people.

"My dad was a gunner in the cavalry, and fought against the Japanese on Los Negros Island. Dad had a long scar from a bullet that traveled all the way up his arm. His right hand was deformed from it – permanently in the shape of a claw. Here's his Purple Heart.

"When he returned to the mill, they told him he would never lay brick again. He said, 'Give me a chance and I'll show you I can still lay brick...' They gave him a chance. My father laid brick for another 42 years. I'm in my senior year at IUN now, majoring in communications. It's like a gift from Dad."

(Patty opens up a shoe box of nostalgic keepsakes)

"I have some of Dad's original pay stubs from Carnegie Steel (Southworks)... Look, this one says he grossed $51.14 on Nov 30, 1939. He netted $50.63."

Well, Patty, the good news was they only took half a buck out taxes.

"He collected all these from the 30s and 40s..."

Campaign buttons... 'If I were 21, I'd vote for Willkie!' Wow, Wendell Willkie from Elwood, Indiana – ran for president of the United States... SWOC CIO, June 1937... You know what happened in your neighborhood a few days before the date printed on this button...

"The Memorial Day Massacre – when ten steelworkers were killed outside of Republic Steel. There's a plaque in front of the union hall with their names on it."

Patty, three of those names, Handley, Popovich, and Reed were from what would be Local 1010 (Inland Steel). Those Hoosiers were simply showing their support. They stood toward the front of the line, holding nothing but picnic baskets and picket signs. The Chicago Police shot them in the back, then finished them off with billy clubs. What do you plan to do with that sheepskin?

"I hope to tell more positive stories. I think the world has too many negatives stories about bad things that are done by a small fraction of the people. The other 95 percent of the population is probably doing good things, but we don't hear about them that much. Therefore, the perception of our world is that it's nasty. I've done some short documentary work.

"In January, I started filming and interviewing different people of Northwest Indiana. Race is the main subject – dialogues about diversity. I've learned things from this project at a deeper level, just by sitting down and really talking. On the other hand, I think some of our problems are more about socioeconomic situations than race today.

"I moved out of a white neighborhood because of white drug dealers. My friend moved out of a black neighborhood because of black drug dealers. It's not always a case of white flight anymore. It's a flight away from crime and drugs. I still want to remain positive with my documentary. I want to look at the people who are doing positive things."

(Patty and I take a stroll in her Porter County backyard. She reflects.)

"Gene and I had both been living in separate trailer parks on Chicago's East Side on the edge of Wolf Lake. The area was starting to get economically depressed because the mills had gone down. Gun shots were being fired into people's trailers – I mean bullets lodging in their trailers. I had a teenage daughter at the time..."

* * *

I notice an overturned trampoline frame. The swimming pool is bone dry. I mention it. Patty says the trampoline was sliced up and the pool was punctured – there was a rash of vandalism and robberies.

From Chicago to Union Township, she continues to remain positive.

Anne Herbert *(Nov 2009)*

"Activism is my rent for living on this planet."
– Alice Walker

After living in Washington D.C. for 30 years, Anne Herbert took a severance package at MCI Telecommunications. She moved back home to the Pullman area of Hammond in 2003 to take care of family. She lives with her mother, Bessie Manley. Herbert, who graduated from Hammond High School in 1968, said she didn't like what she saw in her old neighborhood. She's doing something about that.

* * *

Is this the house in which you grew up?

"No, we moved here when I was about 14. The other house was about seven blocks away."

You were born about a decade too soon to compete in sports sanctioned by the Indiana High School Athletic Association.

"I didn't compete for Hammond High, but they had what was called the Hammond Jaycees. They had all kinds of different sports for the children of the community. I was a good sprinter and long jumper."

You've become quite an activist.

"I basically was trying to reacquaint myself with the community because I'd been gone so long. I did that by attending things like city council meetings and school board meetings."

What really got the ball rolling as far as volunteering?

"It started with (Hurricane) Katrina in 2005. I decided I needed to do something. So, I joined the American Red Cross as a volunteer. I was sent to Biloxi, Miss. It was a tremendous experience for me to be able to give so little, it seemed, to so many people who really appreciated it.

"That experience got me thinking about the people in my community who really needed some type of support."

What did you do first?

"I became very active in my church's kitchen ministry."

What church is that?

"New Hope Missionary Baptist Church at 1117 Merrill Street. My minister, Rev. Herman Polk, started a group called the East Hammond Pullman Crime Watch."

Are you a part of that?

"I'm president; we've been in existence for a little over two years. The crime watch is currently working with the Hammond Ministerial Alliance."

Tell me more about the group and what you do.

"We've had signs made up for anybody who wants one. One side of the sign reads, 'Crime Watch Member: We Call the Police.' If residents witness crimes being committed, they don't have to search for the number because the police station number is printed on the portion of the sign facing them."

Is yours the only group of its kind in Hammond?

"No, there are now 11 different crime watch groups in Hammond. More have formed since we formed."

Strength in numbers.

"Yes; we are very much supported by the mayor and the police chief. There's always a police officer at our crime watch meetings. We love the officer, Sgt. Moore, assigned to us. He provides our monthly crime statistics. Occasionally, we have a crime map printed up."

Crime map?

"Crime maps show the nature of every crime and the address where the crime was committed. That helps people visualize where the crimes are happening.

"Our group is pretty much attended by the same individuals every month. We have a lot of older females. I'd hate for anybody to approach them with a crime; they are vigilant."

You've been a board member of PACT Bradley House in Michigan City for the past two years. What's that?

"Transitional housing for people going from prison to society."

A halfway house.

"Correct."

Anything else?

"For the last six months, I've been working with the Hammond Parks Foundation. They take on projects in the city of Hammond that are not included in the city budget. We do things like chop down weeds and put down mulch. A couple weeks ago we were at Oxbow Park."

Are you paid for any of the good deeds you do?

"No, the organizations I'm affiliated with all boil down to just being helpful to someone or something. I've come up with my own motto: 'Instead of reaching for a handout – lend a hand.'

* * *

On Sunday, Oct. 11, the East Hammond Pullman Crime Watch held a rally at Martin Luther King Park (formerly Maywood Park) because there had been a rash of crimes within the community. Herbert told me their goal was to get more of the community involved to help stop the violence.

About a week after the rally, Hammond residents Milton and Ruby McClendon were gunned down, possibly in their home, which is located a few blocks from where the rally against crime occurred.

On Oct 22, Herbert was presented the Outstanding Adult Volunteer of the Year Award by Hammond Mayor Thomas McDermott, Jr.

As a young girl, she ran a good race thanks to the Hammond Jaycees. Today, Anne Herbert fights the good fight for her Hammond community.

She just needs a little more help from her friends.

Valorie Cady Dunn *(Sept. 2012)*

*"Ooh that smell
Can't you smell that smell
Ooh that smell
The smell of death surrounds you"
– the band Lynyrd Skynyrd*

I knew her as Valorie Cady. She was a year ahead of me in school. Before we attended school, Val and I caught tadpoles together and made hamburger patties out of mud. We preferred mustard with our french fries.

Today, Valorie Dunn lives a Jay Cutler spiral from where the Chicago Bears once conducted their training camp, near St. Joseph's College in Rensselaer.

Dunn, 56, is a widow who raised two adult children from her first marriage.

During our interview, she curled up on the couch with Buddy, her lab-mix. Barefooted and casually dressed in a pair of sweats and a Meatloaf T-shirt, she nursed a cold can of beer or two while we talked. It marked the first time we'd seen each other in more than 30 years.

* * *

"I loved the column you wrote about Ron (Robinson); that had to be a tough one for you," Dunn began.

Yeah, I miss Ronnie. The mill can be a dangerous place; I was working right next to him and Norm Brown when the fatalities occurred.

"I knew Norm, too. Both were from Lake Village."

Val, let's switch gears. I always felt bad for girls your age as far as high school sports. I mean, you just missed it. You were an in-

credible athlete. I remember when you were in sixth grade high jumping 5-feet 4-inches and you were only 5-feet 2-inches tall!

"I didn't even know how to do it right; I kind of scissored over the bar. No one taught me the Fosbury Flop. I did play in a softball league from ages 17 to 30."

You're part American Indian.

"Yes, my maternal grandmother was half Sioux. Grandma Brown was the apple of my eye. She passed away the day before I turned 19."

I remember your grandfather, Walter Brown. He ran the grocery store in Lake Village. Val, your brother Skip and I used to take returned pop bottles that he kept behind the store and turn them in so we could have some penny candy. He knew what we were doing and never said a word.

"Grandpa Brown was good-hearted."

I'll tell you how good-hearted he was. When my mother was in school, her class was slated to take a field trip to Washington D.C. Ma was the only kid that couldn't go – the fee was $40 per student. Walter Brown got wind of the situation and wrote out a faux grocery tab, knowing my grandparents were good for it. Ma got to go to D.C.

"I didn't know that."

Val, our mothers were always close. You know how my mother was into astrology and that kind of stuff. She once told me that you had extra sensory perception. Why did she say that?

"I knew when someone was going to die. It started just before my Uncle Ronnie died; I was in eighth grade. It just hit me. I told my mom.... .It was a smell. Honest to God; I could smell death. When Uncle Ronnie died, the smell went away.

"The same thing happened when Brenda McGraw died. I smelled that smell for a week or so before she was killed in that car wreck. I got the smell numerous times after Brenda died. The last time was when my grandma died. I'm glad it doesn't happen anymore; it kind of creeped me out."

That is eerie. How long have you lived in Rensselaer?

"About 20 years."

When did your husband pass?

"This February; Paul was 15 years older than me. Buddy is on Prozac because of Paul not being around."

Man's best friend. What did Paul do for a living?

"He was a pressman at the Rensselaer Republican for almost 37 years. That's where I met him; I was the mail room supervisor.

"When a new company purchased the newspaper, management called Paul into the office and told him they had evaluated his position and that he was making way too much money and they would have to cut his salary in half."

Paul's reaction?

"He told them: 'Save your money; I'm gone.'"

While in your late 30s, you became a college student.

"Yes, I started in August of '92. It was a rude awakening; in high school, I didn't study, but always made good grades. Within the first week, I'd shout, 'I'm quitting!' Paul would look at me and say: 'No, you're not.' He kept me going. I ended up graduating from St. Elizabeth with honors and graduated cum laude from St. Joe in '96 with a GPA of 3.48. Right now, I working on my masters in nursing education; I have about a year to go."

Good for you, Val.

"I've also been invited to be inducted to the Sigma Theta Tau Honor Nursing Society in Minneapolis."

Impressive. Who do you work for?

"Franciscan St. Elizabeth (Health) in Lafayette; I'm the home infusion pharmacy's therapy coordinator. It's my job to make sure the home health hospice nurses are using proper techniques.

"I'm board certified in infusion therapy; it was a very hard test to pass. There are only about 3,400 of us worldwide who are certified."

Hey, Val, any other childhood memories?

"A few weeks after the Blizzard of '67, it was around Valentine's Day, I remember playing baseball in a pair of shorts at Lake Village Elementary with some of the boys like Bob Love, John Bruner, Randy Belt, John Turbyfill and Skip.

"Well, somebody working for the Chicago Sun-Times saw us, turned around, and took pictures of us. Our photo appeared in the Sun-Times because of that."

* * *

In May, a Purdue engineering student was involved in a horrible crash on Interstate 65 near West Lafayette. The young man has no recollection of the crash that left him trapped below his vehicle except that of someone talking to him while holding his hand. That good Samaritan was a nurse named Valorie Dunn who just happened to be in the right place at the right time. I guess she smelled life that time.

The student, David Rankine, initially was told he'd never walk again, but has since made a miraculous recovery. On Sept. 4, Rankine and Dunn reunited. The Purdue Boilermaker just wanted to thank the kind soul who watched over him in his time of need.

A plaque hangs on Valorie Cady Dunn's wall. It reads: "Let it be known that in the recognition of her contributions to family, career and community, Valorie Dunn, RN, BSN, CRNI is hereby registered as a woman of outstanding leadership by declaration of the executive committee of the International Women's Leadership Association."

Not bad for a kid from humble beginnings who had to quit school at age 16 because she was with child.

Yes, the diminutive tomboy who waded in the creek near the railroad tracks while collecting pollywogs has adult grandchildren now. But let it be known, in her day, Val Cady always hit the cutoff man and her jumpers were nothin' but net.

It's been a long, strange trip for both of us.

Educators

Robert Petyko *(Feb. 2008)*

"...Here's to the kids who are different,
The kids they call crazy or dumb,
The kids who don't fit, with the guts and the grit,
Who dance to a different drum..."
-Digby Wolfe

Robert Petyko is a teacher. He's a nice guy who lives in a nice house located in a nice subdivision in Cedar Lake with his wife of 37 years, Karen, also a nice person.

Robert, 58, grew up in Cedar Lake; things weren't always so nice.

* * *

"I was raised on the east side of the lake – Cedar Point Park," Petyko began. "We lived in seven different houses. I'm a Lake Rat – that's the name they gave us kids who went to MacArthur Elementary. It's part of the Crown Point school system. MacArthur kids don't go to Hanover Central High School."

Tell me about your childhood.

"I remember my third-grade teacher at MacArthur giving me a bag of clothes because I had only one pair of pants to wear to school everyday. I wore an old pair of dad's shoes – size 11s. That was embarrassing. But, at MacArthur, there were a lot of kids like me. It was when I went to Taft Middle School that I became more self-conscious."

And your family life?

"I had five brothers. We'd prop a garbage can inside the front door so we'd know when the old man came home drunk. My dad was the kind of guy who would hit you while you were asleep.

"I remember my parents complaining about why we were poor; I was like 12 years old at the time. They said it was because I was a cripple and my brother had Down syndrome, and they were burdened with medical bills. We never went to the doctor for anything. I told them, 'If we lived in the poorest part of Africa, we would be the poorest of the poor because of your mind-set.'

"Everything was someone else's fault. My oldest brother went to the Navy and then he went to college. He doesn't know it, but he was a big influence. He got out. I found that it was possible to change."

Did you attend college right after high school to become a teacher?

"No, I worked minium-wage jobs. Then, I worked a couple of different sales jobs. In 1978, I got a job at a small plant located near Michigan Avenue and Dickey Road in East Chicago called Standard Forge. We made railroad axles."

Robert, I was working about 200 meters northeast of you back then – at Inland's #3 coke plant. My old beater was parked under the Cline Avenue extension the day part of it collapsed and all those construction workers were killed.

"I was working day-turns that day, too. We saw what looked like a cloud of cement dust coming into the backside of the plant.

"Working at Standard Forge was the best education I ever had. I was ignorant of a lot of things. My parents never owned a vehicle.

"I had limited experiences. Back then, Cedar Lake was all white. I never considered myself a racist, but I did have these prejudices. I went to Forge, and all that melted away.

"What it's all about is money. I was out there with working poor people, just like I was. Actually, it was decent money – a couple bucks an hour less than you guys made at Inland. I still hold those guys as dear friends."

How long did you stay at Standard Forge?

"I came back from vacation and there weren't any cars in the lot. I had to go home and tell my wife that I didn't have a job. That was back in '87 or '88.

"The union held onto us for a long time. We picketed that place 24/7 everyday for more than a year. The United Steelworkers helped maintain a picket out there. They'd help us to pay our electric bills at home. We were locked out.

"Finally the union said, 'This is it fellas. Your jobs are never coming back.' Here I am, 40 years old, I got this limp... ."

"I became a 41-year-old freshman at (Indiana University Northwest.) I got a degree. Working at Forge was the only job that has come close to being as fulfilling as that of a teacher. I can hardly talk about my teaching job – I'm the luckiest guy in the world," says Petyko as traces of tears well up in his eyes.

Why are you so emotional about your profession?

"People always ask, 'What do you do?' I always had to explain, 'Well, I'm in the mill, and I run this machine sometimes, but I'm not a machinist... .' I just wanted to be able to tell somebody, 'I'm a teacher.'

"There are at least three or four times every day that I laugh out loud. How many jobs can you say that about? I teach fourth-graders at MacArthur Elementary."

Is that some kind of fancy water you're drinking in that green bottle?

"Yes; my kids tease me at school, and say, 'That's beer.' I'll say, 'Yep, that's the only way I can teach this class.' I play right along with them. Kids like that. They know you're real. I've found that the worst thing you can do is show favoritism or disgust. You can't set up unrealistic competitions. I used to coach softball. I believe in that kind of competition."

How does baseball translate into the classroom?

"Kids think they know who the smart kids are and who the dumb kids are. And those are terrible politically incorrect words. But that's what kids do. They place themselves.

"I want every kid to hit a triple. Anybody can get lucky and hit a home run. There's no luck in a triple. You gotta leg it out. You have to do everything just right. And anytime that happens, I tell the class, 'Look what Bobbie Sue did!' And they know Bobbie Sue struggles. And, Jeff, they will applaud that kid. Isn't that wonderful?"

Indeed, it is.

"That's what a class is about. Teaching them how to learn and about life's experiences. I have a couple of kids who might be considered upper middle class, and then I have all these kids who are poverty. That's why I don't give out homework. Besides, moms don't like getting Cs. My kids work for me. From the time they sit down until the end of the day. They owe that to me."

Tell me about your colleagues.

"The people at MacArthur have genuine love for the kids. MacArthur is a special place. Our custodian has a thing called Carnahan's Helpers; the kids love and respect him.

"Jeff, I'm a product of MacArthur. Some of my methods are a little bit different."

* * *

The mother of one of Petyko's former students told me about him delivering a Christmas present to a student living at St. Jude's shelter. She also told me of how he made sure that a student was not ostracized during a Christmastime party, all the while respecting the beliefs of that student's family, who were Jehovah's Witness faith.

The Petykos have raised two children. Like his father, the son became a fourth-grade teacher. The daughter works at MacArthur with her father; she's thinking of becoming a teacher.

David Lane *(May 2012)*

"That's me in the corner
That's me in the spotlight
Losing my religion
Trying to keep up with you
And I don't know if I can do it..."
– From "Losing My Religion" by R.E.M.

I imagine it's tough trying to follow in the footsteps of a well-known father.

The actor sons of John Wayne and Robert Mitchum come to mind – Will Rogers Jr., too.

And don't even get me started with Frank Sinatra's daughter, Nancy.

David Lane teaches English at East Chicago Central High School and coaches boys and girls tennis. He also is the son of Indiana University Northwest professor emeritus of history James B. Lane who still churns out his periodical, "Steel Shavings."

After talking to David, I think Northwest Indiana might be blessed with a genuine chip off the old block.

Lane, 42, lives in Portage with his wife, Angie. They've been married 14 years and have two children, James, 11, and Rebecca, 9.

* * *

"We grew up on the Porter County side of County Line Road, but we considered ourselves 'Millerites,' Lane began. We were four blocks away from Wells Street Beach."

Did you attend Portage High School?

"Yes."

Play sports for PHS?

"Tennis and golf. I didn't go out for the golf team my senior year, which really upset my coach. But, I wanted to get into the fall play and the spring musical. I also was in a band all through high school."

Dave, you can't do it all; sometimes something has to go.
"Exactly."
College?
"I went to Indiana University in Bloomington. I earned a double major in four years in history and English. I had a lot of fun my freshman year, so it was tough. I decided to get serious the last three. I worked full time for a landscaping company after my sophomore year. It was hard, hot work."

I'm sure it was.
"My parents had set aside some money for me. I kind of blew it all my freshman and sophomore years, assuming they'd give me more. They explained that was it. I learned the value of money and a very good life lesson."

Life after IU?
"I to West Lafayette of all places (home of IU's major rival, Purdue University)."

What did you do?
"Worked as a substitute teacher at West Lafayette High School by day and played in a band by night. WLHS is an awesome environment to teach – great school."

Your teaching degree?
"I looked into the (urban teacher education program) at IUN. Growing up, I always had an interest in civil rights. I wanted to work in an urban environment.

"I chose to do that not because it was the only job available. UTEP was perfect; I could work in graduate-level classes and get my teaching degree at the same time. It's an accelerated year-and-a-half program."

Let's switch gears. A couple of your favorite bands?
"The Replacements, kind of an '80s alternative band, and 'R.E.M.' That's while I was playing in high school bands. Before that, I was a Beatles guy all the way.

"My dad always was into music; the cool thing about him is he got me into punk rock. I was a Ramones fan and liked The Sex Pistols as a 12-, 13-year-old kid."

Really? I'd have wagered your peacnik pops from the psyche-

delic '60s would've turned you on to Led Zeppelin and Jimi Hendrix.

"Dad definitely evolved with the times."

Back to scholastics – E.C. Central?

"I've fallen in love with the school and its students."

How long have you taught there?

'This is my 18th year. One of the reasons I got the job was because I was willing to take on the newspaper and yearbook, which no one wanted to do because it's a lot of work."

What classes are you teaching this year?

"Right now, I teach nothing but honors kids which includes five sections of dual-credit English, one of which is an Advanced Placement class. I have about 60 kids who are taking my class for college credit, which is really cool.

"But for years, I taught remedial kids. I really miss working with the kids some teachers gave up on. If you can reach a kid who struggles; if you can make a difference, it's special.

"The honors kids are great, but there's something to be said about turning that kid around who wasn't always successful."

Do you miss teaching history?

"My students always tease me because I incorporate a lot of history in my lessons. First of all, I think it goes hand in hand with the literature. I probably put more history into it than your average English teacher because of my background."

Anything else besides teaching and coaching?

"I sponsor the senior class, I'm site-coordinator of the AVID program, public address announcer for all football and basketball games... ."

Do you sweep out the place at night?

"I keep myself busy."

Dave, I interviewed E.C. Central's choir director a year or so ago – nice guy.

"Leon Kendrick – an amazing man and teacher. Leon is one of my best friends."

Is there anything I didn't ask you that you wish I would have?

"I don't know if you want to go in this direction, but when my wife was pregnant with my son, we had this home invasion."

I vaguely remember; was your dad involved?

"Yes, he was. My mom went to visit my brother, so dad came

over to have dinner with us. It was a snowstorm and three guys broke into the house, tied us up and held us hostage for two hours. It was when Angie and I lived in Miller."

The outcome?

"I told them, 'This $200 is all I have; I'm a school teacher.' I guess they didn't believe me; it angered them. I begged them to not hurt my pregnant wife. It was the only humane thing they did; they didn't mess with her too much."

You and your dad?

"They put my father in the hospital for a week with a punctured lung and gave me a brain concussion with a claw hammer."

Dave, I don't know what to say. Actually I do, but it would never make the newsstands; we're a family newspaper.

"I wasn't sure how I was going to mentally recover. My school and my students really made me feel good about returning to work. There was an assembly in the auditorium; they put me on the stage and gave me a standing ovation. Jeff, excuse me, it's difficult to talk about this."

* * *

Quite a family, the Lanes. Dave told me his mother, Toni, is an artist, photographer and a teacher who is one of the most creative people he's met.

Dave's older brother, Phil, is a producer and a director for a PBS television station in Grand Rapids, Mich. He has won four or five Emmy Awards.

Glowingly, Lane mentioned many students, fellow teachers and administrators. Space does not permit listing them, but I would be remiss not mentioning one young fellow who was senior class president three years ago and the captain of Coach Lane's tennis team. Lane worked closely with Emmanuel Mendoza, close enough to help him get into Harvard where he has a 3.5 grade-point average.

Two years ago, Dave Lane was named Lakeshore Chamber of Commerce Teacher of the Year and, last year, was named E.C. Central's Teacher of the Year.

A chip off the old block.

Dorothy Bishop *(Sept. 2012)*

"Imprimatur." (Let it be printed.)
– Ancient Latin saying

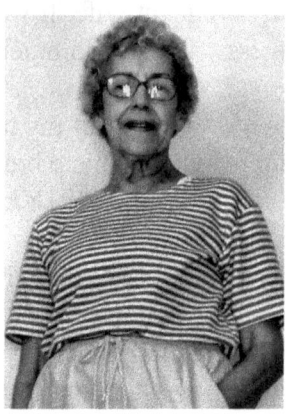

My friend, Tom Spencer, invited me to a Great Decisions meeting three weeks ago at the Central Branch of Lake County Library in Merrillville.

The discussion group included about 15 brilliant free thinkers. I was easily the least intelligent person in the room. Spencer, like Homer, is a blind poet; he needed a ride.

Dorothy Bishop was one of the 15 on hand that night. She recognized me from my photograph in the newspaper and told me she enjoys this column tremendously. I thanked her for the compliment.

Bishop, 76, retired from the Lake County Public Library almost two years ago; she was a reference paraprofessional librarian and was the person who started the Great Decisions group in 2002.

Dorothy lives in Merrillville with her husband, Jerry. They have raised two children and have been married 50 years.

* * *

Dorothy, I really enjoyed the discussion on the global financial crises and its effects the other night; everyone was very interesting, informative and friendly, too. This afternoon, I want you to talk about you. It's not everyday a blue-collar guy like me gets to rub elbows with the literati. You're probably a ballet or opera afficionado, huh?

"I was born and raised in Detroit," she said. "That's why I fell in love with hockey; Detroit is a hockey town."

Hockey, as in professional ice hockey and cross-checking and goons with missing teeth?

"The Blackhawks won the (2010 Stanley) Cup – God love 'em for it – but the Red Wings are my team. I live for hockey season and go berserk during the playoffs. It was an exciting game when (Patrick) Kane got that goal in overtime (to win Game 6 at Philadelphia and clinch the Cup)."

I'm sure you enjoyed Gordie Howe's illustrious career.

"Oh, Gordie! All of us girls in high school loved all the players on the Red Wings team; especially cute little Alex Delvecchio."

Where did you go to high school?

"Dominican, an all-girls Catholic school. Then I went to Marygrove, an all- girls Catholic college."

Graduate school?

"The University of Michigan in Ann Arbor."

Maiden name?

"Vince."

Italian?

"Yes, on my father's side. My mother was Hungarian. It was considered a mixed marriage back then. My father's parents wanted him to marry a nice Italian girl, and my Hungarian grandparents weren't too thrilled their daughter married an Italian.

"My parents were originally from mining country in western Pennsylvania. I've heard the stories about the mines before they got the unions. My parents met in the company store. The mine owned everything.

"When I first got out of college, I was a teacher. Back in those days, a woman could only be a teacher, nurse or librarian. When they started unionizing teachers, I was right there. The teachers were mortified."

Why?

"They were professional white-collar people who didn't want to be associated with unions. But, I'll tell you, when we got our first union contract they went right along with it; they didn't turn down the added benefits."

What did you teach?

"Latin, in Wyandotte, Mich. After a few years, it was decided they didn't need foreign languages; they were more about math and science. It looked like I was going to be teaching Caesar's Gallic Wars for the rest of my life."

And?

"I quit."

Where did you meet your husband?

"In a barn."

Come again?

"When I was teaching in Wyandotte, I got involved in community theater. We were part of the same summer stock company. I love acting; I'm just a ham."

Tell me more about you two lovebirds.

"Jerry is a Buckeye from Newark, Ohio, and since I'm a Michigander, we'd tease each other about which one of us is a hillbilly – the Michigan Farmer or the guy whose family says they hail from 'Nerk, Ahiah.'"

You're killin' me.

"It's ironic; Jerry worked for a small print shop in Chicago and played the clarinet in our brother-in-law's bar in Gary on weekends. My son is a percussionist on weekends in a band called Ripple who works for a small print shop in Munster."

How did you and Jerry end up in Northwest Indiana?

"Actually, we moved to Chicago first. Both of our children were born in Chicago; we were in Chicago for 12 years. We moved into my parents' house in Gary at 8th Avenue and Hayes Street when they retired to Arizona. My dad had transferred from the Budd Plant in Detroit to the brand new plant in Gary.

"Eventually, we bought a townhouse at 35th Avenue and Tyler Street in Glen Park. My daughter graduated from Lew Wallace High School and my son graduated from Calumet High School. I was a housewife while the kids were in school and was very active in PTA and things like that.

"We moved to Merrillville in '86; that's about when I started at the library. I worked at Lake County Library for 22 years."

Great Decisions?

"The Great Decisions discussion group follows the program set up by the Foreign Policy Association, a national, nonprofit, nonpartisan, nongovernmental, educational organization founded in 1918 to educate Americans about the significant international issues that influence their lives. It's an informal discussion facilitated by a library staff member."

The Lake County Library group?

"Our group was started just before we were going into Iraq; Colin Powell had just addressed the United Nations. One of our first topics was Iraq. It was a time when the American people were debating whether or not we should go into Iraq. Little did we know that the decision had been made for us.

"One of our regular members was a Syrian-born doctor. He brought about 10 members of the mosque he belonged to, including the imam, to that meeting."

Did sabers rattle?

"No, it was a very exiting and interesting meeting, filled with great discussion; nobody got hot-headed or anything like that. They just wanted to explain what their beliefs were."

Of course, that meeting was held in 2002, before the advent of the tea party movement. What are some other topics your group addresses?

"Global crime, U.S.-China security relations, international security, global warming, immigration problems. Immigration doesn't just happen in the United States."

Example, please.

"The Netherlands has had their problems with the Muslim community. The Netherlands is very liberal; they allow their people to do almost anything. But now, the Muslim population is creating its own enclaves in The Netherlands and keeping other people out."

And?

"The Dutch are saying, 'No, no, no; that's not how we do things in The Netherlands,' and the Muslims are saying, 'But we must.'"

Other personal interests?

"Besides reading, I enjoy listening to programs on (National Public Radio) and watching old films on (Turner Classic Movies)."

I like classic silent movies.

"Jeff, how about the 1920 version of 'Dr. Jekyll and Mr. Hyde' that John Barrymore did without makeup?"

Barrymore pulled out all the stops for that one.

"He becomes Mr. Hyde. I mean, you can almost see his fingers growing and his jaw dropping down and lengthening, and then his eyes pop open! It's delicious."

* * *

Dorothy Bishop might not be your mother's librarian, but she's probably someone with whom your father would enjoy attending a fight – especially if a hockey game broke out.

Paul & Angie Lowe *(Feb. 2005)*

*"All the world's a stage,
And all the men and woman merely players;
They have their exits and their entrances..."*
– William Shakespeare

For Valentine's week I opt to interview a couple rather than an individual. As I pull into Paul and Angie Lowe's driveway, Paul stands outside of his two-car garage. He has begun the daunting task of straightening it up. No automobiles are parked in it. A tricycle wouldn't fit inside the structure. It's filled from floor to ceiling with a mishmash of past props. The Lowes are theater people.

Paul and Angie have been wed for 40 years; they became engaged when Angie Cremonie was 15. Paul Lowe was sweet 16. They grew up in Terre Haute. After college the newlyweds eventually moved to Cedar Lake where they lived for 36 years. They have recently moved into a beautiful home in St. John.

The three of us sit at the kitchen table. Paul fixes me a cup of coffee; he is a kind soul who has been plagued by ulcers since he was a boy. Angie is quick to attest that he had ulcers before they met.

Angie catches me glancing at some photos sitting atop her piano. One is of a very young and beautiful Katherine Hepburn. The other is a baby picture of Angie. A thick shock of black hair covers her head – Angie's father was of Italian descent. In the picture the baby is making a pouty face. Angie says, "Hey Jeff, look, I can still do it." Ever the actress, the 59 year-old uncannily makes the exact face.

Wearing a pony tail, and possessing mischievous gem-like eyes, Ms. Lowe is quite youthful in appearance even today. An incredibly bright woman, she can rattle off the years and seasons of every show Paul and she have put on in the past 40 years. I ask her the impossible...

* * *

What's your all-time favorite play that you and Paul have produced?

"Always, the one I'm currently working on." She adds, "We like to stay busy. So many shows. So little time."

Were you married when you moved to Cedar Lake?

"Oh yes, we were married when we were in college," answers Paul.

Oh yeah, that's right, you've been married 50 years.

Angie corrects me: "40."

Paul: "Seems like 50."

Angie: "I was 18. Paul tells everyone he was 12. We've been happily married for 26 years. Which isn't bad, out of 40. We double-dated at the prom when I was a sophomore and Paul was a junior – with different people. Paul's date was too shy to dance and mine was too much of a klutz. We both liked to dance. That was the beginning."

It seems you two have a lot in common.

Angie: "We have a lot in common, but were so different. That's what attracts. Being the children of alcoholics, we both had crappy childhoods. That's why we became engaged at such young ages. We needed each other."

Paul: "Our dates comprised of trying to find Angie's mother – which tavern she was in."

Angie: "She was a brilliant woman but never happy."

Paul: "My dad was a mean drunk.".

Angie: "I have four brothers and a sister, but I'm an only child. My siblings were a combination of step-brothers and a sister from her mother and father's various marriages."

Paul: "I'm the youngest of five kids. My brothers raised me, which was great, until they moved out of the house. Then it was a nightmare. My grandmother was full-blooded Cherokee, by the way. And coincidentally, me and Angie's mothers shared the same maiden name and it's not that common of name."

Angie: "We've both worked since we were 12. I started out as a carhop at the Arf and Barf."

Arf and Barf?

Angie: "Dog and Suds."

How did you end up in Lake County?

Paul: "Two of my brothers had previously made their way up here and were teaching at Dyer High School. A job opportunity came up and they loved my brothers at Dyer, so all I really had to do was apply. My name got me the job. I came here as a speech-debate coach.

"I was about 21 or 22 years old back then, Angie stayed down at Terre Haute finishing up her last semester at (Indiana State University). Part of my contract was that I would have to direct a fall play and a spring play. I remember one paid a $50 stipend and the other $70. My salary was $5,800 per year."

Angie: "There were no unions back then at Lake Central. We were involved in three strikes which were all unpleasant, but we had no children. We sacrificed so that our fellow teachers with large families could get better insurance packages."

Paul: "When the next school year rolled around Angie was student-teaching at Calumet High School and the school corporation was trying to bombard me with French Classes. I wasn't interested in all that French and told them so. They asked me if I knew of a French teacher, and I told them, 'Yes, as a matter of fact I do, my wife.' That was 1967. We worked for Lake Central for the next 38 years.

"I had minimal theater training – whatever was required for me to graduate. My emphasis was public speaking, poetry reading, debate – the heavy stuff."

Angie: "Classical Rhetoric."

Paul: "At least Angie had been in plays in high school. Well, our first musical was 'Bye Bye Birdie.'

"Ironically, our boy who played the lead was from Lowell; his father had passed away, bless his heart, and he had come up here to live with his mother or a relative. His first and only year at Lake Central was his senior year. He was a wonderful kid. Both of his daughters have since graduated from Lake Central. His name was John Cox."

"I knew nothing about tech theater, much less acting. I had no concept of building. I learned from the kids. Ang is so darn smart, she just took the roll of an audience member."

Angie: "That's how I direct."

Paul: "She would see what an audience would want, as a universal audience member. She couldn't please everybody, but if she could please herself, that's pretty damn good, because that's pretty hard to do."

Angie: "I've been a movie goer all my life. Because of my mother's affliction, I was left alone. I'd escape reality by attending two or three movies a week. They cost a quarter back then."

Paul: "There are talented kids everywhere. No matter where you go. They're crying out to do things. There is a creative seed in a lot of kids that is never germinated, never touched, because either the school is too big or the people who head the programs might not possess the personalities that the kids can relate with.

"In the early days, theater was bland, it was really hard, especially for a young man. Acting wasn't looked on as a 'manly' thing to do. Finally, I discarded speech and debate and totally focused on theater. I ended getting my masters in theater. Had we not worked together, we wouldn't have stayed together. It takes up all of your time. No way we could do what we do without each other, but we were also blessed with great students, and anyone who doesn't listen to the kids, in my humble estimation, is a fool. They taught us."

* * *

Mama and Papa Lowe, as they have been known for nearly 40 years by their students at Lake Central, never had children of their own because of the scars left from their childhoods, they figure. Yet, they have had children, many children indeed. Children that eventually became artists, scientists, actors, writers, set designers, the head of Neonatal at Riley Memorial Hospital, and the Commander of the USS Alabama; just to name a few. Paul told me there were none more honorable than ones who simply went on to become good parents.

Down through the years the Lowes have helped their kids out financially with college and they've stood up at their weddings – Paul has given brides away. Many of their kids are in their will, and heartbreakingly, as for any parent, they've buried a few, too.

Leon Kendrick *(March 2011)*

"It is easier to build strong children than to repair broken men."
–Frederick Douglass

Leon Kendrick was born in '55 and he is 55. He and his wife Yvetta have lived in Merrillville for 15 years. Four of their five children have left the nest; they range in age from 15 to 37.

Kendrick graduated from Horace Mann High School, attended Columbia (Mo.) College, then did his graduate work at VanderCook College of Music in Chicago. He finished his master's at Valparaiso University and earned an honorary doctorate at GMOR Theological Institute.

Kendrick teaches at East Chicago Central High School.

* * *

Beautiful piano.

"Thanks, I started taking piano lessons kind of late; I was 11," Kendrick said. "But I was playing at church by the time I was 13."

Was there a piano in the house where you grew up?

"No, I begged my grandmother to let me take piano lessons. But I had a brother who had taken piano lessons and hadn't done a very good job, so my grandmother was hesitant. My mother was getting ready to go to Louisiana where my family is originally from, but grandmother didn't want me to go because I spent half of the time at home and half the time at grandmother's."

Leon, I grew up much the same.

"Grandma said, 'Before you go with your mother to Louisiana, look in the back bedroom.'"

And?

"There was a piano. She bought me my first piano."

Wow, what a great gift.

"Besides my grandmother, two other females who have been very important in my life are my mother, Delores Christopher, and my wife. Yvetta is an amazing person. I affectionately call her 'Precious.'"

How long have you been at E.C. Central?

"I started the day it opened, 1986-87. I also spent three years at (East Chicago) Washington."

Your friend, Morrell Roper, told me there is a group of students at E.C. Central called "Kendrick's Kids."

"One of my main goals was to spread love through music. I learned early on the way you really get to these kids, first of all, you have to show them respect. If you show them respect, I don't care where they come from, they're going to give you that respect back.

"We've formed this bond; these kids don't want to go home. Home is my classroom; they've labeled it on their shirts – M 139. It is a number of unity."

That's great to hear.

"They tend to find a sense of family here. They call each other brothers and sisters. They call me dad, uncle and godfather – whatever they feel in their hearts that I am to them. I allow them to do that."

Teachers can learn from students.

"You can't fool them. They know if you're really serious or not. Once they know that you really care, there is nothin' they won't do for you."

Most men and women I worked with in the mill who went to either East Chicago Roosevelt or Washington were proud to be from the city. There was a bond between them. It's hard to explain. Kind of like Marines.

"Jeff, their culture, race and religion doesn't matter; they just come together. I had somebody ask me, 'How can you teach in East Chicago?' My answer was, 'How can I *not* teach in East Chicago?'

"When we go on the road for performances and stop at restaurants, I have people tell me they've never seen a more well-mannered, respectful group of kids. At a Cracker Barrel, I had a lady ask me where we were from, I said with pride, 'We're from East Chicago, Ind.'"

What's your job title?

"Well, my title is choral teacher, but I do all of it: choreography, drama, stage design – I wear many hats."

You are also producing Roper's "The Voices of the Silent Lambs."

"'Kendrick's Kids' are very inspired to be a part of Morrell's play. It relates so much to them. You're talking about kids in the wilderness who feel abandoned. ...They confide in me all the time."

Example?

"I had a kid just last week come up to me and say, 'Mr. Kendrick, I'm not sure where I'm going when I leave here today.' I said, 'Why aren't you going home?' He said: 'Because our lights have been turned off and my mom is gone to Chicago. I don't want to leave Central because I love this class.' I asked him if he called his mom. He said: 'Yes, but she said she didn't have anyone to pick me up. I asked her what I was supposed to do and she told me she didn't know what I was gonna do.'"

Sad.

"Jeff, I listen to stories like that all the time. ... I had a girl tell me, 'Mr. Kendrick, I'm gonna drop out of school.' I told her, 'This is your senior year; you can't do that. You're on your way to graduation.' And she said, 'My mom's on drugs; our lights are cut off. My sister doesn't want to go to school and I have to take care of her. My mom is not doing her job as a parent... .'

"Jeff, she's raising her little sister, they're abandoned to the wilderness. The lambs are out there fending for themselves. The shepherds are not taking their responsibility. I can't understand it. Yet they become some of the most respectful kids in spite of what they're dealing with on a daily basis."

Babies having babies.

"Morrell and I kind of talked about that. She came from a large family and her parents were always there. Jeff, my upbringing was not like hers. So, I can relate to the kids who have one parent growing up. Everything I missed, I made sure I put it in my family."

Leon, I believe you.

"I remember a kid telling me, 'I feel like I'm going to give up; I can't take it anymore.' ... We went for a walk outside; it was in the late fall. I told him, 'Look at the tree; tell me what's on the tree.' He said, 'Nothing's on that tree; it's just a bad tree.' I said: 'That's correct; you are that tree. You look like you're good for nothin', it's bare and that's what people have told you about your life. Come back with me and we're going to find a tree in our classroom.'

"I asked him what was on the artificial tree. He said, 'That tree has beautiful leaves; it's colorful.' I told him, 'It only looks like a beautiful tree – it's fake; it's dead. Don't allow your eyes to deceive you. In the springtime, the real tree we looked at is going to come back, full of leaves and life, giving nutrition and shade.' He told me he didn't think he could wait until the spring,"

Did the young man make it?

"Yes, and later, he wrote me, saying, 'Mr. Kendrick, thank you for that message.'"

* * *

Some of the wilderness lambs' parents have gone astray, but they have a voice thanks to a good shepherd in room M 139.

They're Kendrick's Kids.

Mary Cusic *(March 2009)*

Caesar: "Who is it in the press that calls on me?..."
Soothsayer: "Beware the Ides of March."
-William Shakespeare

When I called on Mary Cusic, I realized she had taught Shakespeare's "Romeo and Juliet" to freshmen at Lowell High School for more than 30 years. I didn't realize Cusic, 57, was born March 15, the day "the old boys club" stuck it to Caesar 23 times.

She has been married to Ray Cusic, Tri-Creek School Corp. assistant superintendent, for 28 years. Their children – Meredith, Rodney and Robert – are all graduates of Lowell High School.

* * *

"My maiden name is Hodakowski," Cusic began. "My parents were born in Poland. Dad is no longer with us; Mom is 88 and sharp as a tack. They settled in Gary."

Did your father work at one of the mills?

"Yes, U.S. Steel for 18 years. Dad was a dentist in Poland, but wasn't able to practice here. Because of that, we had major issues with sensitive egos while growing up. Life was a little rough; he did our dental work at home.

"We were raised conservatively; church and family were the foundation."

What language was spoken within the Hodakowski household?

"When dad was home, whatever you said at the table had to be in Polish – you got backhanded if it wasn't. He was tyrannical about keeping the culture intact although he wasn't about to live in Poland under communist rule.

"Nuns translated for my older sister, so Annie was bilingual pretty much from birth. I learned English from her."

Did you attend school in Gary?

"No, by the time I was old enough to attend school, my parents moved near Hobart."

Did you become a Brickie or an Andrean 59er?

An Ingot; we lived in New Chicago. I graduated from River Forest High School in 1970."

Then what?

"I attended Ball State University, then did a study abroad program in England for two summers through New York University. During the fall of '74, I began student teaching at Lowell High School, was offered a full-time position and have never left.

"I'm an extreme loyalist. I feel that I found my niche at Lowell High School, and I love the community. Lowell is a great place to raise kids – small enough, yet large enough. What I really like is when I go to the bank or grocery store in town, I know the people."

Mary, you consider yourself an extreme loyalist. After sampling your tortellini salad at the high school a few years back, I consider you a creator of extreme cuisine. I mean, your decadent desserts were so delicious they were excommunicated from the adult bible study classes at St. Edward's.

I have a two-fold question: Have you ever thought of writing a cookbook, and, are you going to eat all that homemade coffeecake wafting there before us?

"No, I've never thought of writing a cook book, but I love to work with yeast. I don't mean a small package from the store; I buy it by the pound. I make an Italian Easter bread that is as light as a feather; it takes 18 hours.

"I developed my love of the culinary art from mother, who every Saturday would bake a coffeecake and every weekend would share it with the nuns in the neighborhood."

Probably the same recipe you used to make that homemade coffeecake wafting there before us.

"I get my frugal nature from my mother, who will deny that I am frugal. For example, this coffee will never turn bitter. Usually, if a pot of coffee stays around for an hour or two, it's like tar. But, because I boil water in a ceramic pot with an enamel lining, mix the grounds and a raw egg with shell, add pinches of salt and sugar, throw the grounds over boiling water, simmer for 20 minutes, which allows the grounds to fall to the bottom, I have crystal-clear coffee for two days.

"Are you with me?"

Sorry, my mind must have wafted on the homemade coffeecake before us...

"Cooking is therapeutic for me."

Gluttony works for me; but let's talk shop.

"I've taught everything from basic English 9 all the way through (advanced placement) literature. I have found that my deep passion is with kids who struggle. It is the essence of education; it is the fountain of youth.

"Every student deserves my best, but there is something about the kids who struggle. When you get them on board it is an educational baptism for them; they will forever push forward.

"I see it everyday. I connect with kids constantly: 'How are you doing? How are your grades?'

"'Oh, Mrs. Cusic, I got another credit at alternative school; I'll be back in the high school next year.'"

Alternative school?

"Alt school is for kids who get in trouble and need credit recovery. We've been able to save many a student by offering them opportunities at alt school. It's a different schedule; they're gaining their credits while out of the regular school environment. They usually come back and graduate with a full diploma; it's a beautiful system."

You are part of a teacher leadership team that works with administration. "Yes; the key is, schools that are successful are focusing on the 'three R's.' It's part of a school-improvement model being touted across the nation."

Readin' 'ritin' and 'rithmatic?

"Rigor, relevance and relationship. Rigor deals with curriculum, making sure you stretch them as far as you can. Relevance is making the subject applicable to life today by using lots of hands-on projects, speakers for the classroom and taking field trips.

"The most important of those three R's is relationship – when a student knows that you will go to bat for him, care about his success and do anything to help him out.

"I also teach the Freshman Academy group, which consists of 50 at-risk kids. Those kids move from F's and D's in middle school to C's, B's and As in high school. The secret of our success?"

You let them eat coffeecake?

"We have a no-nonsense approach; the student will work in class and will do his homework."

Let's waft back to Bill Shakespeare; for 33 of your 34 years at LHS, you've taught "R & J" – you'd think those Montagues and Capulets could iron things out after all this time. Fie!

"There has been a lot of controversy about whether we should teach 'Romeo and Juliet' in the classroom to freshmen, that maybe it's not the right play, because it's a love story."

Somebody might have a point there. All that sex is probably more suitable for a classroom of students in Europe. But on the other hand, there's plenty of violence to entertain American kids. What lessons can be learned from "R & J?"

"There are several. 'Romeo and Juliet' is about choices and relationships. Students tend to remember parts of it. Students can learn about the power of language. The language Shakespeare used is still used today; Hallmark cards often use Shakespeare. His themes are very much alive, unfortunately that includes violence."

* * *

Mary Cusic told me every student can be successful all the time with proper support.

How could I disagree?

Since the early '80s, I've had dozens of kids tell me Mary Cusic was one of the most supportive teachers they ever had.

Barb Arko-Hargrove *(Jan. 2010)*

"All labor that uplifts humanity has dignity and importance and should be undertaken with painstaking excellence."
– The Rev. Martin Luther King Jr.

Barb Arko-Hargrove is a liberal Catholic and a Purdue University graduate who has taught art at Jefferson Elementary School in Gary for nearly 40 years.

Arko-Hargrove, 60, has been married to Wayne Hargrove for 13 years. They live on Coolidge in Hammond near the state line.

She is the sister-in-law of United Steelworkers Local 1010 President Tom Hargrove.

* * *

"My family came to the United States from Slovenia," Arko-Hargrove began. "They were blue-collar – railroad people, mostly. A lot of them settled in Cleveland, but my grandma and her sister settled in Elkhart."

What high school did you attend?

"Elkhart High, Class of '67. It was the only high school in the city back then. The Blue Blazers rock!

"It wasn't until I moved to this diverse area that I really got involved with my family history. After I taught a couple years, I went to Slovenia and met some of my relatives."

Where did you begin your teaching career?

"The old Jefferson School which was the first school in the city of Gary. They actually poured the concrete on the sand dunes when they built the school.

"Then, the new Jeff opened up and I started teaching there. I've also taught middle school and high school for the (severely emotionally handicapped) at Lincoln School. Today, I teach kindergarten through sixth grade and E.H, too.

E.H.?

"Emotionally handicapped – students, who, for whatever reason, have some serious issues. They could be the brightest bulb in the box, but they have emotional issues and are not able to control themselves at times. We do the same thing that we do in my other art classes; we just do things a little more carefully."

Can you elaborate?

"Things can easily upset them. I try to separate them so everybody has their own space. If somebody starts getting out of hand the aide helps me calm them down."

Do they get out of hand?

"Sometimes they banter back and forth. With an E.H. child, there is no, 'I have to stop now.' They just keep going.

"I do a lot of multicultural things. We do Christmas around the world. We talk about Kwanzaa and giving a homemade gift from the heart, like writing a poem or singing a song rather than purchasing presents from a store."

Have you always lived in Hammond since moving to Northwest Indiana?

"No, I lived in Miller from '71 to '89. The wonderful thing about Gary is that Gary still has art, music and physical education teachers who are actually licensed in those areas. Many of the schools in Lake County don't have that.

"The first year I came to Gary, I received a certified letter saying I was being relieved from my job. In '71 and '72, the Gary schools were getting rid of all art, music, phys-ed teachers, nurses and librarians. They said we were unneeded people."

The three R's only.

"We had to go on strike for 4 1/2 weeks, but we kept the arts. I'm on the executive board of the American Federation of Teachers, Local 4. We were the fourth teachers union to incorporate in the United States; that's why we have such a low number.

"I was a precinct committeeman when I lived in Miller. Politics and the union are so important to each other."

Tell me a little about your home life.

"Wayne and I have talked about who would be somebody we couldn't marry. Somebody of a different faith? Somebody of a different race? For me, there is no way in the world I could marry a Republican."

You're a member of Our Lady of Perpetual Help Catholic Church in the Hessville neighborhood of Hammond.

"Yes; after Mass, I had another member of OLPH. ask me how I could be for (President Barack) Obama and be Catholic. I asked him, 'How can you *not* be for Obama and be Catholic?'

"My thing is, from inception until death, you take care of a person. It's not just about making sure a mother has a child; it's all about the mother having different options to take care of the child. To me, the Republicans are all about making sure the mother has the baby. Then, once the baby is born, it's, 'Hey, you're on your own.'

"When Obama was campaigning, I had a field day in the classroom. I don't know if the kids really got it. But those of us who lived through the civil rights movement could really appreciate it."

Wayne?

"I met Wayne at a bar on St. Patrick's Day, and that was it. He had the nicest smile. Yeah, he was one of those – so nice."

Wayne's a fireman.

"He's a battalion chief. For 24 hours at a time, he's responsible for half of the city of Hammond."

Besides Wayne, you also love to travel.

"Oh, yeah. After two years of teaching, I spent an entire summer with a friend in Europe – backpacks and hostels. We started off in Ljubljana, Yugoslavia. All of a sudden, we heard all this commotion. We walk out of the travel agency and there's Marshal Tito about 10 feet from me. What are the odds of that?

"On that particular trip, we toured Italy, Germany, Spain, Monte Carlo and Greece – Greece was the best."

Talk about the bond you have with your students.

"I buy a lot of things for my students, because the school system doesn't supply me with all I need to teach. So, I purchase CD's and videos through this cultural arts company called Crizmac. The young lady who runs the company offers trips that are basically for art teachers. I traveled to Sante Fe (N.M.) where I learned about native art. We also went to Alaska for two weeks."

What are your thoughts about possibly burning out on the job?

"As a teacher, I need to be renewed. During the summers, I try to do things where I learn something new. It's important for me to not get stagnant. It could become easy to do the same lesson plans over and over again.

"To be a good teacher, you have to be passionate about what you do. If not, you need to get out."

Rewards of being a teacher?

"Some of my students come back years later and repeat words of encouragement that I had said to them along the way. It just shows that you never know when something you say or do might help someone. Very powerful.

"Another nice thing about Gary is we have the (Wirt-Emerson Visual and Performing Arts Academy. I encourage talented students to go to Emerson."

West Side Theatre Guild's Mark Spencer is an Emerson grad.

"Absolutely, and what a wonderful guy. Mark continues to give back."

* * *

Barb Arko-Hargrove continues to give back, too. She was part of the Peace and Justice group from OLPH that basically built the Jean Shepherd Community Center in Hammond.

She also received the Viola Briley Service Award from Gary Teacher's Union, Local 4 AFT, for invaluable contributions to unionism and to the education of children in Gary in 2005.

With dignity, she has uplifted humanity.

Verna Schrombeck *(May 2008)*

*"All I am, or can be,
I owe to my angel mother."
-Abraham Lincoln*

Verna Schrombeck lives in Lake Dalecarlia. For those not familiar with the area, Lake Dale is part of Lowell. Think Hessville and Hammond on a smaller scale – sort of.

Verna, 76, she is a widow and stands nearly 5 feet, 10 inches tall. Ironically, her maiden name was Short. I find the retired music teacher reserved and proper but not at all stodgy.

* * *

"I grew up in a large family," Schrombeck begins. "There were 11 children in our family. I was smack dab in the middle – five, me, then five. You never forget the lessons you learned during the Great Depression.

"I was raised on a farm near Toto about 7 miles from North Judson and about the same from Knox. Toto was just a stopping place for the train. I graduated from North Judson High School."

Toto is where people buy discount items.

"Yes, we were told the fellow who wrote The Wizard of Oz had been down in that area and that is where he got the name for the dog."

Verna, as a boy I remember going for a ride with my grandparents and smelling the mint in the fields of North Judson.

"Richard Gumz grew peppermint, spearmint, onions and potatoes. The Kline farm specialized in asparagus. After World War II, those were some of the few jobs for teenagers. The Sakaguchi family grew oriental vegetables. They were from San Francisco, but were sent to a relocation camp during the war. After the war, they settled in North Judson. My niece married a Sakaguchi.

"There were also adults who came up from Appalachia to work in the munitions factories and when those plants closed there was no other work except to go out in the fields. My first experience with the Gumz' mint field situation was when I was placed beside a woman who worked in the fields with her grandchildren – except for the two youngest of them who would babysit their infant sibling in the car all day. I was 14 at the time. The grandmother was 53 years old, on her hands in knees, she'd work all day long in the field."

College?

"I attended Indiana State University for Music Education. I received a scholarship which paid $24 every term (3 months). My tuition was $32."

How did you and your husband end up in Lake Dale?

"Well, Al lost his job in South Bend at Studebaker when the plant shut down. So he got a job at US Steel in Gary. That was a 56-mile drive one way. We moved to Lake Dale in 1956. There were four small adjoining lots available. The house covers two or them."

What was Lake Dale like in the '50s?

"The lake water was crystal clear back then, not silty like it is now. There was still a heavy Swedish influence. I can remember many of the Swedish Americans using cross country skis to get around."

You brought five boys and a girl into this world.

"Jeff, Brad, Steve, Jon and Jan, Patrick. Jon and Jan are twins. After childbirth I'd come right back down to 148 pounds. I'm a healthy eater; I've never deprived myself, yet I've maintained the same weight since high school – give or take a pound."

I know Brad and Jon personally. A couple of rough-and-tumble boilermakers. Good guys.

"Four of my sons are union boilermakers. Steve is not. He lives with me. Looking back, you could see the changes in his behavior as the medication was taking effect. There are better medications all the time that address his condition.

"Jon had meningitis, and because of a hearing loss had to have special training at Indiana University in Bloomington. Can you imagine taking a child 5 years old down there and dropping him off, and saying, 'Good-bye, John. We are leaving.'

"I went back to work because there were no funds to pay for his tuition or room and board. Jon stayed in Bloomington for two years. I would go down there as often as I could. I had five other children, and Patrick was a baby. Plus I was told, 'You either work on your master's degree or you don't have a job.' That was in '64."

Meningitis. That had to be harrowing.

"We all had to get shots a month after he was released. I called the doctor saying, 'Something isn't right, Jon's soft spot is swelling again'.

"The doctor said, 'Jon didn't have much of a chance before and has less of a chance now. Can you get him to the University of Chicago? We're full up.'"

(Schrombeck tells of driving her 3-month-old son, who was in a coma, to Chicago and running into the kitchen of the University of Chicago with Jon in her arms).

Brad and Pat have played in their own rock 'n' roll band since the '70s. Brad's a guitarist and Pat's a drummer. What about you, Verna?

"I've played the piano since I was 4 years old. I also played the violin, trombone and French horn. I love singing around the piano. I would play folk songs and my kids would sing along. Folk songs are so timely – never out of date. Songs like 'Sweet Betsy From Pike' and 'Old Joe Clark.' They contain lessons to be learned. I have this 'Fireside Book of Folk Songs.' The kids loved it."

How long did you teach?

"Thirty-six years all together – 20 years of general music and choir at Lowell Middle School, and 16 years as an elementary, junior high choral band and music teacher.

"I also traveled to Schneider. It was a little old country school way back. I came into the classroom and there was this scruffy bunch of kids – and they ain't nothin' wrong with that. I looked at this one boy and asked him, 'Where are your shoes?' He said, 'They're at home.' I said, 'Okay.'"

What was he, a first-grader?

"No, seventh or eighth grade. One of the boys brought his dog – sat right next to his desk. Schneider was poor, but there was this generosity at school. This quality of genuineness. Every child can learn if discipline, hard work and love is being furnished."

The secret of raising kids?

"I don't really know that there is a secret to it. I just know from my own experience. You have children who are very strong-willed. If you are looking from the outside in, you think it's all the parent. But that's not exactly the case because you have children who do not know what fear is. Like my grandmother said, 'Fools go where angels fear to tread.'

"In raising children you do what you feel is really best. They will make mistakes, but eventually, they will come back to what they have been taught. And with my own, that is exactly what has happened.

"When Brad was 16, he decided he was going to visit his best friend in Arkansas. He was going to ride a horse all the way. When he got to St. Anne, Ill, he decided to sell the horse and hitchhike the rest of the way. He also hitchhiked back with a turtle in his pocket."

Brad? He never told me that!

"No; I bet he didn't!"

* * *

Verna's mother's maiden name was Taylor. Her ancestors on that side of the family can be traced back to the Revolutionary War – hardy stock from Virginia and Pennsylvania. Verna herself reminds me of one of those Yankees whom Norman Rockwell painted.

After teaching music for 36 years, Schrombeck taught English as a second language for eight years at the Lake County Library.

She talked about how her children all pitched in when their father's cancer was deemed terminal and she couldn't lift him anymore.

Today, the former child of the Great Depression wears an experimental device that helps pump blood throughout her body; she has congestive heart failure.

As I pack up to leave, Mother Schrombeck's long graceful fingers glide across ivory keys – "Rustles of Spring."

Greg Easton *(April 2011)*

"Well the names have all changed since you hung around,
But those dreams have remained, they're turned around.
Who'd have thought they'd lead ya,
Here where we need ya.
Yeah, we tease him a lot cause we got him on the spot,
Welcome back, welcome back, welcome back."
– John Sebastian

Like Gabe Kotter returning to Buchanan High School in the 1970s sitcom "Welcome Back, Kotter," Greg Easton has come back home to Morton High School in the Hessville neighborhood of Hammond.

Easton, 50, is the divorced father of three adult children and a big-time Chicago White Sox fan. He lives in Hammond.

After graduating from Morton, Easton earned a bachelor's degree at Valparaiso University, a master's degree form the University of Northern Iowa, and a master's in education at VanderCook College in Chicago.

Easton is the director of Morton's Academy for the Performing Arts.

* * *

Your teaching career began at Hammond Gavit High School
"Yes, I was at Gavit for 25 years," he said.

Back in your high school days did you play sports for the Governors?

"I played some baseball; I wasn't very good. Coach (Greg)

Jancich was the coach; he's still here. He's 74 years old. On my first day of work here at Morton, I told him, 'Coach, I want to forgive you for cutting me from the baseball team.' I loved baseball; it broke my heart."

What was his response?

"He just covered his face with his hands and shook his head. He's a great guy; Coach Jancich is a hall-of-famer."

The Academy for the Performing Arts?

"Jeff, the programs in Hammond had gone way down, for the most part. What we did at Gavit was pretty unique. I wanted to give those opportunities to everybody in Hammond. So, our concept was to put all our eggs in one basket and give the kids at Hammond High and Hammond Clark, the same exact opportunities."

Kids from any of the Hammond schools can attend this academy?

"Yes, we've done four shows already this year – huge productions. We have a huge dance program. I'm going to show you the studio, black box theater, music lab... .

"Now, instead of people leaving to go to other schools in other communities, I have people calling me, saying, 'What can we do to get our kid into this program?' But right now, it's Hammond schools only."

What shows have been performed in this, the academy's first year?

"Our first show was a main stage production of 'The Crucible' by Arthur Miller. Then, in the black box, we did the musical 'You're a Good Man, Charlie Brown,' and then, on the main stage we did 'Hair Spray.' I think we're the first school in Northwest Indiana to get the rights to 'Hair Spray.' Our final production of the year is 'Bus Stop' by William Inge."

Let's talk a little more about Morton.

"Back in '78, we had more than 2,000 kids at Morton. Right now, we're bursting at the seams with 1,200. Some parents say their children don't have the opportunities they could have at, say, Crown Point High School.

"Families move. But, now, in Hammond, we have this new, multi-million dollar facility just for the arts when other schools are cutting their arts programs."

Greg, I worked with a lot of guys in the mill who graduated from Morton during the 1970s. How has Morton changed since then?

"When I went to Morton, we had two black kids in the whole school and they came in from Gary for a special program. Now, it is a completely different dynamic. In our program, that's really cool.

"Clark is heavily Hispanic, Hammond High is heavily black, Gavit and Morton are pretty good mixes. You put it all together in a creative place like this and it adds tremendously. We are a real melting pot of ethnicity which is a super positive thing.

"Jeff, most people know there are a couple of Hammond schools that have been put on the watch list by the state. It's kinda been exaggerated. First of all, the kids I'm dealing with here at the academy are top-level kids. They have to audition to get in the program; you have to have a minimum of 2.0 (grade point average). Last year, when we were auditioning for the program, we had 800 kids in Hammond apply. We auditioned 600 kids; we ended up taking about 170. They're starving for this."

Give me an example.

"A year ago, I had a student from Hammond High; out all those kids, he gave the most incredible audition. But his GPA wasn't high enough. I called him particularly; everybody else got a letter whether or not they were accepted. I said to him, 'You're incredibly talented, but you're not making the grades; in life, you have to make the grade.' He also had a truancy problem. This year, he came back with his report card, put it up on my wall, and said, 'Here's my grades Mr. Easton; I am now eligible to audition for the Academy for the Performing Arts.' He also had his attendance record with no truancies whatsoever."

Great story.

"I have a counselor who talks to one of my students who comes from a different high school. She said that being in this program has literally saved the girl's life. She had suicidal tendencies and all kinds of emotional problems. This is a community of kids who are all artists."

Sounds wonderful.

"I really have to credit the superintendent and this school board who had the guts to say, 'This is what kids need. This is about the kids. We're not here about the political thing.'"

Next year?

"We're going to expand the program to about 300 kids."

Teach, do me a favor. I know there is a new adaptation of Studs Terkel's "Working" playing in Chicago until about mid-May. I can't afford it. Morton and "Working" are the perfect fit. I'd come see that gem in a heartbeat here at MHS.

"'Working' is on our agenda. We're working-class people. In fact, I think that would be a great show in our black box theater."

You are fiercely loyal to Morton and to Hammond.

"Jeff, I learned my craft at this school. Here's how weird I am; I try to always buy my gas in Hammond. I try to do my shopping in Hammond. My lady friend calls me 'Mr. Hammond.' If I can do it in Hammond, that where I'm gonna do it. I want to get an Avalanche; Smith Chevy on the boulevard will be where I buy that vehicle, you know?

"The people around here, whether they work at Ford or U.S. Steel or ArcelorMittal.... They are why I buy American; that's why I live in Hammond. These are the people who have taken care of me. My passion for Hammond and these kids is immense."

* * *

I've covered football games and AAU track meets at Morton High School, but I had never been inside it. Believe me, the beauty is within.

After my dime tour, Greg introduced me to Jenevieve Carrizales, Cassandra Sheldon, Felice Brown, Liliana Brito, Sylvia Rodriguez, Alfonso "Fonzie" Villa and Briana Hernandez. They aren't administrators or school board members; they are seven of the 170 talented, young bohemians who auditioned for, made the grades, and now attend the Academy for the Performing Arts.

Welcome back, Easton.

Jimmy Holmes *(July 2005)*

"The fight is won or lost away from the witnesses – behind the lines, in the gym, running on the road – long before I dance under those lights."
– Muhammad Ali

I was greeted by my high school classmate Tim Myers soon after pulling into the parking lot of the IGA supermarket in Roselawn. He owns the place. The IGA and other local businesses had set up a press conference in support of conquering hero Jimmy Holmes

Holmes, 27, teaches first-grade at Lincoln Elementary in Roselawn and moonlights as a professional boxer. He also lives in Roselawn, but grew up in DeMotte.

While wearing spectacles and a long-sleeved shirt in July, the 6-foot, 1-inch and 160-pound Holmes appears more the schoolmaster than middleweight ringmaster.

Tim Myers' wife, Cheryl, told me a story about a little girl who recently ambled into the grocery store with her mother and pointed at a poster of Friday night's championship fight:"Look Mommy, there's Mr. Holmes!" "Don't be silly, honey. Mr. Holmes is your schoolteacher, not a boxer." "But Mommy, look at the picture..."

And so it goes.

* * *

Jimmy, how did you break into boxing's professional ranks?
"After obtaining my degree, I was hired by Lincoln Elementary; my present-day trainer's wife happened to be a teacher's aide here at Lincoln. We were sitting at the lunch table and somebody brought up boxing. I mentioned that as an amateur I'd won the Golden Gloves title. She said, 'Well, you're going to have to meet my husband.' I asked who

her husband was and she said, 'Callahan.'

"I was like, 'Jack Callahan? *The* Jack Callahan! I used to go see guys like Jack 'Kid' Callahan and Marty Jakubowski box when I was a kid!

"Well, I met Jack. Eventually, he became my coach toward the end of my amateur days. He decided: 'Hey, it's time to go pro. If you wanna do it, do it now.'"

Jack Callahan didn't want you to wait until you were 35 years old.

"Exactly. I started out as an amateur when I was 18, but I had just 10 fights in over seven years. There were no gyms around here. That's something I'd like to do in the future, open up a gym, locally. Maybe a smaller version of what One in a Million has up north. Something to keep the kids occupied; something physical.

"There are so many overweight kids who sit in front of TVs eating garbage and playing games on the computers; they need some type of physical activity.

"Boxing is a form of stress relief. There's nothing like pounding those bags. You can be enduring one of your worst days and you start working on the heavy bag for 15 or 20 minutes, and the next thing you know, you're catching your breath – and you feel better. And if a young person wants to pursue the sport, wants to go farther, he or she can compete."

I hear you. For me, it was running. My ex-wife was always amazed when I told her running six or eight miles relaxed me. But it does. Jimmy, not only are you teaching these children in the classroom, you're also setting a good example by the way you take care of your mind and body exercising. I'm sure that's why you have such a following down here. Everyone tells me the youngsters adore you.

"I try to let the kids know boxing can be done in a place where it's structured. You learn how to box. It's not something you use on the street."

For you, it's a lot of work.

"Yes; the conditioning. It's like having a part-time job. You have to devote yourself to it. I used to play guitar in bands. My old buddies call me: 'Hey, you want to go out and jam?' I tell them I can't. I have to go to the gym."

I think it's great, Jimmy, that you've chosen to teach the little ones in school. There's a scarcity of male elementary teachers.

"Right now, I'm teaching first grade. I've taught sixth grade. I might get moved to fourth grade. I like fourth or fifth grade; the children are more impressionable. I'm just happy to have a job.

"One reason there's a scarcity is the money. It's difficult to support a family. I'm divorced and have no kids of my own, and it's still paycheck to paycheck. My girlfriend has kids. I've been fighting as a professional for less than two years. Boxing has helped me out financially. Starting pay for an elementary teacher is rough. Sometimes I help my father as a laborer putting in septic systems. I'm his gofer. I shovel a lot of rock."

"Excuse me, Mr. Holmes, could I have your autograph?," asks a young fan. "I'm an eighth-grader and I like to wrestle."

"Here you go. Keep working hard, buddy. And keep your grades up."

"Jack (Callahan) was a state champion," Holmes continues. "He told me I got what it takes. He says I'm the most coachable fighter he's ever trained. I work at it. I've improved, improved, improved. I'm tall for my weight class. I've got reach. Jack says I hit incredibly hard for my size – comparable to a light-heavyweight. I'm 10-0-1 since going pro, with six knockouts."

How much does the average guy make for a bout?

"The average club fighter gets about 100 bucks per round. I get significantly more. Especially for the state championship."

You're a body puncher.

"I like the body. If I can hit it, I'll go after it. That's one thing as an amateur, I never did. Callahan said anytime you can hit the body, hit it. He's right. After the body, then, you go for the head."

I used to work with Jack's brother, Terry Callahan, in the mill. We went to many a Sox game together. I kicked Jack's butt once in Cal City, by the way.

"In the ring?"

Well, no, in a half-marathon. We both went the distance. Your PR man, Mike Gonzalez, I KO'd him too, in Highland.

"Club Dimensions?"

Well, no, at Borders, in a poetry slam. Got him the third round; it was brutal.

"Impressive."

You know how it is 'Jimmy Teach;' I took 'em both to school. Don't tell them I said anything. I.. I.. don't want to hurt their feelings. (awkward silence)

Jimmy, tell me about Vance Garvey, the Joe Palooka you're going to destroy on the 8th.

"He's no Palooka; he's a real tough guy. A southpaw from the Bronx. Garvey isn't gonna to simply fall down; it'll be a fight."

Who were some of your favorite pugs growing up?

"Me and my dad were always big Roberto Duran fans. Boom Boom Mancini... I liked a lot of fighters. Dad used to take me to the fights at the Hammond Civic Center before I had my driver's license. I'd watch guys like Jack and Marty and think, 'Wow, I'd like to do this.' And then they'd bring the ring card girls out and I'd tell the old man, 'Dad, I'd really, really, like to be out there.'"

How long are you going to fight?

"After every fight, I ask myself that. I think about it. Is it going the way I want it to go? Do I have the time to train? Do I still have it inside me, the drive? It could be one fight, it could be 20. I don't know. One thing I do know; I don't want to look back when I'm 50, and say, 'I coulda been a contendah.' Win or lose, I'll hold my head up high this Friday night because I'll know I gave it everything I had."

* * *

Jimmy "The Fighting Schoolteacher" Holmes. I asked him to write his cell phone number down so we can keep in touch. While he was at it, I asked him for his autograph. And as I merged onto I-65, I realized what makes Jimmy successful in the ring is what makes him successful in the classroom – dedication.

Sophie Wojihoski *(Aug. 2010)*

"We learn not for school, but for life."
— Seneca

I first met Sophie Wojihoski at one of the archeological digs at Collier's Lodge in Pleasant Township. At this year's dig, we had a better chance to get to know one another. I called her about a week later and asked if and when I could interview her. She said: "Meet me at Lake Station Library in an hour."

The word procrastination is not part of Sophie's vocabulary.

Wojihoski, 90, lives in what is considered Hobart, but has a New Chicago ZIP code. Assumption of the Blessed Virgin Mary Catholic Church in New Chicago is about a two-minute walk for her.

Wojihoski was married to her late husband, Joe, for 50 years. They raised four children.

* * *

Where were you born?

"Gary, Indiana," she said. "My maiden name is Mikolagek. My maternal grandfather, Apolinar Saniewski was the first family member to emigrate from Poland to the United States, but he was killed within a year or so at U.S. Steel around 1912."

Welcome to America.

"My mother came to the United States a few months after her father; she was 15 when he died. Her mother never did come to the United States; she was a midwife in Poland and was on her way to deliver a child when she was killed by a horse and buggy."

What about your dad?

"He also was born in Poland; he died when I was 3. My mother said he was an alcoholic. I can remember my father lying in bed; when a nurse pulled his arm, he moaned out loud in a lot of pain. Mother told me to leave the room. That's my only memory of him."

It's like 1923 when your father passed. Then what?

"I learned to read and write Polish and English in first and second grade because mother sent me to a Polish-Catholic school in Glen Park."

The name of the school?

"Holy Family School. But my mother moved from house to house after my father died. I attended five schools in the first eight grades. One year, she moved just two weeks before school ended. Because of that, I was held back. It wasn't my fault.

"I remember East Pulaski and West Pulaski when I was in about fourth grade. West Pulaski School was for the white kids; East Pulaski was for the black kids. Things were so different."

Did your mother remarry?

"Twice. My stepfathers were cruel; I have scars. My mother had seven children from those marriages. In 1932, one of my half-brothers was accidentally shot to death."

How did that happen?

"My stepfather kept a revolver in a dresser drawer. My second brother called my youngest brother to the bedroom door, and said, 'Stick 'em up' and pulled the trigger. He thought he had taken out all the bullets but forgot about the one in the chamber. He carried our little brother in his arms to the doctor's office. I hate guns."

Sophie, please tell me it gets a little better for you.

"It does, but not for a while. We ate beans throughout the Depression. That's why I appreciate what I have today. The neighbors would sometimes bring us food."

High school?

"I did very well in high school. The teachers were so good to me. I had bad teeth with lots of cavities. One of the teachers sent me to her dentist. Her sorority paid to have my teeth fixed."

At which high school did you attend?

"Froebel. I was a member of the Froebel Girls Athletic Association and was handball chairman.

"The blacks were cheated at Froebel. They weren't allowed to be in the Honor Society. They couldn't hold any offices.

"We had a contest to come up with a school motto. All the students were allowed to participate. The motto chosen was submitted by Eugene Foster: 'Non scholae sed vitae discimus.'"

Translation?

"'We learn not for school, but for life.' Eugene was a black boy."

Life after high school?

"I wanted to be a teacher all my life, but I was too poor. I got married and had four children. The second child is dyslexic. He is very intelligent, but had a very difficult time in school. He also was quite active in sports and when he was about to graduate from high school, he said he wanted to be a physical education instructor. We didn't want to hurt his feelings or deter him in any way, so I decided that I also would go to college and take the same classes he took; that way I could help him like I'd done since he was in the first grade."

How did that pan out?

"My son got a job at Bethlehem Steel for the summer. Meanwhile, at the age of 50, I enrolled at Indiana University Northwest and took seven credit hours.

"In late August, when it was time for my son to register for college, he said, 'Mom, I'm making more money now than I would if I became a gym teacher at a high school.'"

And?

"He decided to stay in the mill. My husband said to me, 'You always wanted to become a teacher, why don't you continue?' And that's what I did.

"My first job was at the junior high school in Hobart teaching reading to special education kids. Then, I went to Ridge View School in Hobart and taught sixth grade for a year. Then, Hobart Junior High School called me back, asking if
I'd start a reading program for the special needs children.

"It was great. I guess the holy spirit touches me in anything I do. We had a program called 'Write to Read.' We used headsets and reading machines. I recorded the books and would read to them slowly. Each child wore a headset and would read to themselves along with me."

That's wonderful, Sophie.

"But then I noticed some of the kids weren't looking at the books while I was reading to them."

Busted.

"I made new tapes and purposely made minor mistakes like misspelling the word 'the' or leaving out the word 'is.' I told the students there were mistakes and if they found the teacher's mistake they would get a point for it."

Yeah?

"They watched those words like hawks."

How long did you teach?

"For 23 years. I retired at age 70 because I thought I had to. When I realized that wasn't so, I tried to get my job back but the School Board members wouldn't allow it because I had signed papers."

What did you do then?

"Ran for School Board and won."

God love you. The secret of being a good teacher?

"Put yourself in the child's place."

"Jeff?"

Sophie?

"I believe the good Lord is giving me back the childhood I lost; I m having fun today."

* * *

In adulthood, Sophie Wojihoski has traveled to every continent with the exception of South America. She has taken part in archaeological digs from the Republic of Congo to Kouts. She loves woodcarving and solving cryptograms, too. And, in conjunction with the Portage Adult Learning Center, she still teaches reading.

Not bad for a nonagenarian.

The Arts

Gwen Calmese-Wright *(July 2008)*

"I've learned that people will forget what you said, people will forget what you did, but people will never forget how you made them feel."
-Maya Angelou

I first met Gwen Calmese-Wright at a poetry slam seven or eight years ago. We shared similar interests and quickly became friends.

It wasn't until a year or so later, while attending one of her plays, that I spotted another good friend, Bernita, who was greeting folks at the door. I'd known Bernita since the '70s; I didn't know Gwen and Bernita were sisters.

A word to the wise: As double-deck pinochle partners, these siblings are all but unbeatable.

Gwen lives in Gary; she has raised three adult children and has been married to Dwayne Wright for 12 years. Dwayne played basketball for Gary West Side High School.

They enjoy tropical fish, but don't always agree on what species should be displayed in the tank. They own an orange chow named Regis, who isn't very fond of me.

Gwen has worked as a general clerk at ArcelorMittal's Burns Harbor plant for 10 years, but is off work because of a minor stroke. It was a relief to find her as quick-witted as ever back in the comforts of home on 17th Avenue.

* * *

Gwen, I need some vital stats for the readers; it's all part of the interview thing. What year did you become eligible to vote in a presidential election?

"Jeff, I'm closer to 60 than I am 50."

What high school did you attend?
"Gary Roosevelt."
Class of?
"You just don't give up, do you?"
Tell me about your childhood.
"I grew up in the Dorie Miller Projects on Gary's east side; I'm the oldest of eight children."
Were your parents originally from the South?
"Yes, my mother's family moved to Gary from Little Rock, Ark., when she was 2 years old.. My father grew up in Mississippi, migrated to St. Louis, and eventually settled in Gary. He was a jazz enthusiast who liked to knock people out."
Pardon me?
"He was a boxer who also sang on the radio."
That's an interesting one-two punch. You, too, have entertained members of the community with your voice – all while juggling various day jobs.
"Yes, I was a paralegal for a while, and I also wrote a theater column for the Post-Tribune from about 2001 to 2003."
You've taught dance, you act, sing like an angel and have published poetry, prose and plays – all without any formal training. What first led this affectation for the performing arts?
"It was probably while attending Charles Drew School in second grade. I won a city-wide contest for my poem, 'Barefoot in the Park.'"
Most of your plays have run several times down through the years here in Gary. How many have you written?
"A dozen, maybe. Let's say 10; I don't want to get caught in a lie."
What do you have going now?
"I've written and directed a musical called 'The Audition.' It will be performed in Munster. I believe it could be the best show I've ever done; the cast is magnificent.

"With that said, I don't want the responsibility of directing anymore; it's too stressful. People are not committed. Since I've had this stroke, I just sit back like an old lady and stare at them while they're fumbling around rehearsing. I don't get as fired up as I used to."
Gwen, please, you've been telling me you're through with directing for seven years. How long did it take you to write 'The Audi-

tion?'"

"I started it a year-and-a-half ago, then I stopped working on it and started writing 'High Rise 19.' When I finished 'High Rise,' I went back and completed *The Audition.*"

How do you come up with ideas for your plays? From your own life experiences?

"Not necessarily; it's more imagination."

You've created a certain feisty, snuff-dipping, Bible-toting character many times. I love that "old lady."

"I've actually done Mother Kooper as a stand-up comedy act on the gambling boats. One of my dreams would be to team up with Tyler Perry when he is portraying Madea; Mother Kooper could be 'her' long lost sister."

Gwendolyn Marie, you've brought me to tears in dramatic as well as comedic roles. Do you prefer one over the other?

"No, I enjoy them both. I believe comedy is more difficult. 'Fences' was a real tearjerker – literally. My character had to cry 15 times."

You've also acted in quite a few of Mark Spencer's productions at the West Side Theatre Guild.

"Yes: 'A Raisin in the Sun,' 'A Lesson Before Dying,' 'Steel Waters,' 'Posin'.' Don't forget you and I did 'Steel and Roses' together at both the Towle Theater in Hammond and in New York City."

Yeah, if we would've been any farther off-Broadway, we'd have been in Jersey. But it was a great experience.

"Jeff, when I retire, I'm just going to read my poetry."

Gwen, Mother Kooper wouldn't stand for that.

* * *

She has fixed me up with heaping plates of soul food on Sunday afternoons. And, at my request, she even tried to fix me up with the beguiling, beautiful Bernita.

Hey, what are friends for?

Gwen Calmese-Wright has entertained folks throughout the Steel City for 25 years. And I can't remember exactly what she said or did in her matriarchal roles in "A Lesson Before Dying" and "A Raisin in the Sun."

But I'll never forget how she made me feel.

Samantha Dalkilic-Miestowski *(Oct. 2008)*

"I do so like
green eggs and ham!
Thank you!
Thank you,
Sam-I-Am!"
- Dr. Seuss

Samantha P.J. Emel Dalkilic-Miestowski is the owner of the Steeple Gallery in St. John. Most folks refer to her as Sam. Her parents liked the 1960s sitcom "Bewitched," starring Elizabeth Montgomery as modern-day witch Samantha Stephens; hence, the first name. Sam's parents were raised in "foreign" countries. Her dad is from Istanbul, Turkey; her mom is from Texas.

Dalkilic-Miestowski lives in Schererville with her husband, Roman. They have a daughter; Alexis, who is 8.

* * *

That's quite a handle you got there, Sam. My Grandma Leona Helena Wilhelmina Rosina Carolina surely would've appreciated it.

"That's one of the cool things about the region – our names," begins Dalkilic-Miestowski.

Sam, I love it. There are better odds of me interviewing a Luigi O'Hara or Mladenka Gutierrez in Northwest Indiana than any other place on the planet.

When you let me into the gallery, I noticed that you have "American Gothic" on display. I don't remember Grant Wood painting such a handsome couple. The pitchfork looks the same.

"That's my husband and I; we've been married for 12 years now."

You graduated from Merrillville High School in '86 and also were named homecoming queen your senior year.

"Yeah, I beat out all the cheerleaders and popular people. The non-jocks, punkers, heads, nerds, geeks and underclassmen voted for me. I wore black when I accepted my crown which caused a stir back then. There was an editorial in the school newspaper; some people figured cheating went on because I won.

"My boyfriends were punk rockers; I never dated jocks. I didn't know Roman was a college baseball player when we started going out; I just thought he was hot."

Life after high school?

"Boot camp at Fort Jackson, N.C. I spent six years in the Army National Guard. I graduated from Airborne School at Fort Benning, Ga., in 1988. I was a second lieutenant by the time I was 20."

You were a "second looey?"

"Yeah, I'll show you my certificate downstairs. I was like the only chick to go to 'jump school.' Getting my wings helped give me the discipline I needed to get through school as an art major."

Just basic training alone had to be tough.

"Tough? I didn't take an epidural when Alexis was born; 26 hours of hard labor – *that* was tough. Yeah, when bullies on the playground tell my kid, 'Your mama wears combat boots,' it kind of sticks."

Where did you go to college?

"Ball State University, I received a bachelor of fine arts degree with a specialty in Sculpture in 1991."

You've been to Europe.

"Yes, I went on a tour with some other artists and musicians to Auschwitz, Poland. And I was selected to go to Edinburgh, Scotland for like a fringe festival theater where they celebrate the arts every year. I met kids my age from all over the world – Poles, Spaniards... We worked collaboratively and basically put a gallery together. That's kind of where I got my inspiration.

"I also went to Southern France and did some post-grad work which included limestone carving. It was very provincial; I washed my clothes by hand. I saw the best artists I knew as instructors struggling in France. I figured owning a gallery was the next best thing."

Do you give tours?

"Sure."

Melanzane!

"Excuse me?"

I was admiring the painting of the eggplants. Makes me hungry.

"That's called 'Escaping Parmesan.'"

Great title. I really like this one, too.

"'To the Light,' by Roland Kulla. It's a 50-inch-by-50 inch oil on canvas, and part of his rust series. I've always been interested in industry as far as art. The thread that defines this gallery is industry; it's the body and soul of it."

The music you've been playing since we've been talking is as eclectic as the paintings you have for sale. I've heard pieces from La Boheme, some Latin jazz, and Bobby Darin snapping his fingers to "Mack the Knife." This is a classy joint you have here, Sam. How long have you been in business?

"Since '98. Making this place into an art gallery was a total renovation. It was a dilapidated Assembly of God church.

"Downstairs, we probably have the largest collection of antique prints in Northwest Indiana. First-edition Audubons, original prints from the 1893 World's Fair... There are illustrations, etchings, engravings, photo gravure... . We've shipped to Belgium, Australia, France, Italy and all over the United States."

But it's more than just a gallery, right?

"I'd like to mention that the gallery is not just a box. We're not just selling stuff. There is a lot of community involvement.

"We do framing, judge children's art contests, appraisals; I put those hats on if necessary. We're open five days a week. I have my regular customers and I have people who come here just to hang out.

"We had a private reception for Miss USA when she came around. We lease the space out for private parties, anniversaries and wine tastings – not like a college frat-boy party or anything like that. We haven't had a wedding yet; I want to. Students have worked here for free to get college credit – just like I did back in the day."

How about aspiring artists in Northwest Indiana?

"We're always looking for new artists; we try to professionally review their portfolios to see if the Steeple Gallery is a good fit for the artist. Sometimes, if we can't help them, we can point them in the right direction or help them in the future. We're creating an art market.

"Here is our Hoosier Salon exhibition. There are a few region artists that we represent who enter shows that are based in Indianapolis. About a century ago, these daughters of Indiana decided that Indiana was a hub of talent – the poets, painters – they thought Chicago and the world should be exposed to Indiana culture. The first ever Hoosier Salon took place at Marshall Fields. Many major players in art started out there. Seven or eight years later it moved back home to Indiana.

"Their goal was to get a piece of art painted by an Indiana painter into every home in America. So, 84 years later, it's still going on once a year."

And how have our local artists fared?

"Two Steeple Gallery artists got in last year and won major awards. Julie Sklar won Best Acrylic Painting; she also won more than $2,000. Highland's Fred Holly got two of his pieces purchased by the Indiana State Museum's permanent collection in Indianapolis."

He's the guy who did the sculpture on Ridge Road in Munster. The one of the American Indian, farmer, and a steel worker.

"That's right. Because of Region artists like them, we were able to secure a spot for Northwest Indiana. We were the only stop in Lake and Porter County last year. There are more than 120 pieces collectively; they break it up across the state. Like, I have 15 pieces, somebody else has 15, etc. Our Hoosier Salon exhibition will be here until Nov. 14."

Sam, do you want to do this for the rest of your life?

"Sure; I think I can affect people's lives on a local level that might not necessarily make art a part of their lives. That's a cool experience.

"Jeff, I had a professor tell me: 'When you do a self-portrait, don't do it of yourself. Paint the friends you hang out with. That defines who you really are, not who you think you are.'"

* * *

Seven or eight years ago Dalkilic-Miestowski invited a handful of steel workers to read from a book ("The Heat") they had published regarding life in the mill.

Gritty tales of pig iron and grime delivered within an immaculate art gallery before an elegant hostess might conger up an incongruous scenario to some. But don't judge a book by its cover; Sam's alright.

She knows how to weld and she's pretty good with a torch – just like some of us who read that day.

Ted Kosmatka *(Sept. 2007)*

"I have been a soreheaded occupant of a file drawer labeled 'science fiction'... and I would like out, particularly since so many serious critics regularly mistake the drawer for a urinal."
-Kurt Vonnegut

Ted Kosmatka is my buddy. We first met via electronic mail (it was not a dating service). I contributed to an audio-book that contained steel mill-related stories. He told me my stories made his mother cry. I told him I was very happy to hear that.

Ted is young. I'm old. He's a reserved big guy. I'm a raucous little guy. But we have similarities. Ted's blue collar. And he writes. We bunked together in New York City before the premiere of his play entitled 'Steel' which played before a packed house. I was honored, albeit type-cast once again, to portray his character Stack, a loose cannon millworker about to lose his job after 29 years service with the company.

Ted lives in Portage with his wife Christine. They have a 5-month-old baby girl named Morgan, a Boston Terrier named Bear obtained from an animal rescue, and a fascinatingly hideous feline of the Sphinx variety that goes by Silas. Ted is the oldest of four siblings. He graduated from Chesterton High School in 1992.

* * *

You're Mr. Establishment now, Theodore.

"A good marriage is the greatest catastrophe that could happen to a writer."

Bite your tongue and count your blessings. You're a college boy, but also a third generation steel worker.

"I earned an Associate's Degree in Biology, then hired in at LTV and, through tuition reimbursement, I went back and got my Bachelors. My grandfather worked at Inland Steel for 30 years. My dad worked at Bethlehem Steel for 24 years – until he died."

Ted, I've known people who have worked for two different steel companies. And I've known a couple of guys who have worked for the same steel mill two or even three different times. But I think you're the only guy I know who has worked for three different steel mills.

"Yeah, I worked four years at LTV, until they went bankrupt. Then I worked at US Steel in Gary for four years, and now I have two years at Inland (ArcelorMittal)."

Why did you leave US Steel?

"Forced overtime. I could probably work 70, 80 or even 90 hours a week for six months or so, but when you're looking at doing that for most of your career, you have to decide if that's really what you want to do with the rest of your life.

"Are you going to be a slave to the money or are you going to actually try to live a whole life? I was being scheduled days, afternoons, and midnights all in one week.

"It was right after they offered early retirement to the older guys. They didn't want to hire anybody new. It was funny; you'd see all these safety slogans posted everywhere. They had no problem with scheduling you 80 hours a week, but they also expected you to 'Be careful where you walk!' although you hadn't slept in 24 hours.

Do you like your job now?

"I love it. I work mostly in the Research Laboratory. I'm scheduled Monday through Friday, 40 hours per week. They've flown me to different mills like Sparrow's Point (Maryland) occasionally.

" They have some great poetry on the restroom walls at Sparrow's Point."

You haven't always had such a spic-and-span mill job.

"I've run the full gamut. I started as a laborer at LTV's sintering plant."

The sintering plant was the backdrop for "Steel" and "Indiana Harbor Jones." When did you start writing?

"I wrote a lot of really bad stuff in high school. I thought it was good at the time."

You've been published a number of times since.

"I've sold three stories to Asimov's. I recently sold a story to The Magazine of Fantasy and Science Fiction, the same magazine that published Stephen King's 'The Dark Tower'."

That's great. I mean, let's face it. The short story saw its heyday decades ago when it served as entertainment before television came along. Some of these literary magazines or sci-fi magazines might get more than 1,000 submissions per month and take two. The competition is fierce.

Asimov's is international; your stories have been read all over the world. Do they pay pretty decent for a story?

"I've gotten as much as $500. Lately, I've been getting rave reviews from magazines that critique the genre of Science Fiction – whether it be short fiction, novels or movies."

Let me read that review by Nick Gevers "...Ted Kosmatka treads interesting speculative paths in his alternate history 'The Prophet of Flores' asking what if anti-Darwinian advocates of creationism or intelligent design had managed to hoodwink the entire world rather than just their own religious constituency into rejecting evolutionary theory right down to the present. ..".

Ted, science fiction and fantasy aren't my cup of tea. But you are very good at it.

"I just sold a horror story entitled 'Doxology' to a magazine called City Slab. Sometimes these critics are vicious. If you write a bad story, they'll go after you. *Favorite authors?*

"For fiction, I like Tim O'Brien; he's a rhythm writer like you. As far as science fiction, I like Orson Scott Card and William Gibson."

Any words for aspiring authors?

"Just write the stories that are in you to write. Don't worry about if you'll find a market or not. The minute you start worrying about the market, it changes your writing, and the soul of the story is lost."

You became a steelworker like your old man and a writer like your mother.

"Yeah, Mom's novel is coming out this spring. It's a collaboration with Eric Flint called 'Time Spike.' Here's what the cover is going to look like. It's got a dinosaur eating a conquistador with a maximum security prison in the background. Mom used to work as a nurse at a death row prison. That's where she got the idea for her book. Mom corrupted me early with books."

Dad?

"My dad missed three days of work in 24 years. One day he got sick and called off. Then he called off the next day. And the next day. He never went back to work. He was 42. My little sister was 7."

* * *

After interviewing Ted, he walked out to my truck with me. I told him it was 30 years ago to the day that I hired into the labor gang at Inland Steel like my father before me.

He knows that I survived two mill explosions; five friends did not. Ted told me it was the eve of the date his father eschewed the option of chemotherapy and left this world.

On becoming a writer, it has been said that a messed up childhood or a traumatic adulthood is a plus.

Mark Spencer *(Dec. 2007)*

"Through my singing and acting and speaking, I want to make freedom ring. Maybe I can touch people's hearts better than I can their minds, with the common struggle of the common man."
– Paul Robeson

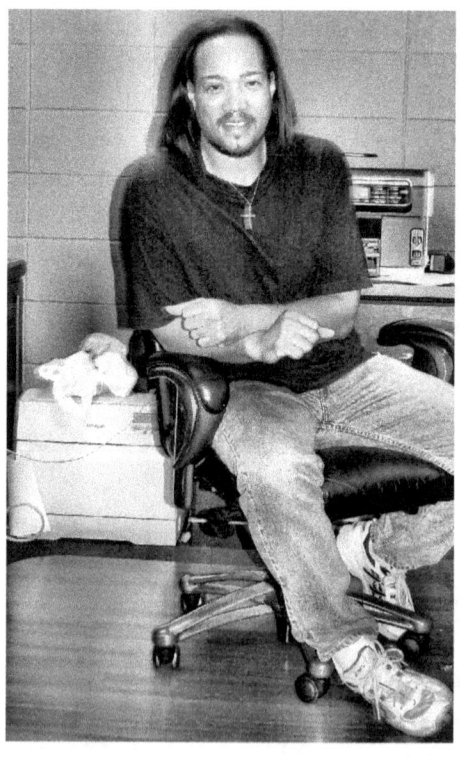

I've held off interviewing Mark Spencer for some time, figuring he's almost too famous for my Salt column. Then I started to really think about it. Who graces this column? Artists, underdogs, and the working class... Hmm...

They don't come much more artistic or altruistic. He surely could have flown the coop for a more glamorous Tinseltown or Chi-town or New YorkCity but remains loyal to his roots. As far as the latter? A harder worker I've yet to meet.

In fact, Spencer hits the grand slam of Saltdom. He's an *eccentric,* hardworking, artsy, underdog!

I call the busy soul's cell phone to confirm our interview at Gary West Side High School – pretty much the home of Mark Spencer.

* * *

Mark, I'm on my way...

"Jeff, do you have a priest's collar? Before we do our interview thing, I need you to read a guy his last rites who is about to get the electric chair. Do you feel me, doc?"

I feel you. You're in the middle of some kind of documentary film. Mark?

"Yes."

I don't have a collar. Could the guy hear the Word from a Protestant?

"That's fine. We're about to shoot the scene. Just wear a suit and tie. You can wear my crucifix. I have a Bible. Just look dignified."

I've portrayed a drunk, the devil, Death, and for you a displaced person of Polish descent in your epic saga of Gary's first 100 years, Steel Waters. But dignified? I'm not that good an actor.

And so it goes. After about 87 takes, I was allowed to do my real job, interviewing someone for my column – but I'll be immortalized in filmdom.

Spencer's brown eyes bestow both compassion and intensity. He resembles a kind of hip maestro with long straight hair. He is wearing his trademark black t-shirt and blue jeans. I once read that Einstein kept seven identical gray suits in his closet – not wanting to waste gray matter on trivial things like which outfit to wear. We take a seat in his backstage headquarters. Three or four guitars adorn the place. They are custom made. Like legendary guitarists Jimi Hendryx and Albert King, Spencer plays the instrument left-handed.

"I'm 37 years old. I transferred to Spaulding Elementary in 1978 from the Lake Ridge school system.

"My music teacher, Mrs. Green, asked a group of us kids to take a part or say a line in a Christmas piece. I volunteered. Afterwards I was offered the monologue of a very distraught wolf who was ticked off by three little pigs. I haven't looked back since.

"I came from a musical family. It all connected. The gospel music at Lively Stone Church of God in Christ, public address and performance: it was a natural fit. I was exposed to things like monologues.

"I was a member of the first graduating class (1988) of Emerson School for the Visual and Performing Arts, grades 7 through 12. Attending Emerson was a blessing for me – divine intervention. Somebody petitioned, got the school board's permission and Emerson became a reality.

After graduation from IUN, majoring in theater, there was an opportunity to fill in as speech and drama teacher for a dear friend who was with child. I covered for her. That was 16 years ago. I'm still waiting for her; she moved to Kentucky.

"I've been promoted to director of art and theater for the district. I assist with all Gary schools as needed. You have to be very careful about impeding others. Their programs are very unique. Our product is designed to be exposed to all students from K through 12."

I've played Beelzebub, Lord of Flies; you've played Jesus Christ.

"Yeah, I had to shed about 30 pounds for 'Superstar'. Otherwise the audience would have been thinking, 'Whoa, the Last Supper must of been an all-you-can-eat buffet!'"

How many plays have you directed at West Side?

"Counting one-acts, probably close to 100."

Do you have a personal favorite?

"'Steel Waters,' because it was conceived from my person – then I collaborated with some very talented people. Writing all those original tunes and pulling it all together was a mammoth task. The abyss of creating from the cuff; it was a mini-'Ragtime' of sorts.

"We had a specific agenda. We had historical content about a specific city, county and time about racial inequality – and we had to cover 100 years in under two hours. That kind of stuff takes six or eight years to do successfully.

"We very naively walked into that and had only sixteen months to prepare. The centennial was upon us. We had to make a world out of nothing. We wanted to talk about blacks; we wanted to talk about whites. We wanted to talk about the melting pot with steel as a backdrop. But by the time it was done, what an incredible diamond. Dude, it worked."

Audience members can be sticklers when it comes to history.

"They lived 'Steel Waters.' So they wanted it right, and I can appreciate that. We wanted to get it right.

"The footage that appeared during the play will be incorporated in the film. Avery Brooks will be our narrator."

"The play was only phase one, you dig? 'Steel Waters' will reach millions of homes – probably in July for Founder's Day. It was Ossie Davis who urged me into making film. He was quite an inspiration. He and Ruby spoke here at West Side."

Mark, the list of past performers and speakers that have appeared here at the West Side Theatre Guild is incredible. Ray Charles, Bill Cosby, Maya Angelou, Coretta Scott King, Wynton Marsalis, Koko Taylor, Ernest Gaines, Cicely Tyson... I was impressed by Spike Lee, but I really regret missing Ossie Davis and Ruby Dee. Such humanitarians.

"Ossie gave up his time and had dinner with me. He was a neat eater, too, man. I was sloppy, dude. He was with the fork and the knife (pantomimes the graceful table manners of Mr. Davis). Since then, I have become more conscious at dinner – I was always rushed."

Which do you prefer directing, plays or films?

"It's like having two kids. Which one do you love more? Dick or Jane? They both have very unique and special qualities. You can't say, 'That Jane, she's the one – as Dick is standing there. They're like my offspring. I love each one individually. I do have more of a discipline/control thing with film. You can illustrate things better with the camera."

Final thoughts?

"Jeff, I have a stake in Gary. It's a wonderful opportunity to work with our young people and so many other talented artists – for the betterment of community and for the idea of using our work as an ex port. There are some great things coming out of this region – and this city."

* * *

That's Mark Spencer's West Side story at 9th and Gerry. Like still or Steel Waters, his legacy runs deep.

Irene Evans *(March 2011)*

"The remarks about my reaching the age of Social Security and coming to the end of the road, they jolted me. And that was good. Because I sure as hell had no intention of just sitting around for the rest of my life. So I'd whip out the paints and really go to it."
– Norman Rockwell

Irene Evans paints up a storm. She also paints barns, portraits, wildlife, bucolic landscapes and has designed her tombstone.

Irene, 80, has been married to Dick Evans for 58 years; they have raised two sons and live in DeMotte.

Our interview took place at noon on Valentine's Day. Dick, a retired farmer, is accustomed to eating big lunches at high noon. Three times I turned down Irene's request to eat homemade meatloaf, mashed potatoes, baked beans, biscuits and blackberry pie. I said that would be highly unprofessional on my part.

* * *

"I moved from Gary, a big city school, to a two-room schoolhouse in Thayer when I was 9," Irene began.

Do you remember much of Gary?

"Oh, yeah, I remember it all. My parents had a business on 12th (Avenue) and Grant (Street). It was called the Spider's Inn. It was a tavern that served food every day.

"It was located right across the street from the National Biscuit Co. We lived behind the business. It was about six blocks south of Methodist Hospital in the Tolleston neighborhood."

What was your maiden name?

"Muraida. My father was from Slovakia; he was married in Slovakia, but my mother stayed there because he could only afford passage for one person. He worked in the coal mines of Springfield, Ill., with other foreigners; that's how he learned to speak other languages."

Tell me more about your European roots; it's fascinating.

"My dad's father was making a wedding for his daughter, Barbara. The wedding ceremony lasted three weeks; it was an expensive affair.

"He went to my mother's dad and said, 'You know, I've got a son who is in the Austrian Army in the ski troop.' Austria had taken over Slovakia. He said, 'My son is from a good family and your daughter is from a good family. So why don't they get married at the same time as my daughter, Barbara?' So, the fathers arranged the marriage of my parents. When my father returned from the army for his wedding ceremony, my mother had never spoken to him before."

Memories of the Spider's Inn?

"They had a basketball team with uniforms and all that. My mother cooked downstairs and my father had a special oven for barbecued ribs. We had a lot of people who came in the evening just to eat."

Your dad probably also had his share of shift workers from the mill who stopped for a shot and a beer.

"There was a lot of that. That's where I got my first artistic thing. All these old men would sit at the bar, and I had a coloring book and would color pictures and show these guys my pictures and they'd give me a penny or a nickel.

"That's how I'd get enough money to get another coloring book. They were all my friends. They were all nice."

Other childhood memories?

"On the other side of Grant Street was a swampy area. My brother and I would play Tarzan and swing from the willows and wild grape vines. We'd also catch polliwogs. We'd raise those polliwogs into frogs underneath our porch."

What grade school did you attend?

"I went to Holy Trinity and Beveridge. Then, in fourth grade, we moved to Thayer where there were four grades in each room. I attended DeMotte High School because Mt. Ayr High School in Newton County was so far away."

What possessed your father to move from Gary to Thayer?

"It was during the Depression and he was tired of the tavern business. He was ready to retire. He bought a very nice place; it was on 40 acres."

How did your family adjust to rural life?

"When we moved to the farm, the city people would come out for picnics. My dad would always barbeque a lamb slowly over a spit. The men drank beer while all us kids played. We'd eat the watermelons that Dad grew.

"We had a lot of fun. But the city people would say: 'How can you stand it here? There are no street lights.'"

Education?

"I went to the college of St. Francis in Joliet, Ill., for one year; I was an art major. Dick and I were going to get married, but my dad had a massive stroke at that time. We didn't know whether he'd live or die. Here was a guy who could speak eight languages, but after the stroke couldn't speak at all.

"I was the baby of the family and the only girl. I had five older brothers. Two of my brothers were married before I was born. I took care of Dad for four years."

You had to quit school?

"Yes. Finally, in 1952, Dick and I got married; I became a farmer's wife. We didn't have any money; nobody had any money in those days. We lived upstairs with my in-laws downstairs and great-grandpa. So, in that house we had five generations. We lived with our in-laws for 15 years."

Did you ever go back to school?

"Yes, to begin with, I went to Indiana University (Northwest) in Gary in the evenings. I had been out of school for 10 years. I went to school for elementary education as long as I could because they didn't have a full program. Then, I transferred to Valparaiso University.

"The first year I taught was at a little country school in Kniman; the janitor would wash my car every Friday. I ended up teaching in Hebron for 26 years. I also got my master's degree while working full time."

Your art?

"While I was teaching, I studied for eight summers under an artist in Auburn, Ala., by the name of Milton Lenoir. I got a white jacket; I'm certified to teach his method of painting.

"These paintings are acrylic, but I've done a lot of work with water colors and colored pencil, too."

Oil painting?

"I have, but a lot of the artists are dying from painting with oil; it's toxic – pastels, too."

How many paintings have you created?

"More than 300. I retired in 1990 and I've been painting ever since. I've tried it all."

* * *

Her artistic career began in a saloon in Gary. After a 50-year hiatus, she whipped out the paints and really got to it in DeMotte.

Irene Evans is an extraordinary woman who also happens to bake one heckuva blackberry pie.

Jerry Edmonds *(April 2011)*

"Love, love me do.
You know I love you,
I'll always be true,
So please, love me do.
Whoa, love me do."
– The Beatles

The Jerry Edmonds spread is nestled away on three acres west of U.S. 41 outside Lowell. He is a retired Arcellor Mittal mechanic.

Edmonds, 59, has been married to Mary for 39 years. They have raised three children.

Edmonds also is a musician and songwriter whose heartfelt sounds and lyrics exude from his pores like the sweat bled from a blast furnace tender's brow in August. His friends say he's a combination of John Mellencamp and John Candy.

* * *

Nice piano, Jerry.

"Jeff, I came up these steps after a 3-to-11 turn and there she was, all shiny and black, looking like some sexy french maid, whispering, 'Play me Jerry, play me... .' My wife surprised me with it. She wallpapered and painted other people's houses – paid for every dime of it. Mary did that, for me."

When did music first interest you?

"I started on the drums when I was in seventh grade. As a freshman, I played in a high school band with all upperclassmen. When those guys graduated, I started playing the guitar."

Who taught you how to play?

"I did. I've never taken a music lesson for any instrument. I can't read music. I can't score it."

How many instruments do you play?

"Drums, guitar, piano, harmonica, banjo, mandolin... ."

Tell me more about your childhood.

"I was in the crib when my dad left. One day when I was in junior high school, waiting for the bus on Hohman Avenue, a man asked, 'Are you Wayne and Jerry Edmonds? I'm your dad.' Wayne got in the car with him. I didn't.

"After about a year, I started visiting him. I didn't know it at the time, but he was a country-western musician. Right before he came back to this area, he had his own TV and radio show in Buckeye, Ariz. He had his own steak house, too. He played with Little Jimmy Dickens and George Jones.

"I had been fooling around on my brother's guitar. Wayne would bring it along when we visited our dad. Wayne told my father, 'Yeah, Jerry plays, too.' I started playing it in front of him. I played Buck Owens' 'Tiger by the Tail.' He almost started crying. Whatever happened between my mother and father doesn't matter, I loved my dad and he was a great musician."

Life after high school?

"I graduated from Hammond High in 1970 and started a band called 'The Yield.' We played for a couple years, then I got married. Then I got drafted; it was 1972. I was sent to Korea in '73. After the service, I started writing more songs. You know, in all these years, I've never quit writing."

You've performed nationwide. Did some of those honky-tonks get rowdy?

"One night, Mary and I were in Danville, Ill. ... I was up on stage; pool cues and bottles were flying... . I was just up there looking at her, making sure she was OK, thinking, 'This is insane.' Barb's was the name of the joint; the stage was up in the window. Mary went into the john to hide. There was a guy heckling me. That's the bad part of playing in bars... ."

Any incidents or injuries?

"I've had a beer bottle busted over my head – 48 stitches. This side of my forehead, it's paralyzed. I can't even lift this eyebrow. That's why I started getting into my writing more. Still, after a while, you start missing playing in front of an audience. I do a lot of weddings and hog roasts now. Stuff like that."

A few of your favorite artists?

"Growing up in the '60s, I'm a big Beatles fans. I like their early stuff best. 'Love Me Do' – such a soulful song. People hear 'Love Me Do' and think of these four snot-nosed kids shaking their long hair. But if you listen to the bass, the harmonica, that could be four highly talented old black guys up there. Some of the stuff they wrote and did was unbelievable."

Who else do you admire?

"The Who. When I'm playing out, I do a 'Magic Bus' that jumps, man. I loved Jim Croce. He had a delivery that's from that place. You can tell when somebody's just singing, or when it's comin' from that place. Ray Charles came from that place. Voices... . Can John Hiatt sing as well as Luciano Pavarotti or Celine Dion? No. Does it come from that place, and is it really great? Yes. Can he sing 'Ave Maria' like Celine does? No. Can she sing 'Slow Turning' like Hiatt? No. Joe Cocker? He comes from that place. Big Time."

Tell about when you were on "The Oprah Winfrey Show" years ago.

"I was in my 30s then. I get this call from a lady by the name of Deborah DeMayo. She was the executive producer at the time. She said I was selected for Oprah's talent show episode. I told her I didn't know what she was talking about. Finally, I realized Mary had sent one of my CD's to Oprah without telling me."

Tell me about the mandolin.

"The mandolin was invented in 16th-century Florence. Mozart and some of those guys wanted a more metallic sound in their orchestras, so the mandolin was invented. Mandolins never really caught on in orchestras. Nobody really wanted to play them, but they kept making them. Mandolins made their way through the shipping lanes into England, Ireland... . The Irish loved them; they made beautiful folk songs...
"

You composed a special song.

"I recorded a tune written for the mandolin called 'Sweet

Tenderheart.' Jeff, do you know an old-timer named George Wesselhoft? He's one-eighth Potawatomi. He's real active with the American Legion. He came by one day selling raffle tickets.... I had my mandolin out, messing around with this riff.

"George told me he had just come from Rochester, Ind. They had had a ceremony there, where the Potawatomi Indians began their march. It was known as the 'The Trail of Death.'

"George told me about a young girl who helped the Potawatomies while they camped on her father's farm en route to the reservation. She went into their encampment and tried to nurse the sick Indian kids. They've erected a monument there. The Potawatomi called her Tenderheart. The story touched me. As soon as George left I wrote 'Sweet Tenderheart.'"

Talk about your creative process.

"The melody always comes first, then the lyrics. Lyrics are hard to come by, but when they do, it's in a flash. Ten, 15 minutes."

The mill?

"I was at No. 3 Cold Strip East the whole time. Never transferred. ... When you start out in the mill, people sort of become your friends. Then they become your good friends. Then some of them, over 30 years, are damn near like family. You know what I'm sayin'?"

Yeah, I know what you're sayin'.

"I want to go to Nashville and get published as a song writer. Getting published is harder than I ever thought. But I'll keep tryin'.

"There are many musicians I consider heroes. But some of the greatest heroes I've known were people like my union president Tom Hargrove and the brave men and women I worked with in the mill."

* * *

Jerry Edmonds is one of the most diverse musicians I've ever met. A lot of talent has wafted in and out of the steel mills.

Scott Brandush *(Oct. 2005)*

"Keep away from those who try to belittle your ambitions. Small people always do that, but the really great make you believe that you too can become great."
- Mark Twain

Scott Brandush lived in Griffith until eigth grade. His mother and brothers moved to Lowell just before his freshman year of high school. Scott is 24 now.

The soft spoken Brandush is a bit of a loner; he reminds me of a 21st century James Dean. His head is all but shaved, but in the past he has sported a Mohawk of many colors. He possesses a tattoo of a tiger that runs along the calf of his right leg.

Starting out as a dishwasher, he has worked at Schoop's for five years. Today, the boss has him cooking and washing dishes. He is a graduate of Columbia College in Chicago.

For the past year or so, Brandush also has worked part-time as a photographer for the Lowell Tribune; he's very good. Scott stops by my apartment to drop off some of last week's football pics. I usually write the cut lines. I shout for him to come on in while I finish up a story. He takes note of the black-and-white photograph hanging on the wall above my computer's monitor. It shows a dozen ironworkers sitting out on a beam about 500 feet up in the air. Depression era... .

* * *

"Margaret Bourke-White to that shot," Brandush began. "She was a great photographer."

Tell me about your schooling.

"I knew I wanted to do something with photography, but there's so many different avenues. There's studio photography, photojournalism, fine art... . All through college, I was just trying to find out what I wanted to do most. Then I took photojournalism my senior year with John H. White and I knew that's what I wanted to do.

"White also works for the Chicago Sun-Times. He won the Pulitzer Prize back in 1983. He was the greatest teacher that I've had in my entire life. Cool guy. Very inspiring. He made you want to work – made you want to come to class. White was all about the passion of photography. He tried to show why he loved photography to everybody else – it worked. I think he also teaches at Northwestern. The man doesn't sleep. He takes a picture of the sunrise every morning. He took us to the Billy Goat Tavern on lower Wabash. That's where all the journalists hang out.

"My other photojournalism teacher at Columbia was Chuck Osgood; he works for the Chicago Tribune. He was really great, too. But he was more about the professionalism of it. How to get a job."

Continue, please.

"I'd drive to East Chicago every day, then take the South Shore into the city. Some days I'd be gone for like 18 hours – 6:00 a.m. until midnight. They were long days, but they were worth it. I'd go to Chicago, even if I didn't have a class that day, just to do my schoolwork – there weren't any darkrooms around here. They wouldn't let us use a digital. They wanted you to learn the analog techniques, to learn how to develop the film – how to process it yourself."

Kind of like a parent wanting his kid to learn how to drive a stick shift before an automatic.

"Exactly. It really helped you to learn more about how light works."

Do you use mostly digital today?

"Yes, now that Mr. Pilcher purchased that long lens. It saves a lot of money. It's a lot faster. You're not limited to how many pictures you can take. You can just keep shooting."

Any particular subject that you like to shoot most? Nature?

Sports?

"I like sports because there's a lot of action. A lot of movement. Nature, landscape – not so much. Ansel Adams is one of my most hated photographers of all-time. I loathe the zone system that he created. It's like from the whitest white to the blackest black. All the different tints and shades of black-and-white. That's why all of his prints look so perfect. So 'beautiful.'"

What would be the ultimate job?

"Working for the Associated Press. Covering assignments all over the world. Whether it be the running of the bulls in Spain, or where they have that huge tomato fight in that one town. I've never been in a war. Don't know if I'm cut from that stone. But I'd like the chance to cover some kind of conflict."

You've told me you were thinking of joining the Peace Corps.

"It's an option – a way of traveling."

It's also a 2-year commitment. You play the guitar and like to paint, too.

"Yeah, I prefer acoustic guitar, I suppose. I just finished a painting yesterday. I stumbled onto a pair of canvases for six bucks at a yard sale. Thought I better use them. I don't watch TV, with the exception of Comedy Central – 'The Daily Show.' It's the most realistic news program in America."

What kind of music do you like?

"I like fast punk rock, but enjoy all types, including oldies like The Beatles, Pink Floyd, Bob Marley..."

You've gambled in Windsor, Canada and deep-sea fished in Pensacola, Florida. What's next?

"I'll head for Amsterdam this winter. I'd like to spend New Year's Eve in London. And I will have my camera."

Tell me about your family.

"I have four brothers. My dad retired from Inland Steel quite a few years ago. He works somewhere in Ohio now. My parents divorced when I was 6. But dad used to pick us up every Wednesday and take us to Stardust. He was in a bowling league with his steel mill buddies. My mom works at different hospitals as a surgical technician. I live with her."

When did you get bit by the shutterbug?

"When I went to Lowell High School, they didn't have photography classes or film classes. Not much of anything art-oriented. Which is bullshit. But I took yearbook at Lowell with Mr. Charpentier, which was a good class. I got to use cameras in that. But that's about as close as it got. I had to go to Northern Indiana Arts Association in Crown Point. That's where I took my first black-and-white photo class."

How was Mr. Charpentier?

"He was one of my favorite teachers in high school. I really liked Mr. Sufana and Mrs. Magley, too. None of my teachers probably remember who I am. Well, those three probably do.

"We had to write a children's book in one of my classes. I remember talking with Mrs. Magley about it. Come to find out we both had the same all-time favorite children's book – 'The Stinky Cheese Man and Other Fairly Stupid Tales.' They were these off-the-wall stories that rip on all the old famous children's tales, like the 'The Gingerbread Man' and 'The Ugly Duckling.'"

Still keep in touch with some of your childhood buddies from Griffith?

"Not too much. We kind of drifted apart. My brothers are my best friends. When I'm not working, I spend most of my time with them."

Schoop's pretty tough?

"Nine-hour shifts. No breaks. You can't leave. Sunday mornings are the worst. I'm not greedy, I just need whatever it takes to get by. I'm not materialistic at all, unless it comes to something for my camera. Pretty much everything else, hey, things come and go. There are more important things to worry about.

"I need to get an internship. But first I have to get a portfolio together with a resume and cover letter. Newspapers don't care where you went to school. You just need to be able to take good pictures. I've waited long enough."

Probably so, kid.

"You know, Professor White would never single anyone out. He'd leave the room. Everyone would have to put their pictures on the wall. He would come back into the room and say: 'This is great' or 'This sucks – and this is why.' He would critique every photograph, not knowing whose was whose. He gave me an autographed copy of his book. It was comprised of photographs he did of that Cardinal that died. White was good friends with him."

The Final Journey of Joseph Cardinal Bernardin.

"Yeah, that's it. I'm not a religious person, but there are some great shots of him. I have John White to thank for steering me into photojournalism. What he taught was the responsibility of being a photojournalist, of being the eyes for the world."

* * *

Scott Brandush. A bachelor with a bachelor of arts degree. We've
chowed down on chow mein at China Koon before covering a football game and we've sat in $100 ringside seats covering professional prize fights. I like working with him. Photography is his passion.

And I hope he sends me a photo of Big Ben.

It'll be too cold to cover cricket.

"Little Chris" Pabon *(Feb. 2010)*

"I think I go down,
To old Kansas stew
I'm gonna bring back my second cousin,
That little Johnny Cocheroo"
– "Mannish Boy" by Muddy Waters

I'd interview Terri Tarquinee just for her name. But when she e-mailed me about interviewing "Little Chris" Pabon, a red flag went up. Little Chris is Terri's grandson. Moms and grandmas can be biased.

I mean, when a reporter questioned Mama Capone about the antics of her son, "Scarface," her reply was, "Alphonse is a good boy."

And she meant it.

But when Tarquinee told me "Little Chris" has played the blues with the likes of "Pinetop" Perkins and Buddy Guy, well, a green flag went up. "Little Chris," 15, lives in Chesterton with his parents, Val and Nick Simic. He has a younger sibling, "Lil' Joe" Simic.

* * *

How long have you been playing the guitar?

"Since I was 10," "Little Chris" began. "I was playing heavy metal back then. But when I started playing out around town, a lot of guys were playing the blues. I got into it. But I play a little bit of everything. I really like listening to the country station 105.5 out of Valparaiso."

What kind of guitars do you have there?

"This is my Takamine acoustic, and this one is a Takamine acoustic-electric. I also have a Fender Telecaster and a Fender

Stratocaster.

Which one gives you that bluest note?

"Probably, the Strat; the Telecaster is more for country and stuff. Some guys, like Albert Collins, use a Telecaster to play blues."

Name some musicians who you enjoy or ones who have possibly influenced you.

"I have a wide range of artists I like listening to: John Mayer, Stevie Ray Vaughan, Johnny Lang, Stevie Wonder, Martin Sexton, Jimi Hendrix, Stanley Clarke, Hans Zimmer and Opeth come to mind. I like all the old blues guys like Eric Clapton, B.B. King, Muddy Waters and Howlin' Wolf. Robert Johnson was awesome."

How did you get hooked up with those world famous bluesmen?

"It all started when I was jamming with a house band called Funky MojoDaddy. Then, I started playing with other bands, and they would refer me to other people.

"I met Marty Sammon, Buddy Guy's keyboardist, at a bar and lounge on the South Side of Chicago called Artis'. I'd go there and play with Billy Branch & The Sons of the Blues once in a while. Marty was filling in for Billy's keyboardist. He asked me to play with him at Rosa's in Chicago. Then he asked me if I wanted to play with Buddy Guy."

What did you say to that?

"Cool."

How old were you at the time?

"Thirteen."

"Pinetop" Perkins?

"The J. C. Smith Band was putting on a Chicago Blues theme thing in California; he got me, 'Pinetop,' Willie 'Big Eyes' Smith, and James and Mike Wheeler to go out there. That's how I got to jam with 'Pinetop.'"

"Pinetop" is 80 years older than you.

"Yeah, he's little bit out of it; but still plays amazingly well. He's a really cool guy."

For the most part, you perform solo. Name a few venues where you've done shows.

"In Chicago, I've played at the Blues Festival, Buddy Guy's Legends, and Rosa's, to name a few. I've also performed at Villa Montalvo Art Center near San Francisco and in Hawaii."

What about locally?

"I play at Leroy's Hot Stuff in Porter a lot."

You're too young to drive. How do you get to Leroy's?

"Mom and Dad take me there. They always stick around for the show and help me unpack and pack stuff. They're very supportive."

You didn't go on stage until 10 last night at Leroy's; you had school the next morning. Wasn't that past your bedtime?

"I was done playing by 11. In Chicago, a minor can go into any bar with a parent or guardian. In Indiana, it has to be a bar-restaurant. When I perform at a place like Leroy's, I have to sit in the restaurant section until I play. When I'm done performing, I have to go back to the restaurant section."

I've been to Leroy's Hot Stuff a time or two; once covered a poker run there for the newspaper.

"They have benefits there all the time; Leroy's a good guy."

Have you ever been jamming on stage and spotted, say, your science teacher, having a beer?

"Yes, I've actually seen a few of my teachers in bars; it's kind of weird. But, hey, everyone has their own lives, you know?"

When they see it's you, do they stick around to listen to you play?

"Sometimes."

How do you fare in the classroom?

"I usually get on the principal's honor roll, but this time, I just got honor roll because I was playing out at the Anaheim Convention Center by Disneyland for four days and I got behind in my studies. I was out there for a whole week."

What do the school girls think about you? Are you a rock star at Chesterton High School?

"Not really. A lot of people know I play guitar, but they don't really understand it because I play music that's not mainstream any more. They're more into rap and hip-hop. I like all that stuff too, but I play mostly blues."

Do you sing?

"Oh, yeah."

Has your voice changed in the last year or so?

"Yeah, that's been a weird thing. I had to change the keys to all my songs because my voice got a lot deeper. I think my voice is getting better."

Height and weight?

"I'm almost 5-feet, 7-inches tall and weigh 125 pounds. When I go to a blues club for the first time, everybody is kinda weirded out when they see this little white kid. But they like it when I play."

Have you written any songs?

"About 13; I've been recording with a guy named Donald Hayes from Los Angeles. We send tracks back and forth over the computer. Musicians from all over the country have been playing my songs because they all have home studios. They'll record something, put it on the track and send it back to Donald."

Still take lessons?

"Yeah, from Mark Hague; he's a member of Mr. Blotto, a jam band out of Chicago. Mark gives me lessons once a month; I'm trying to learn more theory right now."

"Little Chris," could you uncase that Strat and bend a few blue notes by the late, great Stevie Ray Vaughn? "Pride and Joy" is one of my faves.

"Sure.

"...Yeah I love my baby... heart and soul

Love like ours wont never grow old

She's my sweet little thang... she's my pride and joy.

She's my sweet little baby; I'm her little lover boy."

Thanks, I needed that.

* * *

In appearance, "Pinetop" Perkins and "Little Chris" are night and day. But one thing for certain – they sure can play.

The freshman from Chesterton High is the real deal.

Tyler Lennox Bush *(Nov. 2011)*

"Uncommon from a common land
With a fine-tuned mind... a heart
And a calloused hand
Not black
Not white
But skin of tarnished tin
Of Rustedblue
Blue like the collar that I wear
Like my father over there
Like you"
– Tyler Lennox Bush, from "The Tin I'm In"

I believe it was an open-mic poetry thing about 10 years ago, where I first met the brothers Bush, Chad and Tyler. A few months later, they hired me to narrate a piece they had written entitled "The Football Smith" honoring high school football coach, Brad Smith.

Ty Bush, 34, is single and lives in Crown Point; he graduated from Crown Point High School.

Bush has worn many hats, including creative director of Rusted Blue, a production company.

* * *

You're a die-hard Pittsburgh Steeler fan.

"Die-hard," he began. "We're originally from Pittsburgh. Dad was a steel worker. We moved to Northwest Indiana in 1984, but never lost our roots. Our cultural legacy is that of steel people on the hills and valleys of western Pennsylvania.

"We're much akin to the coal mining people of West Virginia

steeped in the oral tradition of storytelling and blue-collar values. It shows up in some of my work."

Did the mill where your dad worked shut down?

"Yes, but he was able to transfer to LTV in East Chicago. The last bastion of hope for the steel industry in this country was in NWI."

Those steel mill scenes in the "The Deer Hunter" were in your neck of the woods.

"Absolutely."

Ty, I can usually tell when someone is from Pennsylvania by their accent.

"The western Pennsylvania dialect is very unique. It has a real indigenous sound to it. They round their O's and roll their L's a lot. There's an eastern European influence with that Appalachian southern dialect."

You were a good athlete at CPHS.

"I was a three-sport athlete – baseball, wrestling and football."

What positions did you play in football and baseball?

"I was a wide receiver and defensive back and a catcher in baseball; I loved that shit."

Did you wrestle for Coach Vlink?

"Yeah, Scott's a good guy. A coached the freshman team at CPHS for one year. I also wrestled and played football at Wabash College. I was fortunate enough to be on some great teams at Wabash. I was an Academic All-American in '97."

Your degree?

"Liberal Arts; I graduated in '99 and also did an off-campus fellowship with the New York artists' program; it was a professional submersion in the arts community. I took some classes at NYU and worked for a theater-production and film-production company.

"I came back to the East Coast after earning my degree at Wabash and spent another five years of my life in NYC. I kind of departed from doing sculpture work and set design and decided to specifically study acting.

"I had been taking classes at Second City in Chicago, but wanted to focus on method training and some bare bones acting training. Second City was able to provide me with a lot of improvisation and comedic sketch writing. But I really wanted to get my chops as far as a real acting education. I took the opportunity to study with the Atlantic Theater Co.; I went on to work for them as a carpenter for a number of seasons."

Rusted Blue?

"I wanted to have a branded concept, something I could use as a platform in order to launch my own career as a storyteller and creator of vehicles. Hopefully, in the long run, media-driven short film narratives on our website."

The name Rusted Blue?

"It's a metaphor for my legacy, which comes from my cultural heritage in blue-collar values and coming from the rusted places like Gary and Aliquippa, Pa., and telling the stories that come from those places – uncommon people from common places. Those are the people I'm most interested in."

You remind me of me.

"I've responded to a lot of your pieces because they come from that same place."

What was your theatrical debut in NYC?

"Sam Shepherd's 'True West.' I like those masculine, virile characters who also are insecure."

Who else is involved with Rusted Blue?

"My two business partners at the top of the tree are Charlie Frasor, who is a local singer-songwriter, and Manolie Pappas who owns the Zodiac Cafe Lounge here in Crown Point. We have a number of other collaborators as well."

Is being the creative director of Rusted Blue a full-time gig?

"I also manage the Country Lounge in Hobart and I still bartend and do hospitality consulting. I also work with Smartmouth Design in Chicago which is a hospitality design company headed up by Alex Morales."

Ty Bush in five years?

"Well, I hope the list of collaborators we work with and the artists we represent will only continue to grow. Hopefully, the company will be shaped by the people who join it. I always wanted it to be a place where people connect and collaborate.

"Also, along the five-year plan, I'm looking at getting an MFA degree. I'd like to get that kind of education and help grow the company. I'm hoping that will happen in the next two years.

"In the meantime, we're also giving birth to a non-profit with

Rusted Blue called Dream Grind Give."

Tell me more.

"We hope to do a camp in the summers with at-risk kids from NWI. We want to create an opportunity for them to become cross-cultural. We want to bring kids from places like Lake Village, East Chicago and Gary and getting them to all work on a collaborative art project every summer for two weeks. We'll use the artists at Rusted Blue to facilitate that camp."

Possible summer project?

"Creating a mural in downtown Gary or Lowell – a theater production, perhaps. We want the kids to talk about their issues and overcome the racial boundaries and create something.

"Dream Grind Give will be headed up by Andrew Knies of Hobart. We're putting together a board of directors."

* * *

Bush might not have been born in NWI – he came here when he was 8 – but he has fused well. He's a grass-roots guy who gets things done by rolling up his sleeves and doing the work.

He's bona fide sodium chloride – salt of the earth.

Ty Bush has iron oxide runnin' through his veins.

Mary McClelland *(Dec. 2010)*

"Ain't no man can avoid being born average, but there ain't no man got to be common."
– Satchel Paige

I interviewed gallery manager Mary McClelland in the waning days of South Shore Art's exhibit "We Are the Ship: The Story of Negro League Baseball" at the Center for Visual and Performing Arts in Munster.

The memorabilia on display from a private collection was historically fascinating, and the portraits by Kadir Nelson were breathtaking.

McClelland, 43, lives in Hammond and has raised two adult children, Zack and Leesa. She volunteers for many community groups and is on the board of the Downtown Hammond Council.

Mary also portrays the "Mean Elf" every year at the Hammond Holiday Kickoff and is the owner of a Great Dane and a Chihuahua, both of which are deaf.

* * *

Have you lived in Hammond all your life?

"Yes, I love Hammond. My father was raised in Kentucky, but eventually became a steel worker at LTV. Dad always reminded me of sheriff Andy Taylor from the Andy Griffith Show."

Mary, because I grew up in Newton County, I used to tell my buddies in the mill that I didn't realize that show was a comedy until I graduated high school. I thought it was a docudrama.

"There is something about the steel mills that has always fascinated me. I can remember when it was still Youngstown or J&L and we got to take the tour. I used to ditch school when I was at Hammond High because I was a horrible kid; they had just finished the Cline Avenue extension I'd drive up there and I thought nothing was more beautiful than that industrial landscape.

"I hate the winter. Sometimes, I ask myself, 'Why am I still here?' But there's something about being near a large body of water like Lake Michigan." *Mary, that's the way I feel about the Kankakee River.*

"We all need each other and we all have something to offer each other, whether we're from Jasper, Lake, Porter, Newton, Pulaski, LaPorte or Starke counties. There's no way we're going to survive in this state unless we work together. The people downstate don't like us."

Northwest Indiana is the 51st state of the union.

"Absolutely; even people in Chicago have this mistaken notion that those of us from NWI are like backwater folk."

Hey, I resemble that remark.

"They don't believe we have culture, and anything coming out of this region couldn't possibly be valuable. I have people from Chicago question whether we're on the same time zone. It's tricky, because we're in this weird, um..."

Bermuda Triangle?

"Exactly. It's like the rest of Indiana doesn't look at us as part of Indiana, and Chicago doesn't look at us as a suburb. That's why this seven-county area has to band together."

College?

"Purdue (University) Calumet; I have a degree in English literature. Everybody wanted to take creative writing with the legendary Charlie Tinkham. I finally got a class with Charlie and he ended up getting sick, so he was out that semester."

Mary, about 10 years ago, when I was still in the mill, the folks at a joint labor-management facility in East Chicago set it up so I could take a one-on-one writing class with professor Tinkham. The lady behind the front desk at PUC said that was impossible because the class was for college graduates.

"What happened?"

Once I finished the course, Charlie gave me an "A" in Creative

Writing 501. He was a beautiful person.

"He was a treasure. I did have him for philosophy – existentialism. He could give you great constructive criticism and, at the same time be so incredibly supportive. He believed everybody had something to say."

Tell me about the CPVA.

"The Center for Visual and Performing Arts has several tenants: South Shore Arts, NWI Symphony Orchestra, Munster Chamber of Commerce, Ridgewood Arts Foundation... ."

Do residents of NWI take full advantage of what not-for-profit groups like South Shore Arts offer?

"Jeff, you were just upstairs enjoying that amazing exhibit. The ads have run in the local newspapers; we got the word out, and time and time again, I'm amazed that more people don't come in. This building we're sitting in is a gem."

How long has the Center been here?

"Since 1989. South Shore Arts will be celebrating 75 years in 2011. We started out in the Minas Department Store."

What's next on your agenda?

"Our Salon show, which is a juried exhibit."

What have been a few of the more popular exhibits?

"Well, (Andy) Warhol was our first blockbuster. We had a ton of school kids come out for that. The Salon Show that I mentioned is very popular because you'll have photography, drawings, paintings, sculptures... .

"We have an entry fee and a different juror every year. We give out $10,000 in awards. People love that show because you get everything from amateurs to professionals. It's all anonymous when the juror is judging the work."

When will the Salon Show begin?

"Jan. 9."

Controversial exhibits?

"I had an exhibit hanging up in the atrium around 2005. The artist, Augustine Portillo, is a fabulous oil painter who lives in Mexico. He had created a body of work that expressed what he thought about a certain faction of Americans, let's say. It was sort of a sarcastic look at the 'haves.'"

Interesting.

"One of the paintings portrayed some men in drag; another painting was of men wearing panties and garters only. The rich people in these paintings were portrayed in an ugly way."

Let me guess; the bourgeoisie took offense.

"The elderly patrons loved that exhibit; they'd tell me how funny it was. It was some people my age, in their late 30s and early 40s, who were so offended. Our general manager at the time, the late John Mybeck, was getting negative calls at his office across the street. He came over to see the exhibit for himself and simply told me, 'It's fine.'"

Do you paint?

"Walls; I'm a performance artist. And one day, darn it, I'm going to be a stand-up comedian."

Your next play?

"A musical comedy called 'Ruthless' at the Towle Theater.

When is it?

"The last weekend in February and the first two weekends of March."

I'll have to check it out; I've been in a few plays at the Towle.

"Have you ever been to Beatniks On Conkey"?

Oh, yeah.

"The Towle and Beatniks are gems. Black-box theaters can be phenomenal; you're right there. The first show I did at the Towle was 'The Search for Signs of Intelligent Life in the Universe.' I decided to cast fate to the wind and audition; I got the lead."

Did you "break a leg"?

"I received the Best Actress Award from the NWI Excellence in Theater Foundation. It was a phenomenal experience and cast.

"Jeff, there are actually things going on in Hammond."

* * *

I arrived a little early for my interview with McClelland. That gave me a chance to take in the Negro League Baseball exhibit. I was the only person in the gallery although the parking lot of The CVPA was nearly full.

Mary informed me that a lot of people come to the Center for theater or brunch, and because of that, they get a huge cross section of people.

Eventually, an elderly man of color entered the gallery. Like me, he was blown away by the exhibit.

McClelland told me, "Art is not something people should fear; it is not an elitist pastime."

And I know the gallery manager with the blue-collar roots is correct because that old timer and I had a great conversation about our national pastime. He let out a belly laugh when I told him I had read that "Cool Papa" Bell was so fast he could be under the covers of his bed before the room got dark after flipping the light switch. We also had a heart to heart about how some people consider Josh Gibson the black Babe Ruth, but there are other folks who consider Ruth, the white Josh Gibson.

And that's the NWI Mary McClelland is talkin' about.

The Good Earth

George Bunce *(Nov. 2008)*

"Good company in a journey makes the way seem shorter."
– Izaak Walton

George Bunce came into this world the same year (1919) the Chicago White Sox threw the World Series. It was a scandalous affair – the rigged series, not the birth of Bunce.

Bunce is a retired Griffith High School science teacher; he has been married to Evelyn for almost 62 years. They raised five children.

* * *

"I grew up in Bippus, a small town of 200 people," Bunce began. "It's near the Fort Wayne area. The late sportscaster, Chris Schenkel came from Bippus."

Earliest childhood recollections?

"I remember when Warren Harding died; I was about 3 1/2 years old. My granddad had a cousin who lived a few miles south of Harding's hometown of Marion, Ohio. We were out there on a visit at the same time that Harding was lying in state.

"Soldiers stood on guard in front of one of those big houses situated close to the main part of town, the kind of house local businessmen usually lived in. There was a wreath hanging in the door; there was a big crowd of people.

"I was miserable because I had to wear shoes and dress clothes – it was hot weather. All I could think of was getting in where the chickens were dusting themselves off. Back home, I liked to play in the dust.

Of course, I'd get a few chicken lice on me. A chicken louse won't bite people; it'll eventually fall off. But my mother wasn't one to wait for nature to take its course. Her delousing station was located on the back porch; it consisted of a galvanized washtub and a bar of Fels-Naphtha."

A bar of what?

"Fels-Naphtha; it's a potent brand of laundry soap.

"I remember the campaign of 1928. Al Smith was a Democrat. He also was a Catholic – that was the big reason he was defeated. The church we belonged to did not approve of politics from the pulpit – some denominations did. Certain preachers would wave their arms while shouting to their congregations, 'Save our homes, save our church, save our country – vote for Herbert Hoover!'

"My dad was a Republican, but he did not vote for Hoover. We had good Catholic neighbors; we were not worried that they would ruin the country. But there were people who were afraid Smith would turn the place over to the pope."

George, this column will run near Veterans Day. You served in World War II.

"Yes, I tried to get in the Navy, but I was too near-sighted. I waited for the Army to draft me, which it eventually did.

"Being a member of the Church of the Brethren, I was eligible for public service (as a conscientious objector), but I figured not to fight the likes of Hitler and Mussolini was like committing suicide.

"I carried a stretcher rather than a rifle; I was a surgical technician in an Army general hospital. We had the same basic training as the infantry. Eventually, I was sent to Camp Carson (now Fort Carson) in Colorado Springs. From there, I went to North Africa, then Italy, then Southern France, and then Eastern France, near Dijon. Those fields of bright-yellow, flowering mustard grown in a checkerboard pattern was a beautiful sight."

Tell me about sunny Italy.

"I was in Italy about the time the Italians told Mussolini he was through. We were about five miles from the front lines and were barely set up when our first patient came in. A piece of shrapnel had taken his entire chin off. While we were stationed in Colorado, some of us had purchased silver dollars as souvenirs. We donated them."

To what?

"The soldier's missing bone was replaced by melted-down silver.

We had some outstanding surgeons in our outfit."

The natives?

"The Italian people that we were in contact hated Mussolini and the Fascists. After landing us, the Navy was anxious to get their ship out of there because the Germans still had some air force left. There was an Italian woman standing by a fence hollering at us. We had some Italian-Americans in our outfit who could understand her. She was desperately trying to tell us there were mines on the beach. Boy, we froze.

"The woman risked her life by walking through that minefield; she showed our engineers where the mines were; she had watched the Germans put them there. That saved a lot of time; we didn't have to use the detectors. That was my first impression of the Italians.

"I remember this Italian man, probably in his 50s; he had a donkey cart heavily loaded with broken-up cement and stone from a bombed-out building. The cart was stuck in a rut. Donkeys know their own strength; they're not about to exert themselves beyond that.

"The Italian was cussing out the donkey. Four of us Americans joined in by also cussing out the donkey in our broken Italian. That amused the Italian; his anger changed to laughter. Then he started cussing out the donkey in broken English. It was quite a cultural exchange. We put our shoulders into the cart and got it out the rut; the donkey had to move then.

"As far as I know, that Italian man is still walking about half sideways going out across that field, waving at us, shouting, 'Grazie, grazie!'

"In World War II, we had an advantage over today's soldier. We knew who the enemy was, where he was at, and why we were there. And we were surrounded by friendly people – sometimes they were Germans. Not all Germans were Nazis."

After retiring from teaching you became a full-time environmentalist.

"Yes."

Tell me a little about Dunes State Park and National Dunes Lakeshore.

"Some of the same people, or their sons and daughters, that helped get the state park (1925) also were involved in adding the national lakeshore to the state park. We had a lot of help from Illinois because the (Indiana) representative from that district opposed the park.

He wanted to build steel mills.

"Whether old codgers like me like it or not, the younger generations are taking our place. Hopefully, we've trained them well. I have a feeling today's environmentalists are going to go farther than we did – they already have."

* * *

Don't let him fool you; Mr. Bunce went to Washington. He testified at eight different sessions of congress, in both houses, to their subcommittees that dealt with national parks.

Thanks to combined efforts by the Izaak Walton League, the Audubon Society, Sierra Club, and The Nature Conservancy back in 1976, the state of Indiana was able to purchase a 300-acre tract of land known as Hoosier Prairie. Bunce was a major player. In 1977, Hoosier Prairie was named a state nature preserve.

Bunce is an authority on the Kankakee River and has been named Griffith's Man of the Year. He has been honored for his many years of service by the Izaak Walton League, the Audubon Society and the AFL-CIO; he was a union rep for his fellow teachers.

Also hanging from a wall within his modest Griffith home is a plaque he received more than a decade ago: 50-year member of the American Legion.

George Bunce is an inherent pacifist, but he will go to war for his planet and its people when the chips are down.

You can bet a silver dollar on it.

Barb Dodge *(Jan. 2011)*

"If you come down to the river
Bet you gonna find some people who live
You don't have to worry if you got no money
People on the river are happy to give"
– John Fogerty

Barb Dodge, 76, is one of the best birders I know. And you can bet your sweet-singin' dickcissel (Spiza americana), I know more than a few bird watchers.

On my way to Dodge's home, I turned left at the only stop sign in Sumava Resorts and soon drove by the spot where I learned to swim, Sumava Beach. Barb lives three houses upstream from the beach and about 25 feet from the Kankakee River.

Looking out her back window is like looking into an aviary. While we chatted, slate-colored juncos, white-breasted nuthatches, tufted titmice, pine siskins, hairy woodpeckers, chickadees, goldfinches, blue jays and cardinals dined on suet, thistle and sunflower seeds a few feet from us.

Dodge's family moved from Chicago to Cedar Lake when she was 14. She has lived in Sumava since 2004. Her son, Devin, lives upstairs and she lives downstairs in a house that a lawyer from Chicago had built in 1934 when Sumava was but 7 years old. The living room walls and ceiling are beautifully designed and made of knotty pine. The place is heated by several wood burners.

* * *

Barb, I've always thought Sumava as a microcosm of Cedar Lake.

"Oh, yes; they're so much alike," she began. "I love Sumava's history; it's very similar to Cedar Lake's history."

Did a Realtor help you find this house?

"I had been looking for a place on the river for several years. I was driving through here and stopped to talk to somebody. I was told that this house was for sale, but wasn't advertised. So I pulled in the driveway and immediately saw a pileated woodpecker in a tree on the property.

"The owner came out and affirmed they were selling, then took me inside the house. Between the rustic living room created by a master builder and the pileated woodpecker pounding at that big river birch in the backyard, I was sold."

Love at first sight. Barb, I can't believe the amount of birds you have at the feeders.

"Most of the time, I can easily count 200 birds out there at a time. The only time there isn't birds at the feeders is when the Cooper's hawk pays me a visit."

Do you still see pileated woodpeckers in your backyard?

"Oh, yeah. He shows up at the feeder two or three times a day. There's a pair of them. They nest in the woods on the north side of the river."

When did you become interested in birdwatching?

"My mother, aunt and grandmother were casual birders. When we'd go on vacations, mom would make me keep a list of the birds we saw. She told me, 'Some day, you're going to appreciate this list, Barb.'

"As a teenager, I wasn't that interested. But, I kept her Peterson's bird book from 1934 with her bird list in it and just kind of picked it up. After I got married, we lived in a wooded area in Cedar Lake that was full of birds."

Is feeding the birds to this extent expensive?

"I spend more on bird food than I do on my own grocery budget."

Do you own the vacant lot next to you?

"Yes, it's a native wildflower and grass meadow – not an alien out there."

Get any help from The Nature Conservancy?

"Oh, yeah; my son used to work for them. The Nature Consevancy was a tremendous help starting us out on that."

Rare birds you've spotted in Northwest Indiana that appear on your lifetime list.

"Varied thrush, saw whet owl, ibis... The rarest birds I've ever seen on my own were a pair of whooping cranes about seven or eight years ago. Biologists had raised a flock in captivity and trained the whooping cranes to migrate back and forth from Wisconsin to Florida.

"The whooping cranes had to make several stops, of course. Well, lo and behold, one of the stops for whooping cranes No. 1 and 2 (the birds were banded) was Howkinson Marsh in Cedar Lake. I just happened to be there. I have a video tape of them flying right over my head."

On Jan. 3, you conducted the annual Christmas Bird Count.

"Yes, I've been overseeing that since '89. We start out at the Grand Kankakee Marsh County Park and cover an area that has a 15-mile radius. We end up at Howkinson Marsh."

The spring and Christmas bird counts are a lot of fun. I can usually spot the birds, but often need someone like you or Chris Salberg to identify them. Those "LBBs" (little brown birds) can be tough.

"I seem to absorb bird identification more by hearing than by seeing; I go a lot by sounds."

Barb, you mentioned your mother's bird book by Peterson. Roger Tory Peterson once said: "I can recognize the calls of practically every bird in North America. There are some in Africa I don't know, though." Let's drift back to Sumava Resorts.

"I like Sumava because it's a town. I'm not totally isolated and yet I don't have neighbors who are sitting right on top of me, either. In Cedar Lake, they put those condos in next to me on the lake front. They just towered over me; it was like we were living in a fish bowl.

"Here, I have my neighbors for security, but I have my privacy, too. Sumava is charming. No one has a mailbox; we all walk to our own little post office."

Barb, the first three years of my life were spent above that post office when it simultaneously served as a Bohemian bakery. My father had to fork out $30 a month rent, but said the NIPSCO bills were pretty good in the winter living above a bakery. I can still smell the apricot *kolaches and fresh-baked bread.*

"We also have our Duck Festival every summer at Sumava Beach. Tobes has the best pizza I've ever eaten, and I've eaten a lot of pizzas around Chicago. We eat dinner at Lukes Restaurant quite a bit."

I remember that place being packed in the 1960s: frog legs, walleye fillets, fried mushrooms, cole slaw, homemade bread, long-necked bottles of Stroh's Bohemian-style beer... . Venus Lukes told me the worst flood in Sumava history was when the dike broke on Easter Sunday, 1950.

"I was going to Lowell High School at that time because there was no Hanover Central yet. I remember thinking, 'Who in their right mind would ever live in Sumava Resorts and be flooded out all the time?' And here I am."

Barb, it was that pileated woodpecker that got you to move to Sumava.

* * *

Dodge has given me many pointers on birdwatching. She might not be a lifelong Sumavan, but she's fitting in just fine.

Welcome to the 'hood, Barb.

Jim Hitz *(April 2010)*

"'What Grandad!' I exclaimed. 'Planting an almond tree?' And he, bent as he was, turned around and said, 'My son, I carry on as if I should never die.'"
— *Nikos Kazantzakis, from his novel "Zorba the Greek"*

Arbor Day is Friday, so I thought I'd feature a blue-ribbon panelist in Jim Hitz. He's the executive director of Taltree Arboretum and Gardens near Valparaiso.

Hitz, 55, also is a board member of the Kankakee Valley Historical Society who lives a walnut's throw from Taltree in Valparaiso with his wife, Jill. They have raised three children.

Although Hitz was born in Harvey, Ill., and grew up in several other urban settings including Detroit and New Jersey, he swears he's a country boy at heart.

I believe him.

* * *

"When I was 12, living in Detroit, I spent a summer on my uncle's dairy farm outside Kouts," Hitz began. "I worked on the farm and loved being around agriculture and the countryside."

Why the interest in trees?

"Golf."

Huh?

"When I was in eighth grade, my friend lent me a set of golf clubs. I hit the ball so poorly, I always was in the woods. I thought to myself, 'I better start learning how to identify these trees because this is where I spend all my time.'"

But seriously.

"Nature and the environment have always been important to me."

College?

"Undergraduate at Western Michigan University, then I received an agricultural and natural resources teaching certificate at Michigan State University, and then I earned a master's degree in horticulture from Purdue University."

Jim, this green space is gorgeous. How did it come to be?

"Damien and Rita Gabis acquired and gave the land to the foundation. Although Taltree wasn't officially founded until 1998, I started working here in 1995.

"In 1996, we did our first little prairie strip working with the U.S. Fish and Wildlife Service. In '98, we did 35 acres of prairie in the middle section of Taltree, along with 16 acres of reforestation; we planted 7,000 trees. In '99, we did the savanna wetland."

Total acreage?

"About 300 acres. When we first started Taltree, some people thought we were a wildlife refuge."

Why?

"If you build it, they will come. Since we planted the prairies, created the wetlands and reforested on a large scale, we've had a wide range of mammals, amphibians and reptiles that have made their home here. More than 80 species of birds have been sighted and confirmed here; we're listed by the Audubon Society as one of the top birding places in the country. But it's not a refuge for them."

For whom then?

"We're creating a 'people refuge' in an area that is developing tremendously. And we're not anti-development; we all need homes and places to live. That's why a place like Taltree becomes incredibly valuable; it becomes an oasis, in the midst of development."

Most "oases" in the Chicago area have interstate highways beneath them and charge outlandish prices.

"Someone asked me, 'Doesn't it bother you that they're building subdivisions around Taltree?' I said: 'No, the land on the Valparaiso Moraine is not good agricultural land, especially where we're at. Most of the topsoil has eroded away. This is the better land to locate houses on.' You wisely choose what is the best usage of a particular area; that's part of stewardship – and it's not always politically popular.

"People and nature can co-exist. We were created to be part of this and we have a responsibility of stewardship. And stewardship doesn't mean destroy; it means taking care of nature in a lot of different ways.

"Every time I walk out onto the prairies here and see our big burr oaks that are over 250 years old, I'm thankful that 200 year ago, someone left those trees alone. And somebody 100 years ago, left those trees alone."

James, I believe you have an affinity for the mighty oak.

"My favorite genus. There are more than 450 types of oaks worldwide. I'm secretary of the International Oak Society, by the way. Let me show you what we call Oak Islands, it's a collection of oaks from around the world."

I thought you'd never ask. Don't black oaks tend to get diseases?

"They can. If you drive along I-65 and Fair Oaks Farms, you'll see those short oaks in the median. Not that many years ago, there was a massive woods of very tall oaks in that area."

I remember; it was on the east side of I-65.

"Yes; in the early '80s, anything that was on the high ground of what is now Fair Oaks Farms was all black oak savanna. The trees in the median got diseased and died."

Yeah, what about the savanna?

"Three-and-a-half miles of oaks were cut down by Prudential Insurance Co."

Stewardship, indeed.

"At the time, it was very controversial. The young trees in the median are now replacing the dead ones."

What's with all the new construction?

"This is going to be Taltree Railway Garden, our next big garden project. It's scheduled to open in 2011. The depot building will be a replica of an early 1900 country railway depot. Behind it will be an exquisite garden with mountains and water features going through it. The plant populations will feature miniature representations of large ecosystems. G-scale trains will run through it."

Very cool. And what have we here?

"This is the Hitz Family Rose Garden. After my mother passed away in 2003, my father donated the funds to build this garden in her memory. My brother, who is a landscape architect, designed it.

"The gardens of Taltree all meander, with the exception of this one, which is very linear; there's a pattern to it. I'll give you a moment to guess what it is."

I see several 6-foot-square, very well kept, raised beds accented by granite blocks and a variety of fruit trees in full bloom.

"If I showed you an aerial view, you'd pick it up pretty fast. This layout is based on 'Scrabble.'"

It is! And that bed in the center would be the four double-letter squares surrounding the star in the middle of the board!

"Mom loved 'Scrabble' and roses. The Duneland Rose Society has its monthly meetings at Taltree; they've helped out maintaining the family rose garden."

This is interesting, the Native Plant Garden.

"Yes, these are some of the plants you'll see in our prairies, but here, they're all labeled. We're an educational foundation at Taltree."

You've all done a great job.

"Jeff, you come out here and forget that you're just a short distance from the steel mills. You're in a special place. It's been my privilege to help build it."

What's on the horizon?

"We're in the middle of a big master plan that will develop over the next 10 to 15 years. Part of the fun of working here is seeing it come to fruition. It's something my grandchildren and great-grandchildren can walk through and some day say, 'Wow, Grandpa helped do all this.'"

* * *

Jim Hitz is not only a country boy at heart, he's a good man.

And, fortunately for us, he's a bad golfer.

Mike Echterling *(Aug. 2010)*

"If you want a friend in Washington, get a dog."
– Harry S Truman

My first contact with Mike Echterling was through YouTube about eight months ago; he commended a rough-cut video that Pat Wisniewski and I created promoting our documentary about the Grand Kankakee Marsh.

Our interview took place at the Conservation Building at the Lake County Fairgrounds. Echterling is conservation chairman of Lake County Fish & Game Protective Association.

Whereas Mike is a Little Calumet River kind of a guy who was raised in Munster, his second-cousins – Kevin, Scott and John Echterling – are Kankakee River kinds of guys – I went to school with the rough-and-tumble Echterling boys.

Mike, 41, lives in Highland and has been married to Angie for 20 years. He says they have two "four-legged children" – Jack and Blue.

* * *

Tell me a little about Jack and Blue.

"Jack is a Lab-Weimaraner mix and Blue is a Portuguese water dog."

I would've guessed Blue was the Weimaraner

"Jack looks like a charcoal lab – not chocolate, but charcoal gray."

I'm not familiar with Portuguese water dogs; fill me in on Ol' Blue. "Portuguese water dogs were almost extinct. The Water Dog Breeding Association has been real particular about the dogs they allow to breed. Ideally, a Portuguese water dog weighs about 65 pounds."

Are they hunting dogs?

"They were fishermen's dogs. Portuguese water dogs can dive and untangle nets. I buy Blue rope toys and he takes them apart; he doesn't tear them up, he unties them. President (Barack) Obama has a Portuguese water dog; I had mine first."

Jack and Blue sound like "good people," but tell me about when Mike Echterling, the biped, was just a "pup."

"I grew up on Hart's Ditch and Independence Park in Munster. We spent a lot of time at Schoon's Ditch and the Brickyard, too. The Brickyard is an old 20-acre clay pit; it has some really deep spots.

"My friends and I fished every day in the summertime. We'd also fish in a pond at Meadows Park, but the fish wouldn't bite on red worms there; they liked lunch meat – greasy salami skin was the best."

Makes sense to me; I've always preferred salami or pastrami over worms or crickets. Did you play sports for Munster High School?

"No, but a group of us who grew up in the same neighborhood would play tackle football without pads against the high school football team. We got in trouble because a couple of the Mustang players got hurt; we kicked their asses."

You're an Echterling, all right. What happened to your right eye?

"In '95, I was delivering a tanker of vinegar to a salad dressing factory in Beaver Dam, Wis. While pumping off the load, the hose popped off. The pressure from the blast of vinegar washed off my cornea.

"I was wearing my safety glasses, but it hit me so hard my entire face was black and blue. When my wife and friends came to pick me up, I looked like I'd been beaten with a baseball bat. They want to do a transplant, but if the transplant doesn't work, I'll lose my eyeball."

Was your right eye your master eye?

"Yeah, I had to switch hands for shooting; it took a lot of practice. And don't throw anything at me because I won't catch it; I don't have stereoscopic vision – no depth perception."

What do you do for a living?

"I'm disabled because of rheumatoid arthritis; once a month I have to go for Remicade infusions. I'm also immune suppressed because of the Remicade. I'd be a liability to anyone who would hire me."

That's a cruel, crippling disease.

"I started off on a cane when I was about 33; then crutches, then a walker, then a wheelchair just before I got my new knees in 2004. It took about three years before my knees were completely gone – bone on bone, no cartilage. I lost an inch-and-a-half in height. When I got my knees replaced, I regained the inch-and-a-half thanks to a urethane buffer that goes in between the metal parts of my artificial knees."

Lake County Fish & Game?

"Lake County Fish & Game is actually the oldest independent conservation group in Indiana; its been around since 1920. It was first organized to help save Wolf Lake.

"Lake County Fish & Game also initiated the clean-up at Lake George where Lost Marsh golf course is now (in North Hammond). We also help stock Wolf Lake with walleye in conjunction with Perch America every year."

Is yours a paid position?

"No, we're all volunteers. There are about 320 members."

Must members live in Lake County?

"No, we have people who belong within a 50-mile radius. We're all about using natural resources, not just protecting natural resources. Leave it better than you found it; don't abuse it, but use it."

Pet peeves?

"People from Northwest Indiana travel to Potato Creek, Tippecanoe (River) and Turkey Run (state parks) to have fun and to see nature, and we have the Little Cal, Deep River and the Kankakee River right here in Lake County. The Little Cal is full of blue herons, wood ducks, muskrats, beavers, deer, steelhead, bass, pike, crappie bluegills..."

You failed to mention one of Lake County's four rivers.

"The Grand Calumet River is bad. The (Department of Natural Resources) says: don't eat anything out of the Grand Cal."

Can the Grand Cal be saved? More than a century worth of toxins have accumulated in that river.

"The Feds are doing a cleanup, but, in some places the sediment is 11 feet thick; they're only taking off 3 feet, putting down a liner and packing that with sand and gravel. The 'cleanup' is not cleaning up the entire mess."

* * *

Echterling enjoys hunting pheasant and duck, but doesn't hunt quail because there isn't enough of them.

He said, "Leave those birds alone; let them come back."

Echterling also teaches hunters' education courses at Cabela's, maintaining: "I don't have kids, so I teach everybody else's kids. The world's a little safer every time we have a hunters' ed class."

Dan McDowell *(Oct. 2012)*

"That man is the richest whose pleasures are the cheapest."
– Henry David Thoreau

Dan McDowell recently took me on a tour of a 5-acre Eden he calls Ike Prairie.

The property is owned by the Spring Lake chapter of the Izaak Walton League in Hobart near Interstate 65 and 61st Avenue.

McDowell is not a member of the IWL, but he is a member of the Friends of Robinson Lake and the Shirley Heinze Land Trust. .

McDowell, 68, is a retired steel worker who has been married to Margaret for 48 years; they've raised three adult children. Dan is a native of Tennessee, but has lived in the Hobart area for more than 50 years.

McDowell doesn't have a degree in botany, but he really knows his stuff. He could've rattled off the scientific names of every plant on the property, but, for my sake, was kind enough to speak in English rather than Latin.

* * *

How many years were you in the mill?

"I worked at U.S. Steel for 37 years," he said.

What department?

"No. 1 caster; I was an upper hoist operator. I'd raise ladles of molten steel to be cast into slabs. I got out early because I didn't want to be a slave to the clock.

"Out here, there is no pressure. I do this because I want to do it. I live for stuff like this. I get some good help out here, too. It's not entirely me alone. This property will be here a long time after I'm gone."

Are you a self-taught botanist?

"Not really, but after retirement, I did natural land restoration work for three years part-time with the Shirley Heinze Land Trust. That's where I learned everything I know.

"I also I learned a lot from some very educated people like Sandy O'Brien; she's the one who is responsible for getting the burns done here. Sandy not only talks the talk, she walks the walk."

What is Ike Prairie?

"It's an important remnant of the historic silt loam burr oak savanna ecosystem. This property starts off as a dry prairie, going into a wet prairie, going into a natural wetland."

When did restoration at this site begin?

"In 2005, this area was very rough. There was a tremendous amount of autumn olive, purple loosestrife and canary reed grass that had to be eradicated.

"There also was quite a bit of debris such as tires and metal objects that had to be removed. The recovery of this place in seven or eight years has been amazing."

To what do you attribute this recovery?

"Fire. A controlled burn is the most important restoration tool there is. Hands down, that's what makes this preserve successful."

How often do you burn?

"We have burned two years in a row, but usually every other year."

Dan, this is something, and right next to I-65. Most people driving by probably don't have a clue this place exists. Let's go for a hike.

"This prairie looks like it's predominantly sunflowers and goldenrod, but it's much more. This is a rare lady's tress orchid and that is a New England aster."

What is this handsome blue-flowered plant?

"Bottle gentian."

Did you sow the seeds of these prairie plants?

"No, it's all natural. There are more than 200 species of plants on these five acres. This eared false foxglove gets its name because the leaves have 'ears' on them.

"It's nice to have these types of plants scattered throughout the preserve."

Fauna living in Ike Prairie?

"Well, we don't have rabbits anymore because we have a den of coyotes living over there by that tree.

"We do have woodcocks, finches and many other species of birds here. After a rain, the prairie is swimming with frogs. There are butterflies, deer, crayfish, snakes and turtles, too."

Really nice.

"How did you hear about me?"

A former copy editor of mine, Tim Zorn, contacted me. He thought you'd be a good interview for my column. He also informed me that you are reluctant to talk about yourself, but become very passionate when telling people about this restoration project.

"Tim is good people; he's also a member of the Friends of Robinson Lake."

Places like this are important.

"If 10 percent of the population could give just six or eight hours a year doing some type of conservation work, there would be significant improvement to our natural areas.

"Indiana has 250 dedicated nature preserves; I've visited 187 of them."

* * *

Several decades ago, an environmental group called the Grand Calumet Task Force was formed.

Tough duty, the Grand Cal. It might surprise some folks, but most of the GCTF charter members were steel workers like Dan McDowell.

He has done volunteer work for the Department of Natural Resources, The Nature Conservancy and Lake County Parks. But Dan derives no more pleasure than when he traipses through the *daucus carota* and *nepeta cataria* of Ike Prairie, just off I-65.

That would be Queen Anne's lace and catnip to you and me.

Kip Walton *(March 2010)*

"When I was young I wanted to save the world; in my middle years, I would have been content to save my country. Now, I just want to save the Dunes."
– Paul Howard Douglas

When Kipton Walton was young, he wanted to be an Olympic athlete or a park ranger.

He chose the latter.

Walton, 41, was born and raised in Springfield, Ill., and earned a degree in environmental education at Western Illinois University in Macomb.

He and his wife Jennifer Lute live in Michigan City; they have a daughter named Jada.

Walton is the outreach program coordinator a the Indiana Dunes National Lakeshore's Paul H. Douglas Center for Environmental Education in Gary.

* * *

You were quite an athlete while growing up.
"In high school, I did quite well in track."
Sprinter, maybe middle distance?
"You got it; we went to state in the 400- and 1600-meter relays. I also played soccer at the college level; at one time, we were ranked 15th in the nation. After moving to this area, I coached Chesterton High School's girls soccer team for nine years. We went to state three years in a row. In 2000, we lost to Carmel in the state championship."

By the photos thumb-tacked to your bulletin board, it looks like you have other interests as well. Walleye, muskie, bluegill... .

"Yeah, I love fishing."

Who's posing with that largemouth? Looks like that bass probably went about 5 pounds.

"That's my wife; she caught that one. It actually weighed about 3 1/2 pounds, but she'd probably tell you it weighed 5 pounds. And that's one of the reasons we're so happily married. Jennifer doesn't mind if I go fishing and she'll usually fish right alongside me."

Tell me a little more about your early years in central Illinois.

"My grandfather always took me fishing. He let me shoot my first gun. I grew up with kids who did much the same. Instead of hanging out on the street corner, we went hunting. I guess my love for the outdoors just naturally evolved into my profession.

"When I was 10 or 12 years old, I wanted to be either an Olympic athlete or a park ranger. Bruce Jenner (1976 Olympic gold medalist in the decathalon) was doing his thing, and I thought, 'Boy, I'd like to do that; that's really cool.'

"As far as becoming a ranger, I imagined being out in the wilderness by myself, you know, rescuing people out in the wilderness. That's furthest from what I do now."

Where did you get your start?

"The National Park at (Abraham) Lincoln's Home in Springfield. I worked there for three years as a summer job. The Lincoln Home is a historical interpretation, not really my bag, but I did get my foot in the door by doing that – I got paid and everything."

What happened next?

"From there, I got an opportunity to do a three-month internship with Indiana Dunes National Lakeshore during the summer just before my senior year of college. Then, before I even graduated, I got a phone call from Bruce Rowe, who would eventually become my supervisor. He said, 'Hey, we appreciated what you did while you were here and we'd really like you back.'"

And?

"I came back to Indiana Dunes and have been working here ever since; it's been 18 years. They started me out at $17,000; back then, that was looking pretty good.

"You don't see a lot of African-Americans doing the park service thing, especially around here. But I grew up fishing and hunting, whereas a kid from Gary probably doesn't.

"My job is to get people into the park, let them know where we're at and to tell them about the programs we have here. We have plans to extend our trail all the way out to the lake. We're also going to make a bike trail going all the way from West Beach to Miller Woods. This entire area is going to be much more accessible in the next few years.

"I want people to become interested in the park. Basically, I want them to have a love for the park."

Working with children.

"I really enjoy bringing kids to the park. It's a passion of mine to not just tell them about the park, but to actually take hikes with them. Jeff, it's really something to see those kids' faces light up when they see something cool."

Examples.

"There have been a few times when we've walked up on a snake; I'll catch it and, at first, they'll be scared of it. Then, pretty soon, they'll be like, 'Can I touch it?' 'Sure, you can touch the snake.' And then we let it go.

"Just walking out in the dunes and having a covey of quail jump up – exploding in the air. Growing up, I jumped coveys of quail all the time, but kids in the inner city, they don't know what's going on. A quail jumps up at their feet and they're about ready to pee their pants.

"The other day, I had a bunch of little kids. I showed them coyote tracks in the snow; they were enamored by them. 'Oh, that's so cool.' Then, I showed them the coyote scat and they we're like, 'Oh, that's so gross.' But then we talk about the coyote's lifestyle and so forth, and it's just a great learning experience for them. I love it."

Your workmates.

"The rangers who work here have the same kind of passion I do, not only in teaching kids, but also their love of the outdoors. In fact, these two guys in this photo, Ted and J.P., are like my brothers.

"It's amazing how J.P. and I think so much alike as far as the park itself, working with kids, being outside, fishing and love for our families. People will call here at the park and think they're talking to me and it's J.P. – and vice versa. He's white; I 'm black, but everybody mixes us up for some reason."

You're birds of a feather.

"Jeff, when I was in high school, we raised enough money to

drive to Alaska; I was president of our science club. On the way, I remember seeing the (Grand) Teton Mountains for the first time. Tears welled up in eyes. It was so beautiful to me, I cried.

"And I see that here in this park every day. The Indiana Dunes National Lakeshore is one of the jewels of the Midwest; it's a 15,000-acre diamond in the rough.

"When a lot of people think of Northwest Indiana, they think of steel mills and things like that. Those same people need to come out here after a fresh snow or when the sun is setting down upon these interdunal ponds; it's one of the most beautiful places in the world – right here in Gary. It's so beautiful, what God has created."

* * *

Kip Walton is quite a piece of work, too.

Alyssa Nyberg *(April 2010)*

"Amie what you wanna do?
I think I could stay with you
For a while, maybe longer if I do"
– Pure Prairie League

The Nature Conservancy's native plant nursery is nestled near North Newton High School, between the intriguing ghost town of Conrad and the hamlet called Enos.

The nursery is an integral part of TNC's 7,800-acre Kankakee Sands Prairie Restoration project in Newton County, along both sides of U.S. 41. Alyssa Nyberg, 37, is the nursery manager; she also is my Earth Day interview.

Nyberg lives in Lake Village with her husband, Gus, the executive director of Niches Land Trust in Lafayette where he does land protection work along the Wabash River.

Conservationists at heart, the Nybergs named their 5-year-old daughter Savanna Rose and 2-year-old son Forest Burns.

With, Marley, her pound-rescued dog, at her side, she was busy in the nursery greenhouse transplanting Scirpus acutus, more commonly known as bulrush.

* * *

Are you from Lake Village originally?

"Indianapolis," Nyberg said. "I went to Bishop Chatard High School."

College?

"Indiana University; I have a master's degree in environmental science and did my college internships in organic farming."

Did you go to work for TNC right out of college?

"No, I spent 2 1/2 years in Nepal while in the Peace Corps. But I've worked here since the beginning of this project –1999. When it was decided not to put an airport here, TNC bought a big block of land from Prudential.

"Initially, this area was marsh. Then, it was drained for grazing. Then, it became farm ground. Prairie soils have fertile soils and are fairly easy to turn over because there aren't a lot of trees. In '99, this was a soybean field."

How big is the nursery portion of Kankakee Sands?

"About 120 acres."

How many beds?

"A lot. Some are only 6 feet by 6 feet, and some are as big as 5 acres. The point of the nursery is to germinate seeds for our restoration.

"We'd like to have 400 to 500 different kinds of plants at Kankakee Sands. The magnificent thing is they're all from Newton County. For us to plant something here, there has to be some kind of historical record of the species being here in the past."

Thank goodness the tongue depressors designating these flats use the common name. All that Latin is Greek to me. Besides, I like the cool names: Jacob's ladder, black-eyed Susan, rattle snake master... .

Alyssa, these bulrush seedlings you're transplanting from germination trays to individual plugs aren't ornate bloomers or fruit bearers, yet they must produce some sort of pod.

"Yes, they have a little seed head; in the fall, we'll go out with a pair of scissors and clip the seed heads. Then, we'll take them to our seed barn where we let the seeds dry out."

Separating the chaff from the grain as it were.

"That's right. Direct seeding can be tricky; you hope they hit soil, don't get eaten and receive the right requirements to germinate.

"Some people tell us to be patient, 'Your restoration is still very young; you need to wait 50, 60, 70 years.' I think there's a lot to be said for that."

Summer help?

"I hire five high school kids every year; most are from North Newton. For many of them, it's their first real job or opportunity to be around science and nature. Last year, everybody who worked for me wanted to come back. It's wonderful.

"At Kankakee Sands, we don't have someone on our staff who

is dedicated to public education or public outreach. But there is group called Friends of the Sands who have decided to get these native plants into the community; they encourage people to incorporate them into their landscapes. The FOS has planted some of these species at area libraries and also by the old log cabin on display at the government center in Morocco."

What are "Work Days"?

"Work Days are when the public is invited to volunteer time here. That's how a lot of this stuff got transplanted. I had 12 people show up for each of our last two Work Days; I was really pleased. We transplanted more than 10,000 plants."

When is the next Work Day scheduled?

"Saturday, May 8. We'll transplant violets into our prairie restoration. Violets are food source for the larvae of the regal fritillary butterfly. The violet is a good example of why the project is here. We're re-creating the system here, not only for plants, but for the insects, amphibians, reptiles and mammals.

"Jeff, it's an honor to work on this prairie restoration; it's so much bigger and richer than any of us."

* * *

Nyberg grew up in the city, but now lives just five miles north of the nursery where she works and next to the northeast corner of TNC property.

I grew up with LaSalle Fish and Wildlife Area in my backyard.

Nyberg not only has seen a glass snake, a type of legless lizard, but has held one. She has one up on me there.

The glass snake probably was extirpated from my boyhood stomping grounds by then. But, they're coming back, thanks to people like Alyssa Nyberg.

Forty years ago, I once saw a badger while exploring the woods of LaSalle. I've never seen one since.

Nyberg saw a badger not long ago on the Kankakee Sands.

Stop by TNC office, along U.S. 41 in Morocco. Ask about the hiking trails. Take in the beauty of blooming bergamot, boneset and black-eyed Susan. You might even spot a badger in the bulrushes.

It's pure prairie league.

Chris Salberg *(May 2010)*

*"Bluebirds
Singing a song
Nothing but bluebirds
All day long."
– Irving Berlin*

Chris Salberg, 60, is past president of the Indiana Bluebird Society, Dunes-Calumet Audubon, and the Friends of the Kankakee who received an Environmental Achievement Award from the Indiana Division of the Izaak Walton League in 2001 and the IBS Bluebirder of the Year in 2000.

Salberg is a retired computer specialist and a native of Conneaut, Ohio who has lived in Cedar Lake for 20 years. A bout with uterine and colon cancer in late 2008 slowed her down in 2009, but she's back in the pink and again is doing her green thing.

Our interview began at Salberg's house, but concluded at Lemon Lake County Park where she monitors a bluebird trail.

* * *

"I grew up on the shores of Lake Erie," Salberg began. "As kids, we were always in the woods or the lake. You get a love of nature that carries into adulthood."

Lake Erie has made quite a comeback since many people feared it was a 'dead lake" years ago.

"A lot of work was done to clean it up."

Chris, I didn't even know what a computer was back when you started working with them in the early '70s. From what company did you retire?

"The Federal Highway Administration. When we'd get new computers, I'd set them up. When there were problems with the computers, I'd repair them. When they wanted programs written, I'd write programs."

Before you lose me with high-tech computer speak, let's veer off toward the bluebird trail.

"About six months after moving to Cedar Lake, I read a notice in the Dunes-Calumet Audubon newsletter, asking for help monitoring bluebirds.

"That's how I met Gene Bissing of Crown Point. Gene took me out to Lemon Lake on Easter Sunday of '91. He said, 'I'll show you what a bluebird house looks like, and if we get lucky, maybe we'll see a bluebird.' And, by God, there was a bluebird sitting on a fence not 40 feet away. I've been hooked ever since."

Tell me a little about the bluebird.

"The Eastern bluebird, the bluebird in this area, is a member of the thrush family and a cousin to the robin. They feed mostly on insects in the summer. Bluebirds return to our region in late March and early April."

These bluebird trails consist of several nest boxes in a particular vicinity.

"Yes, I monitor seven trails ranging from six boxes to 22. The trails should be checked weekly."

Where are your trails?

"Willow Slough Fish and Wildlife Area, Buckley Homestead County Park, South Shore and Summertree golf courses, Lemon Lake and two at the Grand Kankakee Marsh County Park. At the GKM, the trails are near water to attract tree swallows, which also use bluebird boxes to nest in."

Problems on the bluebird trail.

"Cracks in the box can create a wet nest. If the birds are less than eight days old (featherless), they can get hypothermia. The larvae of blow flies will attach themselves to the young bluebirds and suck the blood out of them. The non-native house sparrow will get into nests and kill both young and adult bluebirds. It's called crowning; the sparrow will peck at the bluebird's head until it fractures its skull."

Any other duties?

"You also monitor the box to see how many eggs were laid and how many fledged out. Bluebirds lay an egg a day. They don't start incubating until all the eggs are laid. Clutch sizes ranges from four to six. The first clutch, in late April or early May, is the bigger clutch. There's usually a second clutch in late June."

Are the eggs blue, like those of a robin?

"Usually, but 4 percent of the time, you'll find a nest with all white eggs."

How long do the young ones stay in the nest?

"About 17 or 18 days; then, they'll fly to a tree."

You restarted the defunct Indiana Bluebird Society in '96.

"Yes, along with Ann and Jim Auers, formerly of Goshen."

How many members today?

"About 200; I recently sighted an immature bald eagle while monitoring one of the trails at the GKM. I also saw indigo buntings and a woodcock with three babies at the GKM.

"That's the thing about monitoring bluebird trails, you get to see so many other things in the wild that you don't see while sitting on the couch, watching a bird feeder."

Chris, Patty Wisniewski and I just took a 15-mile round trip on a pontoon boat up and down the Momence (Ill.) Wetlands along the Kankakee River. Pat captured an incredible amount of wildlife on film: pileated woodpeckers, huge softshell turtles with long snouts, beavers, blue herons, green herons... . The bayous were the best.

"I just kayaked from Cedar Lake to Lake Dale via Cedar Creek. While cleaning up the stream, we spotted three black-crowned night herons and a pair of Caspian terns. All people have to do is take a walk in the woods and they can see so much.

"When I'm out on my trails, I often wonder how much habitat loss our birds and plants can sustain before they disappear from our area.

"Jeff, I hope the Grand Kankakee Marsh National Refuge will be established. It's our chance to protect a small remnant of the old Grand Marsh while providing recreational opportunities for the growing number of people coming to this area.

"And, of course, it will benefit the birds."

* * *

Inside Salberg's house is a bird clock that chirps on the hour and plethora of
of field guides on birds, insects, wildflowers and trees.

At Lemon Lake, she opened up a box that had three babies in it. At another nest box, a female bluebird exited as we approached. When Salberg opened that particular box, she said, "Well, look what we have here."

It contained five white eggs.

John Barenie *(June 2008)*

*"I come to the garden alone
while the dew is still on the roses
and the joy we share as we tarry there
none other has ever known."*
-C.A. Miles

John Barenie, 51, doesn't give his colossal Cucurbita names, but he does take it pretty hard when they split. He is one of Northwest Indiana's premier growers of big pumpkins.

Barenie also is a lifelong bachelor and Griffith resident who retired from ArcelorMittal's East Chicago plant three years ago where he worked as a mechanic-welder.

* * *

"I'm from a big family," Barenie began. "There were 10 of us kids. My parents always gardened. Mom still cans vegetables.

"I started growing pumpkins in 1999 for the county fair. I found out some information on the Internet about growing giant pumpkins; I always wanted to try it."

John, it's June 12. How we doing so far?

"May had cloudier days and colder nights this year; it seems like things are a little bit slower. We had a warmer May last year.

"The biggest pumpkin I have right now has an estimated weight of 180 pounds. It's 28 days old – 28 days ago I pollinated it. It's gaining 25 pounds a day now – it's picking up speed. Normally, my big pumpkins are about 400 pounds at 30 days. I'm behind, but it could catch up some. It depends on how long the growing cycle holds in there.

"I have six plants going. Three are my plants; three are seeds from other growers – we swap seeds. But I did pay $250 for the seed that started the plant growing there in the middle of the patch."

That's a lot of money for a pumpkin seed.

"It came from a pumpkin that weighed over 1,500 pounds last year – I wanted it for genetic purposes.

"I started these plants in my house in late March. They were transplanted outside, but with a greenhouse over them, around April 5. I take the greenhouse away in late May."

Tell me more about pollination.

"All my pollination is controlled. You get a feel for when the flowers are going to open up. I'll go out the night before and cover them with 3-ounce Dixie cups.

"The female blossoms look like they have a miniature pumpkin underneath them. They're the ones that are going to grow, but I'll protect the male flowers the same way. I do the cross pollinating by brushing the pollen from the male flower inside the bulge of the female flower – then I'll tie it shut. That way the bees can't get to it."

Why would that be a problem?

"Actually, the bees could probably do a better job of pollinating than I could, but you also could end up with up with mixed pollen from other flowers in the patch."

You were grand champion at the Lake County Fair last year.

"Yes, I've won it every year since '99 with the exception of 2003 when Joe Richards of Steger, Ill. won it."

John, after the county fair comes the state fair competition, but the big daddies aren't harvested until later in the season when a pumpkin can reach its ultimate weight, correct?

"Yes, we have the state championship weigh-off in October. Any grower from any state can enter the county or state fair contests. But to vie for the Indiana state championship or in order to break the Indiana state record, you have to be a Hoosier – and the pumpkin has to have been grown in Indiana.

"The state record holder is a guy from Grovertown, Ind. – about 50 miles east of Merrillville. It weighed 1,273 pounds."

What's your biggest pumpkin?

"Officially, 1,154. I had a 1,236 last year, but it went bad. When growing these things you have to keep an open mind because you might have something huge, but if you don't make it to the weigh-off, it isn't any good."

What happened?

"It was cool in the mid-September last year, I covered the pumpkins with blankets every night. We had a night that got down to about 40 degrees. I took the blanket off about 9:30 in the morning – a half hour later the pumpkin split open. I don't think it could handle the temperature change. Once they split – they split. They're goners.

"I've had a lot of ups and downs in my growing. I set a state record with an 896-pounder in 2000. In '01, the best I grew was like a 500-pounder. In 2003, I had a state record of 916 pounds – it was beat a week later by a 952. In '04, I had a state record of 1,068. Then, I broke my own record with an 1,136."

What's the world record?

"A guy from Rhode Island grew a 1,689-pounder last year."

John, do you think we'll ever see a one-ton wonder in our lifetime?

"Yes. Last year about 10 people beat the 2006 record of 1,502 – three went over 1,600."

Is there a certain breed of pumpkin that year in and year out is head and shoulders above the rest as far as weight?

"They are all Dill Atlantic Giants – named after the legendary Howard Dill of Windsor, Nova Scotia. Howard just passed away a couple weeks ago. If it wasn't for him, we might still be growing 400-pound pumpkins. Howard got a hold of an heirloom seed that came from a world-record pumpkin back in 1904. Down through the years, Howard just kept working on crossing it..."

John, I'm sorry to hear about Dill's demise. Shall we lighten up the topic of conversation a bit? Do you ever give your individual pumpkins a pet name like, oh, just off the top of me head: Big Red, Egg Yolk, Orberta May, Mr. October, Old Sol or the Orange Blossom Special?

"I don't, but a lot of growers are doing that now."

I noticed a small fan mounted to a particular pumpkin in one of the photos from your scrapbook.

"Sometimes you develop problems – like when you get a crack in your stem."

Sounds like some serious shit to me.

"You have to put a fungicide in there and keep it ventilated."

That's logical. Any other preventive maintenance or tricks of the trade?

"Once a week, I foliar feed my plants calcium, fish emulsion and a seaweed fertilizer. I tilled in maple leaves last fall and I've used horse manure. I also take soil samples every year in the fall. And I brew up about 50 gallons of my own compost tea per week – adding six cups of worm castings to the mix."

Castings?

"Worm manure. It really helps process the roots so they can take up more nutrients.

"Jeff, I spend $2,000 to $3,000 a year on this hobby. I get a little bit of money from the fair – not a lot. It isn't about the money."

John, let me play devil's advocate. You could probably make a good chunk of change with your own strain of seed. Think about it. It's all about marketing. You're the man around here. All you'd need is an attention-getter of a name for your product. Something like, say, 'Berenie's Brobdingnagian Behemoth'. Huh?

"I don't want to do that."

Yeah, probably wouldn't fit on the seed packet anyway.

"For me, this is fun. You can spoil a hobby, you know? The folks who grow big pumpkins are friendly; we share information on the Internet.

"During the summer, when I'm out tending my garden and the pumpkins are getting bigger, interested people stop by almost every day and talk to me – they ask me questions.

"In the fall, my sisters, nieces and nephews carve about 40 or 50 pumpkins – we have a different theme every year. Last year it was characters from 'The Little Mermaid'. We had about 10,000 people come out and look at them on display in front of my parent's house. We don't charge admission or anything like that. It's nice."

* * *

For three decades he made a living working shift work in the mill. The nape of his neck still gets hot and gritty. But he's not turning wrenches within the bowels of a basic oxygen furnace anymore.

With tanned and callused hands sunk deep into the good earth, he raises big pumpkins in the town where he was raised. And he is content.

John Barenie is a down-to-earth kind of guy.

Kim Ferraro *(April 2008)*

*"I'd put my money on the sun and solar energy. What a source of power!
I hope we don't have to wait 'til oil and coal run out before we tackle that."*
    -*Thomas Alva Edison*

The first Earth Day was April 22, 1970. Today more than a half billion people participate in Earth Day Network campaigns.

My travels take me to beautiful downtown Valparaiso. At Valparaiso High School, Kim Ferraro's eldest daughter wears a green singlet for the Viking track team.

Kim E. Ferraro Esq. is a green lawyer, not green as in inexperienced. Kim is the founder and executive director of Legal Environmental Aid Foundation of Indiana, Inc. (L.E.A.F.). She also started the Northwest Indiana chapter of 'Green Drinks' where 'eco-freaks' flock together once a month to let their hair down and discuss environmental issues.

Ferraro, 44, was born and raised in Austin, Texas. She and her husband moved to the Midwest 22 years ago so she could attend Valparaiso University School of Law. Her husband also is a lawyer.

They live in Valpo with their two daughters, ages 16 and 12. In October of last year, Ferraro opened her not-for-profit law practice in Valparaiso.

* * *

"I've been an environmental activist for more than a decade," Ferraro begins. "That is the sole reason I went to law school and opened my law practice. Before I went to law school, I was a paralegal. I was very unchallenged and unhappy at work, but certainly recognized how lawyers can effectuate societal change for the good or bad depending on the types of cases they're involved in and what side they're on.

"There are laws in the books that are not being enforced because most environmental lawyers go to work for companies like BP."

You work for PB – pro bono.

"Yes, I don't charge my clients for the cases that I take on. My funding comes from private donations and grants. The only way that you can really do effective public interest law is to make your services available to those who need it, not based on whether or not they can afford it."

Typical clients?

"Most are the local activist organizations such as Save the Dunes Council. For years, they have been trying to do good things to protect the environment on a legislative level, but they have not had good access to low cost attorneys. So I'm filling that need for them."

You represent urban and rural communities. You go up against both Davids and Goliaths. Let's start with a giant – BP. Jobs versus the environment.

"That is a very false choice. Regarding the BP air permit, they framed that very issue. We don't want to stop the BP air permit. All that we want is for that air permit to have the most stringent standards, as it's supposed to under the Clean Air Act. This is not about stopping the Whiting expansion project.

"So for the people of BP to come out at the hearing and say, 'This is for national security and our jobs are going to be lost' – no. You can have your jobs and we can have environmental protection.

"Study after study shows that when you have a clean environment, the economy benefits. We'll have green jobs. You can have people working on projects that are good both economically and environmentally; get me off of my soapbox."

You got my attention.

"How is a multibillion-dollar company like BP going to be put out of business just because it has to put in stringent environmental pollution controls at its new plant? Look at the price of oil. They are raking it in. They are making record profits."

Counselor, to paraphrase the late great Carl Sagan, 'BP's

makin' billions and billions of bucks. Why 60 clams to gas up our trucks?'

"Sagan really said that?"

No, but I saw an opportunity to speak in rhyme and took it. An idiosyncrasy some find annoying – editors in particular.

"I have a case fighting a local ethanol plant from being built in San Pierre. Ethanol is not a renewable energy source, in fact, it's very polluting to the surrounding communities. Ethanol made from corn is a horrible thing. Even the small plant that we're fighting uses 250,000 gallons of water per minute. Significant toxins end up in the local well-water supply.

"That's an example of a case where I'm representing the local community. They do not want the plant there, so we are challenging the Board of Zoning Appeal's decision to grant the plant a conditional use. The land where they want to build the plant is zoned for agriculture. An ethanol plant is industry, so you have to get it re-zoned or get a conditional use permit."

Kim, the ethanol plant would probably mean jobs for people residing near San Pierre. It also could be a source of income for local farmers.

"The (company) is basically saying it will hire 32 people. Ethanol production seems like it would benefit local farmers, but the truth is the corn that would be brought in for this plant would not come from local farmers. In fact, they'd also burn wood supply, old tires and garbage.

"OK, it might create a few jobs, but it's also going to cost the community in health problems and water issues. The water the plant uses is going to suck up the water the local farmers need for their own crops.

"I represent more than 200 people in San Pierre as a community action group. Not as sexy as BP..."

It is to the folks of San Pierre.

"The behemoths go out and spend millions of dollars and hire big-time lawyers to fight the things that I'm bringing. We want to slow them down and raise awareness. And if the judge agrees with what we're doing, that's great, too.

"We can go to meetings and bitch all day long about the way things are, but to effect change against the powers that be respecting the environment, you need to educate yourself, know what your politicians' views are on environmental issues, and support organizations like mine that do legal work for the environment. The only way to hold corporations accountable is to bring them into a court of law.

"At some point, we have to look at how we have become consumers at our own expense. At what point do we recognize that what we are doing is not sustainable? At what point do we say enough is enough?

"At some point we're going to run out of oil. And we will have ruined the earth in the process so that our children's children's children have no place to live.

"At what point do we say, we can still have a good way of life and we can still maintain our existence on this Earth? We have to do it in a way that is not just for the almighty dollar; the environment always loses, and ultimately, we all lose."

* * *

One small planet, trashed by billions.

Dan Plath *(March 2010)*

"Travel 1,000 miles by train and you are a brute; pedal 500 miles on a bicycle and you remain basically a bourgeois; paddle 100 miles in a canoe and you are already a child of nature."
– Pierre Elliott Trudeau

Dan Plath, 34, has lived in Indiana and Illinois his entire life, but I had a sneaking suspicion his people originally were from north of this neck of the woods. He pronounces words such as "about" like the late Peter Jennings, the Canadian-born former ABC News Anchor.

Plath lives in Westville with his wife Vicky; they've been married 10 years. The Plaths have two children, Eric, 2, and Katie, 5 months.

There isn't a blade of Kentucky bluegrass or red fescue to be found on his 5-acre spread; his "yard" is planted in tallgrass prairie.

Plath is the Environmental Health & Safety Coordinator - Water Program Leader for NiSource. He's based out of Merrillville, but coordinates NiSource's water programs corporate wide. He also manages NIPSCO's Karner blue butterfly habitat conservation plan and is president and founder of the Northwest Indiana Paddling Association.

* * *

"My family is originally from Minnesota and Iowa," Plath began. "My dad wrestled in college and for the Navy. My four brothers and I all wrestled for Rich South High School in Richton Park, Ill."

Were you born in Illinois?

"No, we lived in Rochester (Ind.) until I was 5 or 6 years old. But I kinda grew up back and forth between Rochester and Matteson; my parents always had a place on Lake Manitou; I spent a most of my weekends in Rochester."

Wasn't there a terrible horror movie made back in the '70s called "The Manitou"?

"Yeah, I believe Manitou is a Native American word meaning, 'lake monster.' Legend has it that the Indians often saw lake monsters in the area.

"What's interesting, 150 years ago, Lake Manitou had super pristine water like the Grand Kankakee Marsh once had.

"Today, it's believed what the Indians saw through the clear water were huge filter feeding fish of the sturgeon family. I believe they still exist in Lake Michigan, but they're rare. Some people call them paddlefish or spoonbills."

That is interesting; a lake sturgeon does look kinda like a sea serpent.

"Lake Manitou recently got known for something that wasn't a good thing, but it had a positive outcome. It's probably one of the few places where an invasive species, in this case, hydrilla, was stopped."

What is hydrilla and from where did it come?

"It's a real nasty invasive plant that will take over everything; it came from Florida and was probably transported on somebody's bass boat. If hydrilla would've spread to the Great Lakes system, it would have devastated shipping."

What had to be done?

"All boating on Lake Manitou was banned for three years. It was treated, and I don't believe they've had any hydrilla since then. It makes for a good case study regarding the Asian Carp issue."

Were you involved?

"Yes, up until two years ago, while still working for the Indiana Department of Environmental Management. It was primarily a Department of Natural Resources project but, IDEM was involved, too."

How long did you work for IDEM?

"About 10 years."

What are some of your duties at NiSource?

"Making sure all their water-related permits are in place; there's a tremendous amount of new rules coming down the pipe. I also make sure we're in compliance. Beyond that, I do a lot of outreach type things."

Such as?

"The Grand Kankakee Marsh Restoration Project, for one. NIPSCO and NiSource have been involved since the beginning, probably 12 or 13 years ago. I actually did my thesis on the GKMRP."

Cool.

"I'd done a lot of paddling on the Illinois side of the river; it's very scenic and meandering. Then, I saw the Indiana side for the first time; it's a drainage ditch and straight as an arrow.

"In '07, I was a member of the Trail Creek Watershed steering committee in Michigan City. We cleaned up a 3-mile stretch of Trail Creek by getting the log jams opened up without messing up the wildlife habitat and the good fishing spots; it's called the Palmeter Method. Near the bridge, there was a ton of steel and debris. We took the metal out of the creek and got like $1,500 worth of scrap fees."

Tell me about the NWI Paddling Association.

"We've only been in existence for a year or so, but we're already 225 members strong. The NWIPA is a not-for-profit organization dedicated to promoting the region's paddling resources and opportunities, providing environmental stewardship of the region's waterways, education and to be a link between the region's paddlers."

The education outreach aspect of it?

"We've worked with the Gary School Corp, Boys & Girls Club in Michigan City, and a troop of Girl Scouts out of Illinois; Roz Varon from ABC 7 News was their scout leader; she's real interested in the Indiana Dunes."

Give me an example of an NWIPA excursion.

"In June of '09, we were part of the Burnham (Ill.) to Marquette Water Trail Expedition; it was a two-day, bi-state sea kayaking event from Chicago to Michigan City along the coast line of Lake Michigan."

Like Joliet and Marquette did back in 1673.

"Yes; at the end of the first day, we camped along the lakeshore at Marquette Park in Miller.

"This year, we're going to pick up where we left off in Michigan City. We'd like to make it a national water trail and not just Indiana; we want to go all around the entire lake."

When you're on Lake Michigan, you prefer the kayak, but many members of NWIPA also are canoe enthusiasts.

"This summer, we're going to do a paddling event to draw awareness to the Kankakee River. We're not sure exactly which stretch of river yet, definitely the LaSalle area. We'll probably start somewhere around Starke County."

Back to the kayak and "The Big Lake" that turns tempestuous in the blink of an eye.

"I feel the sea kayak is the most seaworthy boat there is. Eskimoes have paddled across the ocean. Let's say you get in heavy waves and rollover."

Not me.

"You can right-side your way back up if you know how to Eskimo roll."

Is that like an Eskimo Pie?

"I have a brand-new kayak hanging up in the garage; it's still wrapped in plastic. Come on, I'll show it to you. ... It's made out of Kevlar, carbon and fiberglass. I got a good deal; they're usually about $3,000, I paid $2,000. The guys who made this kayak were aeronautical engineers for Boeing, but quit to form their own company designing these kayaks. Jeff, this baby is super fast, but still stable for a beginner."

Dan, I'd feel much more comfortable tipping your Objiway hunting canoe in the Kankakee in July, when it's 3 feet deep.

* * *

Dan Plath is vice president of the Shirley Heinze Land Trust, a charitable trust that preserves and protects the unique ecosystems of the Indiana Dunes region.

In 2009, Plath was inducted into the Northwest Indiana Society of Innovators, and received the Northwest Indiana Quality of Life Council Sustainability Award.

And kudos to Plath and NiSource for their efforts; more area industries should follow suit.

Larry Davis *(June 2011)*

"I'd put my money on the sun and solar energy. What a source of power! I hope we don't have to wait until we run out of oil and coal before we tackle that."
– Thomas Alva Edison

I recently met Larry Davis at a presentation of "Carbon Nation" at the Memorial Opera House in Valparaiso.

Davis was a co-chair of the joint Safety & Health Committee at ArcelorMittal's Burns Harbor plant. He also was chairman of the Energy & Environmental Committee.

Davis has been on the board of the Hoosier Environmental Council and is currently on the executive committee of the Hoosier chapter of the Sierra Club and vice president of the Save the Dunes Council.

Davis, 53, is a single steel worker who was raised in Wheeler and lives on 20 acres in Hebron.

* * *

High school?

"I was part of the last graduating class of old Wheeler High School."

College?

"I attended Purdue in West Lafayette for a year-and-a-half while studying to become an electrical engineer. Then, I applied for a job at Bethlehem Steel in Burns Harbor. The plan was to work two years in the mill and go back to Purdue; that was 33 years ago."

What's your job title?

"I'm an electronics repairman at No. 1 and 2 Caster. It's where they take the molten steel from the basic oxygen furnace and cast it into slabs.

"The Burns Harbor plant was the last ingot steel made in the United States. Now, you have to go to China to get ingot steel. Some of the special grades of armor plate can only be made with ingot steel, so we get are armor plate from China."

Do you think America is keeping up with China in steel making?

"The short story is that China, right now, is closing down and consolidating, not just their steel industry, but across the board, starting with all the heavy hitters like energy, chemicals, paper, glass, primary metals... .

"Within 10 years or less, you will see a complete transformation of the Chinese industry and manufacturing base, and they will have the most energy-efficient and productive technology in the world. China has actually curtailed steel production because they don't produce enough energy."

But you say that's going to change.

"China has put in every kind of energy you can think of, including alternative energy – solar, wind, onshore wind, offshore wind. China is investing six times what the United States is as far as alternative energy. And despite all of those efforts, China still can't produce enough energy to meet the needs of their expanding economy."

What are they going to do about that?

"What's left? Energy efficiency. They are closing down all their old, inefficient and polluting industries and replacing them with new, modern efficient and less polluting plants. Pollution is a gross inefficiency. Along with energy efficiency comes quality.

"The bottom line is, China, in 10 years or less, is going to have the most modern steel industry in the world. The United States has been the most productive workforce in the world. But you can't make up for not having the proper technology."

What about American steel mills?

"The thing that concerns me is, are we going to clean up our mess? We have created quite a legacy along the shoreline. There are literally millions of tons of toxic waste that we've dumped in and on the lake. That could be cleaned up and turned into raw materials. It could be a positive resource instead of a liability if we put in modern technology."

You're well-versed on the subjects upon which you expound.

"I went back to school and got two associate degrees in water and waste-water treatment and pollution control. I've done a lot of research and investigation on my own. I've read a lot, taken lots of photos – including aerial photography – and I've done samplings of landfill leachate runs into the creeks and streams."

Tell me a little about energy efficiency.

"That's the low-hanging fruit. Make products and use energy in the most efficient way you can. It doesn't require altering your lifestyle, just using the energy smarter."

The future, environmentally speaking?

"We don't have to invent new technology, we've got it. Are we going to do what's necessary at scale to change? We can set the example for the rest of the world like we used to or we can be a declining world power that over-extends ourselves militarily and tries to make an economy based on speculation and paper instead of tangible goods that we manufacture.

"Are we going to fail to adopt the next energy source? Those are the mistakes every declining world power has made since the Romans.

"Jeff, we're at a fork in the road here, and we don't have a lot of time left."

* * *

I don't always agree with Larry Davis, but I have to like him. He calls 'em, like he sees 'em.

Kindred Spirits

Josie Sturgill *(Nov. 2005)*

"Sweetest little fellow, everybody knows
Don't know what to call him, but he's mighty like a rose
Lookin' at his mammy, with eyes so shiny blue
Make you think that heaven, is coming close to you"
– Paul Robeson

I was told she was a fighter. But I'd already interviewed a fighter, a middleweight by the name of Jimmy Holmes – although a woman boxer would be interesting.

"She's not a boxer, Jeff. She's a realtor. But make no mistake, Josie Sturgill is a fighter," said Lori Clark while cutting my hair.

Hey, thanks. I'll give her a call. And Lori, be careful with those scissors.

* * *

Josie Sturgill's birth certificate reads Giuseppina Roberto. Her parents moved to the United States from Italy when she was 9. Thirty years later, the married mother of two makes her home in Lowell.

Other than setting up the interview over the phone, we were total strangers. While I unlaced my boots, we introduce ourselves. With her arms akimbo, and her head slightly cocked, Josie Sturgill studied me while I spoke. I knew what was coming next... .
***

"Who are some of your relatives?"

Jason is my brother.

"I knew it! I didn't put two and two together. But now that I've seen you, my goodness, you two talk and wave your arms exactly the same way. We've known Jason for years."

Josie, it happens all the time. I come from a family of excitable gesticulators. Jace is the prosperous, good lookin' one – Ma always liked him best.

"My family came to America when I was 9. It was January. That April, I turned 10."

April what?

"April 6^h. I'm a stubborn Aries – the Ram."

Aries, the God of War.

"I had this wonderful young teacher named Miss Catton who helped me tremendously that first year when we moved to Blue Island. I spoke no English. Not, 'I'm hungry,' 'I'm sick' or even 'I have to go to the bathroom.' Miss Catton stuck with me. She would come to our house after school. She gave up her free time to help out. I was placed in third grade. From that January, she did everything she could to make sure I was able to go on to fourth grade the next school year."

Was she of Italian descent?

"No. She spoke no Italian. I spoke no English. We connected. She found an Italian version of 'Peter Rabbit', and gave it to me as a gift. I think of her often. I want to get in touch with her. I haven't seen her since fourth grade."

Which high school did you attend?

"Eisenhower in Blue Island."

Where did you meet your husband?

"South Padre Island in Texas. It was spring break. I met him at a party. We've been together ever since. John graduated from Lowell High School. We have two children, one girl and one boy. Nicolette is in seventh grade and Jordan is in fourth grade. We lived in Crown Point when we were first married and then moved to Lowell in 1990."

Does your famiglia call you Josie?

"No, they call me Pina."

What part of Italy were you from?

"Near Naples. I used to work as a waitress at the Stork's Nest on Friday and Saturday nights. I loved it. I loved the rush. The madness. My desire is to do that again. I liked it for the exercise. You never stop. It also exercised your mind. You had to remember so many things. That's what I want to do, exercise my body and my mind. It's better than a gym.

"I've been with Langen Realty since 2000. I love working with the Langen Family. They are awesome people. Very understanding. Jim never gets mad or shouts. He never talks down to anyone. He's a fabulous man. The people in Lowell have been unbelievable. So many good, loving people. Everyone stops and asks, 'How are you?'"

When did you find out that you were sick, Josie?

"I was diagnosed October of '02, my last treatment was June of '03. I've been back on chemo since March of this year, and I've been on it every single week since. It started out breast cancer, but it has spread. I just started a new chemo treatment Mon., Nov 14. It just got passed by the FDA. I'm only the third or fourth person at my clinic in Tinley Park to use it. At 4 a.m. this morning, I was crying my head off; I was in so much pain."

Josie, you should have cancelled ... .

"No, I want to do this. It's just, I feel, well, my hair is falling out again. I can't put on make-up because my skin is so sensitive. I used to have long hair. There were times when people thought I was Nicolette's older sister. I always hung out with her friends. I'm a goof ball. I like to have fun with all the kids. It's tough for my kids."

You're very brave to try out these new medicines and treatments. It has to be a scary thing, you're sort of, well, a guinea pig.

"It's not so much a guinea pig as it is surviving. I have an extremely aggressive oncologist. Very knowledgeable. The drug that he was giving me prior, was working really well. And then it stopped working – I just wanted to stop. I didn't want to do it anymore. I was going through a really tough time in March. I was in terrible pain. I called my mom; that night she had a massive heart attack. She survived. The two of us battled it out together. Slowly, they brought her out of a semi-coma. I told her, 'We're going to fight together, Mom.' I went back for more chemo. She had another heart attack. She survived that one, too. It's been a tough year.

"I've never been interviewed before. I wasn't sure what I was supposed to do. I wrote this last night... ."

Read it to me.

"OK: *'This Thanksgiving I am very thankful to all of my family, and I would like to give special thanks to my wonderful, caring, loving, and supportive husband John, daughter Nicolette, and son Jordan; also my loving parents, Joe and Michelle Roberto; my brothers, John and Pat Roberto; my in-laws, Bob and Janet Sturgill, Jason and Kristen Hughes and family; cousin Karen Savoy and family. My thanks to my uncle Gerardo Coppola, who traveled from Switzerland twice to visit, and my Aunt Ida Coppola who came from Italy to support my family and me.*

'I would also like to thank my co-workers and friends at Langen Realty, and so many other special people in Lowell and the surrounding area.

I was diagnosed with breast cancer in Oct, 2002. I went through several surgeries, and began chemotherapy in December, 2002. My treatment ended with radiation therapy in June, 2003. I was in remission until earlier this year. On February 25, 2005 I became aware my cancer had returned, and metastasized to five lymph nodes, innumerable tumors and lesions on my liver, and lesions to the bone. I have been going through chemotherapy since the first week of March and am still fighting.

I want to give special thanks to Dr. Kahn and staff and my oncologist, Dr. Baridi and staff who keeps me well, strong, and living.

We should be very thankful for our life on earth; to see and smell our world is a beautiful thing. To share time with our friends and family is a blessing; to love and receive love is a gift.

Thank you to everyone who has touched my life with so much love and support.

Happy Holiday Season with a cheer, a smile and love.

– Josie Sturgill

* * *

And yes, Lori, Josie "Pina" Sturgill is a fighter.
And she's mighty like a rose.

Harvey and Alice Johnson *(Feb. 2011)*

"I've fallen in love many times... always with you."
– Author unknown

In honor of Valentine's Day, I interviewed Harvey and Alice Johnson.

In autumn 1919, eight Chicago White Sox players took a bribe from Arnold Rothstein and threw the World Series to the Cincinnati Reds. In February that year, Harvey Johnson was born.

Harvey, 92, married Alice, 88, on May 21, 1938 in Charleston, Miss. "Gone With the Wind" had not appeared on the silver screen.

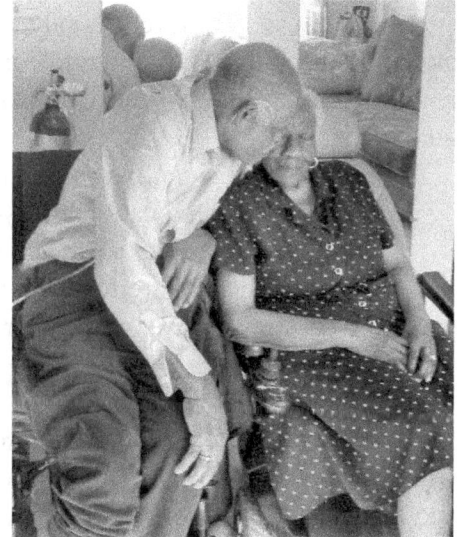

Harvey and Alice Johnson live in the Tarrytown neighborhood of Gary. They have raised 10 children and are the grandparents of former Chicago Bears defensive tackle Terry "Tank" Johnson, now a member of the Cincinnati Bengals.

Both Harvey and Alice are sharp as tacks; Harvey still doesn't wear glasses.

* * *

You two are really something. I mean, in this day and age, 72 months is quite a spell to be married, let alone, 72 years. Harvey, how old were you when you tied the knot with Alice?

"Nineteen," Harvey said.

Wow, that means Alice was only about 16.

"I like your math," Alice said.

Harvey, when did you and Alice move up north?

"In 1940; we lived in Chicago for 25 years before moving here."

What did you do for a living?

"Automobile painter."

What year did you move to Gary?

"In '55. This house was built for me," Harvey said. "We're the only people who have lived here."

Harvey, what's the secret to a long and happy marriage?

"Love."

Do you visit Mississippi?

"We used to have a family reunion in Mississippi on my grandmother's birthday," Harvey said. "Since she passed, we've had a reunion in a different city every year. Last year we went to Texas; this year we'll go to Chicago."

Harvey, do you have emphysema?

"Paint; I painted cars for 40 years."

Harvey, are you or were you a smoker?

"I quit when cigarettes went to 65 cents a pack. It costs $5 for a pack of cigarettes today. I remember when you could buy cigarettes for a penny a piece."

Are you a sports fan?

"Oh, yeah. I like the National League in baseball. I remember when Jackie Robinson (of the Brooklyn Dodgers) stole second, third and home off (New York Yankee pitcher) Whitey Ford."

You're a World War II veteran.

"I was in Africa, France, Belgium, Italy and Germany."

Are you a member of the American Legion?

"No, I didn't want any connection with the Army whatsoever. I threw all my GI clothes away the first day I got out. I didn't get to come home until the time I was discharged – never had a weekend pass."

How long did you serve?

"Three-and-a-half years."

They say the way to a man's heart is through his stomach. Can Alice put on some pots?

"You better believe it."

What's one of your favorite meals?

"Whatever she has on the menu. I used to raise all my vegetables. Homegrown produce is so much better than store-bought. Tomatoes taste better picked off the vine."

Harvey, I have sunny Italy in my veins; I love tomatoes.

"I like 'your country.' They was friendly, down-to-earth people.

Italy was my favorite country. I was in Naples and Sicily. I saw that volcano (Mount Vesuvius) erupt. They accidentally dropped a bomb in it.

"But I will say that Royal Air Force was out of this world. They could put the heat on the Germans in a hurry. The British came back and got us out of there. They shot those German airplanes down like they was birds."

Memories of Mississippi?

"I wanted out. At 18, I was a grown man and gone. Even as a kid, I hated the farm. Sharecroppin' is bad. You work the whole hot summer and the man would always say, 'You almost come out of the hole.' I also worked at a service station in Mississippi for $1 a day – seven days, $7."

Alice, when you first saw Harvey did you think he was the most handsome man you'd ever met?

"No."

What is the secret to such a long, wonderful, romantic marriage?

"Don't disagree with him. Make him think you agree with whatever he says, whether you believe it or not. Just let him talk."

Do you and Harvey go to church?

"New Revelations."

Your memories of Mississippi?

"Work; Harvey and I got out together. We weren't the cotton pickin' kind. We didn't know what the destination was gonna be, but we got away from it. It's been mostly good times ever since."

Harvey says you're a great cook.

"Collard greens, black-eyed peas, biscuits, peach pie, blackberry pie – all that. Sweet potato pie is our favorite."

Harvey, when you were a kid living in the Deep South, did you think it possible that a black man could become president of the United States?

"No, and you didn't, either."

Well, you have a point.

"In the school books, we were taught about George Washington, but not about George Washington Carver," Alice said. "But the older generation would hand those stories down to us. It never crossed my mind what I couldn't do."

Alice, the way you talk with your hands reminds me of some of my older relatives.

"I might have some Italian mixed in me; I don't know," Alice said.

Talk a little about raising your children.

"We did a pretty good job with the kids," Alice said. "They all graduated from school and got pretty good jobs. No drugs and no drunks. We all have a few drinks, but don't overdo it."

Added Harvey, "Three kids went to college."

A lot of kids today have children, but don't get married.

"They couldn't make it like we did," Harvey said. "Times is too fast today. When I was young, very few women had babies without being married. The women stood guard over their girls; they didn't trust anybody. The mothers would take care of their girls."

Added Alice: "Harvey and I have love and respect for each other and our family. We wanted to make sure our family stayed together."

* * *

And that's when Harvey leaned over from his wheelchair and gave her a peck on the cheek.

Alice smiled.

Bill and Barb Peterson *(Jan. 2010)*

"About six sections of this marsh land in the southeast corner of our county are covered with timber... some sycamore and gum trees. The balance of these wetlands, running west to the state line, is open marsh, covered with a luxuriant growth of wild grasses and flags (wild iris). It is the home of waterfowl and muskrat, and a paradise for hunters."

– Lake County Auditor John Brown, 1884.

Thomas Childers became the first settler in Lake County back in 1834, when he staked a claim due north of the present town of Schneider. The area was known as School Grove.

Although the Kankakee River was a couple miles south of Childers' homestead, the waters of the Grand Kankakee Marsh surrounded him.

For the past 50 years, Bill and Barb Peterson have lived in a nice brick house nestled atop a sandy, 15-acre knob shaded by white oaks and black oaks. It used to be an island in the area known as School Grove.

The Petersons are 81 years old, have been married nearly 60 years and have raised three children. Bill is a retired farmer who earned a degree in forestry from Purdue University. Barb was a nurse; she also was a Schneider.

* * *

"The town of Schneider was named after my grandfather, Fred Schneider,
in appreciation of the labor and material given by him when the New York Central north and south rail line was built in 1905," Barb began.

"He was a large landowner."

Added Bill: "That lady who owned all the land south of Lake Village wanted this area named Conrad. When that didn't happen, she was quite perturbed."

You speak of Jennie Conrad.

"Jennie and my Grandpa Fred didn't get along very well," Barb said. "I believe our school was built in 1910. There was a statute that a town had to have a population of at least 100 to get its own school. I was told grandfather moved a few families in because we were just shy of 100 people.

"The Presbyterian Church was built in 1911. Today, it looks about the same as it did back then."

Your dad?

"My father's name was John Schneider," Barb said. "I also have an Uncle Fred. The whole family was named either Fred or John. You didn't know for sure who you were talking about – maybe that was good. My father's two siblings never married, and I'm an only child."

How many acres do you and Bill own?

"I believe it's 1,260. Grandfather paid about $20 per acre for most of it."

Where were you born?

"Right across those railroad tracks. Originally, they called this area School Grove, then it became known as Oak Grove."

You have a Lowell address.

"This is where the mail carrier turns around. Everything south of us is Schneider. See that old carriage house about 100 yards south of here? The Cumberland Lodge sat next to it. So did the boathouse and outhouse, but we've restored and relocated them closer to our house."

Barb, those old hunt clubs like Cumberland Lodge, fascinate me. Wasn't there some sort of unsolved mystery concerning Cumberland Lodge?

"Yes; two Englishmen, William Parker and Captain Blake, had the lodge built in 1872. But they were called back to England and were never heard from again."

Added Bill: "There was a mechanic's lien put on it. The list of materials to build the place came to about $1,200."

That's amazing; I've seen photographs of that behemoth of a building.

"Before Parker and Blake sailed away, they gave a local man power of attorney," Bill said. "The Cumberland Lodge belonged to several hunting clubs out of Chicago until Barb's dad bought it in 1937."

I didn't know your family owned the Cumberland.

"We lived in it from 1937 until it burned down in '46 when I was a senior in high school," Barb said. "It had 21 rooms; there were eight bedrooms upstairs and one downstairs. And it had an English fireplace with warming ovens and a cook stove – very unusual."

Bill, what about Indian artifacts?

"Thousands of them. This former island has never been disturbed by agriculture. Let's go downstairs; I'll show you my collection."

"Jeff, look at what I call Grandma Schneider's bedroom," Barb said. "It includes her bed set from 1888, including her bed warmer, bowl and pitcher, commode, lamps... ."

Bill, Barb, your thoughts on the proposed bioethanol plant that would be located about a mile due south of this riparian Garden of Eden.

"If you can believe what the promoters of it have promised, it could be nothing but good," Bill said. "But if they have lied to us in any shape or form, we're going to have a problem."

That's the problem I have; it's being billed as a panacea, yet it's such a new technology. Barb?

"Our land will not be sold."

* * *

The Peterson home is a museum of antiques that were all handed down rather than purchased from a dealer – cool stuff like eel spears and wooden duck decoys.

Barb and Bill are members of Three Creeks Historical Association and two of the nicest people I've ever met.

Sally Burns *(Nov. 2011)*

"...The syringe injected. I lean over to whisper goodbye; unexpectedly, his gray muzzle meets me halfway. I receive a lick on the cheek like so many times before. Last kiss.

"A peculiar noise forces its way from my body, a noise one might render when trying not to sneeze in a library or church, only to worsen matters. I gnash my teeth so intensely they should hurt, but oddly they don't.

Salt water drizzles down from my cheeks onto Shep's coat. I use the back of my head and shoulder as a shield; hopefully my wife hasn't witnessed this – the dog licking my cheek – it would break her heart.

She's one of those animal lovers."
– Jeff Manes, Jan. 2000

Sally Burns helps run Burns' Pets Remembered Crematory & Cemetery in Crown Point.

Burns, 60, is the wife of Jim Burns, a third-generation funeral director. The Burns family operates funeral homes in Hobart and Crown Point.

Sally and Jim live in Hobart and have been married 34 years; they've raised three adult children, one of whom has become the fourth generation of Burns to become a licensed mortician.

Our interview took place at the "Pets Remembered" Crematory & Cemetery behind the funeral home in Crown Point.

* * *

Maiden name?
"Schleicher; it's a common German name," she said.
Did you grow up in Northwest Indiana?
"I did. We lived in (the) Miller (neighborhood of Gary) until eighth grade; then, we moved to Merrillville. I graduated from

Merrillville High School."

Memories of Miller?

"Miller was the greatest place to grow up. I was in seventh grade; I had a boyfriend – you do that sort of thing. You hang out at the lake. My three sisters and I all hated to leave; we lived on Lake Shore Drive."

Has Merrillville High changed through the years?

"Absolutely; now, it's the 'University of Merrillville.' When I was there it was all on one floor and we had about 360 people in our graduating class in 1969."

Did you go to mortuary school?

"No, I'm not a licensed mortician or funeral director, but I do whatever I need to do. You wear a lot of different hats when your name is on the sign."

College?

"Indiana State University; I have a teaching degree, believe it or not."

How long have you and Jim lived in Hobart?

"We've been in our 'starter home' for the past 32 years."

Sally, let's switch to the family business. Wasn't Burns Funeral Home the first in Northwest Indiana to have a crematory?

"Yes, but, as time went on, people were coming up to us and saying, 'C'mon, you guys, cremate my dog; nobody has to know. So, we established 'Pets Remembered' in April 2007."

Are humans and pets cremated in the same crematories?

"No, completely separate buildings. We have two crematories for the pets. One can accommodate 750 pounds of pets.

"We use that one basically when we pick up from the veterinarian. They'll have people who will bring their dogs to them and the pet owners don't want the cremains back. We'll put all those together and cremate them as a group."

Then what?

"We'll scatter the cremains in the pet cemetery. We also have a smaller crematory – up to 250 pounds."

Do most people take home the ashes of their pets?

"Absolutely; that's why they come to us. Their pets are their family. They're not just a dog, cat, bird or even a mouse; we've had mice."

You mean like those little white mice?

"Yes, we have a little container for the pet mice because you don't have much left after you cremate them."

Other unique pets you've cremated?

"Snakes, ferrets, macaws... ."

Sally, let's say a duck hunter comes to pick up Duke, his black lab. Are the dog's remains stored in a generic container or some kind of fancy urn?

"They can purchase an urn from us, but a lot of people opt for a temporary tin – what we call our 'paw print tin.' It's a keepsake with gray and black paw prints on it. Probably about half the people who have their pets cremated purchase an urn. We also make a clay paw print."

What's the largest animal to be cremated at Pets Remembered?

"I've done a small horse."

Sally, when I was a kid, the neighbor shot my dog. Caesar made it to our back yard and then collapsed. My dad had to finish him. My brother and I buried the Doberman-shepherd mix out in the woods behind the house.

"It's illegal to bury a dog in your backyard. I've heard it from more than one vet, but I've never seen the 'pet police' out there arresting people for putting their dog in a hole. I have two dogs in my backyard."

The pet cemetery?

"My husband was approached by a minister who didn't want his dog cremated. He said: 'C'mon Burnsy, you've got all this property back here. Why don't you put in a cemetery so I can bury my dog?' Voila. We did. The pet cemetery has been a great comfort to so many people."

Gravestones?

"We have one marker that we use a lot; it's a granite marker that starts at $160."

I've talked to a number of folks who grew up in the Great Depression; they've told me they didn't even think of taking a pet to the vet when it was sick. The animal either made it or it didn't. Those old-timers are amazed that people spend, say, $900 on a pet operation.

"I know people who have spent like $20,000 on a dog. But it's not a dog; it's their 'child.' We have a lot of pet parents who have no (human) children. Usually, when a pet dies, it happens in less than 20 years. That's not a very old person; it's like burying a child."

Sally, there was an elderly music teacher from Lake Village who lived next door to my family; she never married. When her dog died, she wanted to have it buried in Lake Village Cemetery, but she was denied.

"(The other day), we buried two cats with a lady in her casket."

* * *

Sally Burns was easy to talk to and very down to earth. I'm glad I met her and glad the Burns family had the vision to create a pet cemetery for pet "parents."

As so often happens, the words of a song popped into my head during the drive home. It was a song by the Nitty Gritty Dirt Band called "Mr. Bojangles."

'He danced for those at minstrel shows throughout the South

He spoke through tears of 15 years how is dog and him traveled about

The dog up and died, he up and died

And after 20 years he still grieves... .'

Alice Gray *(Oct. 2007)*

Editor's note: In honor of Halloween, Jeff Manes is dedicating this week's column to deceased – rather – ghostly – interviewee.

"...In solitude when we are least alone..."
-Lord Byron

Gulls escort me in the gloaming along Lake Michigan's sandy shore. Goldenrod has become pregnant with galls. Cattails are but burst fluff. Clumps of sagging sedge drown while bulrush wisps morose. I veer off onto a path less traveled...

Nearing a windowless shack not more than 10 feet square, I spot movement in the midst of a black raspberry thicket. Barren red canes like serrated grasshopper legs cling to a khaki-clad woman as she patrols. She appears approximately my age. She is leather brown, weatherbeaten.

* * *

Ms. Gray?

"Yes. And who might you be?"

Jeff Manes is my name. I write a human-interest column. I'd be honored if I could interview you.

"I don't seek publicity, Mr. Manes. And I don't care for nosey newspaper men. Why should I feel any different regarding you?"

I've admired what you've stood for.

"I've read your column. I read many things. You're an odd duck. As you can see, I shoot ducks."

Your prowess as a huntress is widely known. I'm sorry to have intruded.

"Like the red-tailed hawk, I kill for subsistence, not sport. Follow me, Jeff Manes. With you, I shall converse. By the way, you don't appear as youthful as your photograph would have your readers believe."

Well, it was –

"It was this time of year, October, when the oaks are red, the maples yellow, and sassafras orange, that I stepped down off the South Shore and came to live here. I had nothing but a jelly glass, a knife, a spoon, a blanket and two guns.

"For four nights before discovering this abandoned hut, I slept under the stars. Then I began housekeeping. All the furniture I have is made of driftwood. Everything is driftwood here, including myself. I have named this place 'Driftwood.'"

Alice, you're a highly educated woman...

"At the age of 16, I enrolled in the University of Chicago, where I studied mathematics, astronomy, Greek and Latin. I was named a Phi Beta Kappa honor society member. Ah yes, Mr. Manes, I have been educated – and I was born a woman."

After graduation you continued your studies abroad.

"In Germany, I was introduced to a movement called Wandervogel."

Birds of Passing. It was said to be a kind of 'walking commune' involving young people, correct?

"You've done your homework, Mr. Manes. We gave up our material possessions to live off the land in nature."

You returned to your native Chicago.

"I became an associate editor for an astronomy magazine. I was not paid what I was worth. Day-to-day work in the city was nothing more than slavery for someone of my gender. Who were these men to tell me how to behave or what I could or could not accomplish?"

Some say you had a falling out with your father, who was a supervisor in the steel mills.

"My father was a prominent physician. He had nothing to do with my decision to dwell here. I wanted to live my own life – a free life. It was a poem written by Byron that gave me my longings to get away from the conventional world, and I never gave up on the idea, although a long time passed before I could fulfill it.

"At the age of 34, I came here. My salary when I worked was nothing extraordinary, and yet I lived that entire first winter and summer on the last pay envelope that I received in Chicago. I buy only bread and salt now, from money made selling berries."

Without salt we perish, Alice. There were others like you. Artists, writers, bohemian types...

"They came and went like the blue herons. I have never left. I have weathered the harshest of winters. I have weathered..."

You mentioned your interest in reading.

"I've toted books and magazines by the gunnysack to and from the Miller Public Library. Travel, philosophy, biographies..."

What is your favorite book?

"'Apologia pro Vita Sua,' by Cardinal John Henry Newman."

Do you believe in reincarnation?

"No, I do not. When my time comes, I wish to be cremated on a funeral pyre atop Mount Tom. Let the Northwest wind scatter my ashes. I will become compost like the fallen leaves of the high oaks."

You're not only a reader...

"I have written about the dunes, yes. Essays, mostly. I also study wildlife. I am not the hermit the newspapermen make me out to be. I give tours of the area to the children."

I don't believe you are a hermit at all. How could such an activist be a total recluse? You have fought the good fight versus the old boys' club. Elbert Gary had old money backing him. You and he might have shared anagrams for surnames but that is where the similarities end.

"The locals claimed that Hearst exploited me by publishing my diary. They wrote that I should make my life worthwhile by entering the service of the Red Cross and going 'over there' to nurse the boys who have fallen in the big fight. Little did they know five times which perished on the Western Front would perish on the home front from the grippe.

"Here, I have made use of pleurisy root, horehound, boneset. Tea is made from juniper berries, coltsfoot, plantain, sallow bark and wild honey."

They have called you a Venus with gleaming skin who stands nude in the moonlight, with arms outstretched, like a statue of –

"Look at me! Do you see Galatea? Curiosity seekers from Chicago who flocked to gawk were sorely disappointed, wouldn't you say, Mr. Manes?"

Well, I don't know. I mean, ahem, beauty is in the eye of the –

"Backed by industrialists they also wrote that I was but a tool used by A.F. Knotts to advertise his national park scheme. Smokescreens favoring smokestacks, I say! And what about you, Jeff Manes?"

I will write about a hunter's moon that shone down upon a great lake, windswept dunes and a hovel. About seaside spurge and sand reed grass. Jack pines and junipers. Solomon's seal and Dutchman's breeches.

About green-headed drake mallards and majestic bald eagles. Of perch, prickly pear, and Potawatomi.

* * *

We stare at each other in silence. I search. She peers. Alice Gray remains still like the objet trouve surrounding her. I make my exit. An owl hoots. A coyote yowls. Like Lot's wife, a man of salt cannot resist the temptation. I look back...

The hovel is vanished. A luna moth flits into the night – moonbeams her only source of light. I assure the wan sylph... .

And I will write of driftwood, Diana.

Jennie M. Conrad *(Oct. 2010)*

Forbidden Fruit
*"When the moon is full,
In the month of Halloween
The ghost of Jennie Conrad,
Occasionally is seen
And she's been known to rant,
With buggy whip in hand:
'Jace and Jeffy Manes,
You best stay off my land!'"*
–JM

For Halloween, I decided to interview Jennie M. Conrad. She's been dead for 71 years. Our "chat" took place in the ghost town of Conrad which is located about two miles south of Lake Village, just east of U.S. 41.

Jennie was the daughter of cattle baron Lemuel Milk of Kankakee, Ill. Milk owned 40,000 acres in Illinois and Indiana; 12,000 of them in Newton County.

At the age of 23, Jennie married George Conrad. She was a widow by the time she was 40. George and Jennie Conrad had one son, Platt Conrad. Platt was Jennie's mother's maiden name. The Platts were quite wealthy.

* * *

"Get off my land immediately, unless you want a load of double aught buckshot lodged in your ass,"Conrad began. "You would think Conrad was the only place on God's green earth where blackberries grew. Be off with you before I crack this buggy whip across your back."

Ms. Conrad, I'm not here to steal your blackberries, and I surely would've called you from my BlackBerry, but I don't have your cell phone number.

"What in tarnation is a cell phone?"

My bad. I forgot we're in the year 1915. Jennie, my name is Jeff

Manes; I'm a human-interest columnist. I'd like to interview you. Besides, it seems you could use some positive public relations.

"Manes... . That name sounds vaguely familiar. A newspaper man, are you? Seeing how my son has absolutely no interest in farming, I've been mulling over the possibility of putting an advertisement in the newspaper with the intent of hiring an athletic, well-bred, American, college man with nerves of steel who does not use tobacco or alcohol. His main concern would be to prevent trespassers. Do you meet all those specifications?"

Well, ahem, I am second-generation Italian-American and I was a decent center fielder – I just couldn't hit.

"Humph!"

Jennie, I'm not here for a job interview.

"Oh, alright, ask your inane questions."

Thanks; don't let me forget to take your picture before I leave.

"You will do nothing of the sort. No one has ever photographed me. I do not permit it."

Jennie, your failure to use contractions while speaking galls me. "Gall," a word I've always admired. My grandmother used "gall" frequently. Where were you born?

"Milk's Grove, in Iroquois County, Ill."

I was born in Kankakee.

"Good for you."

Tell me about your early years.

"I was privately schooled and speak fluent French. The first years of my married life were spent in Chicago. I obtained this land in 1885; my husband and I eventually moved here in 1891."

It was your father who deeded these 4,400 acres to you for the sum of $1.

"You have done your research, Jeff Manes."

Tell me more about your father.

"We did not speak for years. Some consider him a self-made man, but he acquired much of his wealth with the assistance of my mother's family. After my dear mother and brother passed, he married a woman 46 years younger then he was. The marriage produced a child."

Your half-sister, Mary Milk. Ol' Lem was 68 when she was born.

"That child and her mother were the beneficiaries of his will."

What did you inherit?

"One dollar."

Ouch. This area looked a lot different before your dad arrived on the scene.

"Prior to 1873, my estate, now named Oak Dene Farms, was part of Beaver Lake in Newton County, Ind., and mostly covered with water, in some places 10 feet or more deep and all of swampy character. In '73, what was called the 'Big Ditch' was completed, and the restraining dam opened in the presence of great assemblage, thereby releasing the water of Beaver Lake, which rushed into the Kankakee River, and this well-known lake, home of myriad wild fowl, with island harboring horse thieves and fugitives of justice, was completely wiped off the map, an epoch in the history of Indiana."

Yeah, the annihilation of the largest fresh-water lake in the state. Beaver Lake was soon one-tenth its original size, but it died hard. That last tenth took another 20 years to drain.

"Yes, in 1893; the year my father died."

You didn't plan out your town until 1905, at age 50.

"Correct; I divided the property into smaller units which were rented out to individuals who were willing to work the land and share the profits with me."

I must say, this is quite the bustling little burg: a nice school, church, post office-general store, hotel, depot, ranch houses, outbuildings.... And each and every one of them painted such a hideous of yellow.

"I like yellow. Next question."

Hogs were the ticket.

"Yes; today, a woman who is left widowed does not necessarily have to be planted among her relatives or take in sewing and washing. In pioneer days, women were confined to the interior of the home and from dawn until dusk they toiled. A woman's work was never finished until the grave yawned.

"No more is it considered out of the ordinary for women to engage in the livestock industry. The best asset for any woman of the farm is the hog. If she does take it up, she should stay on the job, for the eye of the master is what prevents loss in this day of independence. So, I say, 'Go to it girls!'"

Get off your soapbox, sister. You can't even vote yet.

"I specialized in the Poland-China breed. The progeny of Paul No. 20, who surpasses in bone and length any boar of the breed, is wanted in every state of the union. Paul No. 20 walks like a Percheron horse and is an absolutely dependable sire of early maturing, big boned pigs with good backs and feet. His docility endears him to all who know him and he is as affectionate as a beloved dog."

You're obviously fond of animals. When your beloved dog, Bouser, came up missing, you laid in bed, grieving for two weeks. Why can't you get along with people, especially the residents of Lake Village?

"Because they are trespassing swamp rats!"

Before your family arrived, they had free access to the shores of Beaver Lake and its bounties.

"Just the other day, I caught two of those ragamuffins carrying pails of my blackberries. I jumped down from my buggy, emptied their buckets in the middle of this dirt road, and crushed the berries with my feet!"

Most of those folks from Lake Village are poor. Besides, you can't eat all these berries; it's a sin to let them rot when so many could be fed.

"Those little heathens hid in the weeds after I ordered them off my property; they waited until I left and then set fire to a 40-acre tract of wheat which was ripe and ready to cut – the field was a total loss."

All over a gallon of berries. Who knows, their mama might've made you a blackberry cobbler in return, if you could've just shown a little kindness.

And there's something else, Jennie M. Conrad; I was born in Kankakee, but I was raised in Sumava Resorts and Lake Village!

"Off my property, swamp rat!"

* * *

The Great Depression took its toll. When Jennie died at Jasper County Hospital in 1939, only 1,200 of her nearly 5,000 acres remained in her possession. A few crumbling foundations are all that remain of the town of Conrad.

Today, Jennie's empire has become Conrad Station Savanna, a nature preserve owned by The Nature Conservancy and part of its Kankakee Sands restoration project.

The public is welcome.